PRAISE FOR

The Tale of the Rose

"Pioneering aviator, bestselling writer and romantic idol, Antoine de Saint-Exupéry enjoyed a celebrity in his lifetime that was surpassed only by his fame after death. . . . Now, Consuelo's side of the story of their stormy thirteen-year marriage has at last become known. In pages weighty with love, passion, betrayal and tragedy, the Salvadoran-born beauty has reclaimed her place in the Saint-Exupéry myth." —*The New York Times*

"[Consuelo] was a gifted writer with a flair for the dramatic . . . she turns a stunning phrase [and] conjures one radiant image after another of daily life in a truly dysfunctional union."
—*Atlanta Journal-Constitution*

"A poetic memoir of their tempestuous marriage . . . Consuelo . . . for all her coquettish bravado and embellishments, writes, with style and courage, for grown-ups."
—*Entertainment Weekly* (Editor's Choice)

"Consuelo de Saint-Exupéry's passionate account of her marriage to the daring French aviation hero and author Antoine de Saint-Exupéry is partly about smothering someone with love. It's also partly about the freedom of spirit that compels an adventurer like her husband. . . . It is a tale . . . full of vigor and intensity." —Associated Press

"Consuelo de Saint-Exupéry looks and writes like Anaïs Nin."
—*Los Angeles Times*

LONG BEACH PUBLIC LIBRARY
AND INFORMATION CENTER

LOS: JI705
NOV 1 1 2005

"Consuelo also had a way with words. . . . In the Exupéry marriage, torment, it seems, cut both ways."

—*San Francisco Chronicle*

"We find in these pages all the tenderness and patience, but also the tenacity, of a woman who loves. Consuelo does not seek to explain or even to understand her husband, she accepts him and leads him to what he must be." —*Elle*

"Consuelo's explosive prose . . . is alternately bitter and lyrical as she struggles to understand her complex husband. . . . Why didn't she leave him? Why did he keep returning to her? Like the Little Prince and the rose of Saint-Exupéry's tale, their bond was inexplicable but inescapable."

—*The Times* (London)

"From Buenos Aires to Casablanca, Paris and New York . . . Saint-Ex repeatedly fled the constraints of marriage, only to find he could not write without his wife's support and inspiration. . . . An intimate glimpse of the strange and passionate life behind his mysterious work." —*Publishers Weekly*

"A passionate, dreamlike memoir that draws you into its reverie." —*Kirkus Reviews* (starred review)

"A great love story that unfolds under thundering skies . . . We are drawn into a tale full of drama and flair, where the dazzle of the high life is entwined with a tender and tragic hymn to mad, passionate love. . . . It is the greatest love story of the year. Consuelo is a writer of true talent." —*Le Point*

CONSUELO DE SAINT-EXUPÉRY wrote *The Tale of the Rose* in 1945. She died in 1979, thirty-five years after her husband, never having published her story. The manuscript, sealed away in a trunk, was discovered in 1999 by an academic doing research for a new biography of her husband. A number one bestseller, its publication in France was a national sensation. It has been translated into sixteen languages.

The Tale
of the
Rose

Consuelo de Saint-Exupéry

The Tale
of the
Rose

THE PASSION THAT INSPIRED
The Little Prince

Translated by Esther Allen

848
S137t

LOS ALTOS

RANDOM HOUSE TRADE PAPERBACKS

NEW YORK

3 3090 00781 5808

2003 Random House Trade Paperback Edition

Translation copyright © 2001 by Random House, Inc.

All rights reserved under International and Pan-American
Copyright Conventions. Published in the United States
by Random House Trade Paperbacks, a division of
Random House, Inc., New York, and simultaneously in
Canada by Random House of Canada Limited, Toronto.

RANDOM HOUSE TRADE PAPERBACKS and colophon are
trademarks of Random House, Inc.

This work was originally published in France as *Mémoires de la rose*
by Les Editions Plon in 2000. Copyright © 2000 by Plon.
This translation was originally published in hardcover by
Random House, Inc., in 2001. This edition published
by arrangement with Les Editions Plon.

This work was originally published in English in hardcover
by Random House, Inc., in 2001.

Library of Congress Cataloging-in-Publication Data
Saint-Exupéry, Consuelo de.
[Mémoires de la rose. English]
The tale of the rose: the passion that inspired
The little prince / Consuelo de Saint-Exupéry;
translated by Esther Allen.
p.   cm.
ISBN 0-8129-6717-8
1. Saint-Exupéry, Antoine de, 1900–1944—Marriage.
2. Saint-Exupéry, Consuelo de.   3. Authors, French—
20th century—Biography.   4. Air pilots—France—
Biography.   5. Authors' spouses—France—Biography.
I. Allen, Esther, 1962–   II. Title.
PQ2637.A274 Z828335   2001
848'.91209—dc21
[B]   00-068850

Random House website address: www.atrandom.com
Printed in the United States of America
2 4 6 8 9 7 5 3 1
Book design by Brooke Koven

"Of course I love you," the flower said to him. "It is my fault that you have not known it all the while. That is of no importance. But you—you have been as foolish as I. Try to be happy. . . . Don't linger like this. You have decided to go away. Go now!"

For she did not want him to see her crying. She was such a proud flower. . . .

—From *The Little Prince*

Introduction

In the decades that followed December 17, 1903, when, on the windy coast of North Carolina, the age-old human dream of taking to the air in a powerful machine at last came true, the aviator emerged as one of the new century's greatest heroes. The progress of each successive feat—a longer distance covered, a higher speed attained, an ocean crossed in a single flight, two new continents connected—was followed with bated breath, and names like Alberto Santos-Dumont, Harriet Quimby, the "Red Baron" Manfred von Richtofen, Charles and Anne Morrow Lindbergh, Amelia Earhart, and Antoine de Saint-Exupéry echoed around the globe. Frequent disaster only heightened the drama of success; every flyer who made it home safe knew of many who had gone down in fiery, or watery, death.

Even more compelling were the stories of survival against unbelievable odds—that of Saint-Exupéry's close friend Henri Guillaumet, for example, who crashed in the Andes in 1930 and dragged himself across the mountains alone for seven days before he was rescued, or that of Saint-Ex himself, who, after his plane went down in the Libyan desert in 1936, was only saved days later by stumbling across a group of Bedouin. But the most haunting stories were the most mysterious ones: the disappearances. The radio falls silent. The plane never arrives. No trace is ever found.

No one knew more than Saint-Ex about the fascination of such vanishings: the nameless pilot who narrates his most famous book, *The Little Prince*, has gone down in the middle of the vast Sahara, his whereabouts unknown. He has little hope of survival, and none of rescue. In the end, the fictional pilot manages to save himself and tell his story, but the remoteness of that possibility, his own near certainty of being lost to the world forever, underlies its every word. Then, in 1944, only a year after *The Little Prince* first came out, Saint-Exupéry himself took off from a military base in Corsica on a reconnaissance mission over Nazi-occupied southern France and disappeared. Neither his plane nor his body has ever been found.

★

A WEEK BEFORE THAT, Saint-Ex wrote a letter to his wife, Consuelo—the last of the innumerable letters he had written her since their first encounter in Buenos Aires fourteen years earlier—to tell her that his only regret if he were shot down would be that it would make her cry. "Consuelo," he wrote in another letter around that same time, "thank you for being my wife. If I am wounded, I will have someone to take care of me, if I am killed, I will have someone to wait for in eternity, and if I come back, I will have someone to come back to." Letters were always an essential element of what bound the two of them together, perhaps the most essential element. He would write to her when he was halfway across the globe and when he was in a café around the corner from their home. The first of those letters, a gargantuan missive, became the starting point for his prizewinning novel *Night Flight,* and through all their wild nomadic years together and apart, the letters kept coming, voluble and impassioned. They were a way of creating space and distance when he felt marooned on the small asteroid of their marriage, and a way of rejoining her when much of planet Earth lay between them. A failure to write her, an interval without letters, was the one thing Consuelo could not tolerate from him.

In some way, *The Little Prince* itself, written during one of the more peaceful phases of their tumultuous marriage, when they were comfortably ensconced in a large white house in Northport, Long Island, was one of those letters. "One never ought to listen to flowers," the Little Prince confides to the aviator about his beloved and impossible Rose. "One should only look at them and breathe their fragrance. Mine perfumed all my planet. But I did not know how to take pleasure in all her grace. . . . The fact is that I did not know how to understand anything!" he continues. "She cast her fragrance and her radiance over me. I ought never to have run away from her. . . . I ought to have guessed all the affection that lay behind her poor little stratagems. Flowers are so inconsistent! But I was too young to know how to love her. . . . " Antoine had many names for Consuelo: she was his little girl, his sorceress, his *Pimprenelle*, his bird of the islands, but finally and most of all she was the Rose, unique in all the world, whom the Little Prince could not live with and could not live without.

A year or two after Antoine's disappearance, when the end of the war had brought no news to banish the agony of waiting and all hope of another letter from him had evaporated, Consuelo began to write a letter of her own, a very long letter, telling the story of their marriage. Perhaps she wrote it in French, which was always harder for her than her native Spanish, because she was writing it for him, and his Spanish was never very good. "Write to me, write to me," Antoine had pleaded in one of his last letters to her, "from time to time the mail comes and brings springtime to my heart." She typed some of it, wrote other parts out in longhand, and then went back over the manuscript, correcting it and making changes; the whole process must have taken many weeks, or months. Finally, she had the pages bound in thick, black cardboard, and put the volume away in a trunk.

Interest in Saint-Exupéry and worldwide sales of *The Little Prince* soared in the years that followed, but Consuelo never published her manuscript. Even in 1949, when the wealthy woman who for many years was Saint-Exupéry's mistress (and source of financial support), Nelly de Vogüé, published the first biography of him under the male pseudonym Pierre Chevrier and, predictably, made scant and dismissive mention of his wife, Consuelo did not release her side of the story. She let it lie, silent and unknown, locked in its trunk. Instead, she sculpted image after image of Antoine and his Little Prince and played her role as his devoted widow, representing him at all the many tributes, memorials, receptions, and conferences held in his honor down through the years. Meanwhile, her trunks, crammed with papers, mementos, bits and scraps of their lives—old flight maps, a life jacket he had used during his experimental flights in a hydroplane before the war, and the manuscript of the book you are now holding—were shipped from New York to Paris and from Paris to the house in Grasse, in the south of France, where Consuelo spent the last years of her life.

When she died in 1979, the manuscript was still buried somewhere in there; it is quite possible that she had forgotten about it. It was his letters that she remembered. "I always tremble when I open the files or trunks where my husband's letters, drawings and telegrams are piled," she wrote toward the end of her life. "Those yellowing pages, spangled with tall flowers and little princes, are faithful witnesses to a lost happiness whose grace and privileges I value more strongly each year."

Two decades after her death, Consuelo's manuscript finally came to light; José Martinez-Fructuoso, who worked for her for many years and was her heir, and his wife, Martine, discovered it as they were making their way through the trunks' myriad contents. Alan Vircondelet, the author of a biography of Saint-Exupéry, edited it, smoothing out Consuelo's French and dividing it into chapters. Its publication in France in 2000, a full century after Antoine de Saint-Exupéry's birth on June 29, 1900, became something of a national event. The great myth of

Saint-Exupéry, the heroic fighter pilot, now had to be altered to make room for the impassioned new voice of his wife, who in the fifty years since his death had been virtually airbrushed out of the picture.

★

BECAUSE SHE WAS TELLING such a private story, intended for an audience of two, Consuelo left out or alluded only vaguely to a great many things. There was no need to say who she was or what her life had been like before meeting him: why repeat what she had already told him so many times, stories he would sometimes beg her for? Those who knew her had fond memories of her weird and glittering evocations of her childhood in the Central American republic of El Salvador. There was the story of how, as a little girl, she decided to make herself the most beautiful dress in the world, so she rubbed honey all over her naked body and ran into the tropical rain forest, where she was soon arrayed in a rustling, luminescent coat of live butterflies. In a variant on that story, she would say that she was born half-dead and to save her a sorcerer smeared her tiny body with honey, which attracted a swarm of bees whose stings awoke her to life. Not without reason did one of her detractors once sum her up in a letter, cited by Saint-Ex's biographer Stacy Schiff, as "Surrealism made flesh"—a description Consuelo would undoubtedly have taken as a great compliment.

When Consuelo Suncin Sandoval was born, on April 10, 1901 (though the year carved on her gravestone, in the

Père-Lachaise cemetery, is 1907), her parents named her Consuelo, or "consolation," because they were in need of it: the four sons born before her had each died in early childhood (later there would be two more daughters, Dolorès and Amanda). Her family were Ladinos, of mixed Spanish and Mayan blood, and she grew up within fifteen miles of an active volcano, Izalco, a perfect cone of ash and black lava sometimes known as the Lighthouse of the Pacific, because its red halo was visible to nineteenth-century navigators. Her father, Félix Suncin, a coffee planter and a colonel in the army reserve, was locally renowned both as a brutal authoritarian and as a healer who concocted plant-based potions with which he treated the neighboring campesinos' ailments. While these two aspects of his character might seem contradictory, they were not: when his youngest daughter, Amanda, developed a white spot on her forehead that was slowly spreading, Félix's treatment was to take the cigar he was smoking from his mouth and stub it out on his daughter's forehead. The resulting scar kept the white patch from spreading any further.

During her student days in Mexico City, Consuelo charmed her circle of friends with stories about an earthquake that she lived through as a young girl, a disaster that, according to her biographer, Paul Webster, is unmentioned in the annals of her hometown (though the country's capital, San Salvador, was destroyed by earthquakes no fewer than seven times between 1854 and 1917). But whatever the truth of her tales, she was a bewitching storyteller, and that, even more than her delicate beauty, seems to have been what captivated the many men who fell in love with her.

José Vasconcelos, a prolific and influential philosopher who was at one point a strong contender for the Mexican presidency, devoted more than twenty-five pages of his autobiography to "Charito" (as he called Consuelo): "Her smile made me dizzy," he wrote. "She had a music inside her . . . and the key to its melodies was in her voice and her diction. To hear her tell a story was to fall under a spell. The words rose to her lips full of harmony and sensuality. You wanted to put a tape recorder in front of her, to capture her stories in her own precise and melodious expression of them."

In the aftermath of a first marriage in 1922 to Ricardo Cardenas, a young Mexican army officer she met while studying English in California and who died less than a year after their wedding, Consuelo moved to Mexico City to continue her education. There she soon embarked on a three-year affair with the very distinguished and powerful Vasconcelos, who was in his forties and had a wife and two children. It was, Vasconcelos says, "the mystery of Charito" that inspired him to write one of his most memorable short stories, "La casa imantada" ("The Magnetic House"), the first manifestation of Consuelo's power as a literary muse. "The most seductive thing about Consuelito," he commented, forgetting, for a moment, her alias, "was her sincerity. She didn't lie or lied very little. And she was as likely to talk about things that showed her in a bad light as about what made her look good."

Late in 1925, Vasconcelos and his family left Mexico to go into exile in Paris, and soon Consuelo wrote him a letter from her family home in Armenia, San Salvador, asking him to send her money for a ticket to Paris. (The Suncins were well-off by local standards, but their funds were no match for Consuelo's ambitions.) He sent the money. She arrived in Paris in January 1926, and not long after, Vasconcelos and his good friend Alfonso Reyes, a celebrated essayist who was then a minister in the Mexican government, took her to dinner at a fashionable restaurant. Consuelo asked Reyes, "Is this one of the best places? Are the women here the loveliest and most elegant in Paris?" When Reyes assured her that she was indeed surrounded by the *crème* of Parisian society, she turned to Vasconcelos in triumph and said, "Well, I think I can hold my own with them."

She did that, and better. Before the year was out, she had broken with Vasconcelos to become the third wife of the wealthy and renowned Enrique Gómez Carrillo, who, though born in Guatemala, had long since established himself in Paris, writing articles for several Madrid-based publications, traveling around the world, publishing books at a dizzying rate, and serving as the Argentine consul. Some three decades Consuelo's senior, Gómez Carrillo was a commander in the French Legion of Honor, and was persistently rumored—though he vehemently denied it—to have been promoted to that rank in gratitude for his services to the famed Deuxième Bureau, the French intelligence service, in the matter of the entrapment and arrest of the celebrated Dutch courtesan and secret agent Mata Hari. His name had also been romantically linked to Isadora Duncan's.

Though the handsome and Byronic Gómez Carrillo was a daunting rival, Vasconcelos did not give up his lover without a struggle; at one point passions ran so high that Gómez Carrillo, who had fought eighteen duels in his life and was known as one of the best swordsmen in Paris, sent a telegram challenging Vasconcelos to a sword fight. The challenge was accepted, and Vasconcelos engaged a fencing master and underwent several weeks of intensive training, but the duel never materialized, though other dangers did, or were said to have. Consuelo loved to act out the story of how, as she and Gómez Carrillo emerged from the church where they had just been married, his second wife, Raquel Meller, a famous Spanish cabaret singer, suddenly loomed before them brandishing a revolver that was aimed straight at the bride. The gun jammed, and Consuelo fainted into her new husband's arms. Eleven months later, it was Gómez Carrillo's turn to lie inert in Consuelo's arms: he suffered a fatal stroke (drained, evil tongues whispered, by the demands of his much younger wife) and left Consuelo all he owned. She was twenty-six years old.

Aside from a brief but memorable visit to Gómez Carrillo's great friend Gabriele D'Annunzio at the Vittoriale, his lakeside villa in northern Italy, Consuelo spent most of the three years after her second husband's death in Paris, living in the apartment on rue de Castellane that she had briefly shared with him, where his death mask, which she had made herself, was prominently displayed and would emit ominous crackling noises "whenever Consuelo flirted or said something out of place," her confidante of that period, Xenia Kouprine, the daughter of Russian novelist Alexander Kouprine, told Saint-Ex's biographer Curtis

Cate. Then, early in the fall of 1930, Consuelo set sail for Buenos Aires, which is where the story of her life with "Tonio," as she usually called him, begins.

★

FOR ALL THAT IT TELLS about the two of them, there are many things Consuelo's story silences. One scene, especially, echoes through their marriage in the recurrent, aching abandonment of every home they ever tried to establish, the strange sequence of nightmarish moments when Consuelo would walk into a house suddenly and inexplicably emptied of all its contents. For they were perpetually unable to find a place where they could stay and be together. All of their paradises were lost: the house in Buenos Aires; El Mirador outside of Nice; a whole series of apartments in Paris, Casablanca, and New York. No sooner had they settled in to some new location than the nameless imperative to move on, to move away, made itself felt once more.

It happened in the summer of 1932, at the château of Saint-Maurice-de-Rémens, the wondrous setting of Saint-Exupéry's childhood, the most vivid years of his life ("I'm not sure I have lived since my childhood," he wrote to his mother from Buenos Aires). He—or the anonymous aviator who tells the story—would invoke Saint-Maurice in *The Little Prince:* "When I was a little boy I lived in an old house, and legend told us that a treasure was buried there. To be sure, no one had ever known how to find it; perhaps no one had ever even looked for it. But it cast an enchantment over that house. My home was hiding a secret in the depths of its heart . . . " A little more than a year after their wedding, the grown-ups with their strange ideas about matters of consequence and the businessmen with their endless, nonsensical figures finally conquered Saint-Maurice. It was sold to the nearby city of Lyons, and emptied out; all the familiar beds, armchairs, stoves, clocks, dishes, and toys that had surrounded him during those buried treasured days were lined up along the main street of the local village and auctioned off on two successive Sundays. Antoine and Consuelo, Comte and Comtesse de Saint-Exupéry—for the Saint-Exupérys were an old and titled family—wandered for a while among the things out on that street. While Antoine said good-bye to the irreplaceable objects of his youngest days, Consuelo, Paul Webster tells us, made a great show of her nonchalance, as if to reaffirm that none of it mattered to her, that she hadn't married him for this, that she could live, as she says, with "never any luggage, nothing at all except my life, suspended from his."

★

AT HER WEDDING to Antoine de Saint-Exupéry on April 23, 1931, Consuelo wore black. It was perfectly understandable. She had already lost two husbands within a year of marrying them, and this latest one was known for his recklessness. Though Consuelo was a small and sometimes frail woman whose conversation, in moments of emotional crisis, was often punctuated with fits of coughing (a trait the Rose would share), it seemed likely, given the dangers of his profession and his passion for adventure, that this was yet another husband she was destined to outlive. And she did. Only this time the marriage lasted thirteen years. It produced no children, but it did produce *The Little Prince,* or was rather the rich, chaotic, and often painful reality from which it grew. Antoine wrote the book (Consuelo was adamant that credit for a work of art goes only to the artist who created it), but it was their marriage that gave rise to its sweetly dissonant and enduring central pair, the Little Prince and his Rose.

Long before that, someone had noticed that Antoine and Consuelo together were like two characters out of a children's story. Henri Jeanson, a friend who knew them during the first years of their marriage, wrote in his memoir, "I have never forgotten the way Saint-Ex looked at her. So fragile and small, she charmed him . . . she surprised him, she fascinated him; in short, he adored her. That little bird never kept still. She perched according to her whim on her huge stuffed bear, that huge flying stuffed bear that was Saint-Ex." People speak of a couple as being happy or unhappy, as if it were ever that simple. In this case, at any rate, it was not. As a young girl, Consuelo told her classmates that when she grew up she wanted to be a princess, and she did become a countess, but her story is no fairy-tale romance. Yet through all the vicissitudes that beset them, the perils from without and from within, the spreading baobabs that threatened to strangle them and the domestic volcanoes whose eruptions brought disaster, across vast distances and amid war and tragedy, something kept bringing them back to each other, sometimes even to their own surprise. In the end, it was bigger than they were. "What moves me so deeply about this little prince," muses that lost aviator, "is his loyalty to a flower—the image of a rose that shines through his whole being like a flame within a lamp."

—Esther Allen

Ou est ma
Consuelo ?

Consuelo ji vous aime

Antoine

Part One

Buenos Aires, 1930

1

EVERY MORNING ON THE BRIDGE, Ricardo Viñes, the pianist with hands like a dove's wings, would say in my ear, "Consuelo, you are not a woman."

I would laugh and kiss his cheeks, pushing back his long mustache that sometimes made me sneeze. He would then go through all the rituals of Spanish courtesy, wishing me a good morning, inquiring about my dreams, inviting me to enjoy this new day of our journey to Buenos Aires. And every day I wondered what Don Ricardo could possibly mean by his little morning greeting.

"Am I an angel, then? An animal? Do I not exist?" I asked him fiercely at last.

He fell serious and turned that El Greco face of his out toward the sea a few moments, then took my hands in his.

"So, child, you know how to listen; that is good. . . . For as long as we have been on this ship, I have been wondering what you are. I know I like what is within you, but I also know that you are not a woman. I have spent whole nights thinking about it, and finally I set to work. I am more of a composer than a pianist, and only in music can I express the way I sense it, this thing that you are."

With the Castilian elegance for which he was so famous in Europe, he raised the lid of the piano in the ship's lounge. I listened. The piece he played was very beautiful. The ocean rocked us gently, prolonging the music, and then, as usual, we started telling each other about our sleepless nights and latest sightings on the horizon, for every so often the sea would yield a glimpse of a lighthouse, an island, or another boat.

I thought Viñes's little greeting would never bother me again, now that it had been expressed in music, and I went to join the other passengers on board the *Massilia*.

There were Europeans on the ship, whose travel agents had persuaded them that the whole young American continent would reveal itself to them in the sound of a tango. And there were South American tourists, coming home from Paris with a sizable booty of dresses, perfumes, jewels, and *bons mots*. The older women talked freely and openly about all the pounds they'd taken off at their spas. Other women, even more brazen, showed me photographs in which the various surgical phases of their pretty little noses could be measured to the millimeter. A gentleman whispered to me about the success of a delicate operation: a dental transplant, using teeth bought on the cheap from people with no money.

The younger women made a game of appearing in four or five different dresses every day. They had to get some wear out of those dresses, for the South American customs officers were very hard on the practice, common among society women, of smuggling luxury items back from Europe. Between each new outfit they would douse themselves in heady perfumes. The Argentine and Brazilian women far outstripped the Europeans in the luxury of their attire. And they were always ready to play the guitar or sing the traditional songs of their countries at the drop of a hat. As the boat progressed, these daughters of the tropics began behaving more naturally and their distinctive character grew more conspicuous. Old and young alike, they twittered away in Portuguese and Spanish without giving the French women a chance to slip in even the briefest anecdote.

Rita, a young Brazilian, had discovered a way of making her guitar sound like a church bell ringing for mass or a carillon chiming from a campanile. She said she had first been inspired to do this during a Brazilian carnival, one of those nights of Negro sorcerers and Indians when women abandon themselves to their desires, their truth, the whole vast life of the trackless, virgin jungle. Rita's bells sometimes fooled the other passengers and brought them out onto the bridge. She claimed her guitar was a magical object and said she thought she would die if any harm ever came to it. Père Landhe, the priest she often confided in, was thoroughly disarmed by her and finally gave up lecturing her about her pagan desires and magical beliefs.

I liked Père Landhe. We would take long strolls together, talking about life, God, the problems of the heart, and how to become a better person. When he asked why I never appeared in the dining room, I told him I was in mourning for my husband, Enrique Gómez Carrillo,* and that I was making this journey at the invitation of the Argentine government, which my poor late husband, a diplomat, had represented in Europe for a time. Père Landhe, who was well acquainted with several of my late husband's books, did his best to console me; he listened while I told him, with all the sincerity of my youth, about the love a fifty-year-old man had awoken in me during the all-too-brief time of our marriage. I had inherited all his books, his name, his fortune, and several newspapers he had owned. A life, his life, had been entrusted to me, and I wanted to understand it, relive it, and go on with my own life in homage to his memory. I wanted to grow for him alone; that gift to him was my mission.

Ricardo Viñes had been one of my husband's close friends. Don Ricardo had paid special attention to me in Paris because, through my mother, I bore the same name as one of his friends, the Marquis de Sandoval, and for Viñes, Sandoval meant storms, the ocean, an unfettered life, and memories of the great conquistadors. Every woman in Paris adored him, but he was an ascetic—his greatest love affairs had never been anything more than musical. One day we heard Rita, the guitarist, say to him

*Enrique Gómez Carrillo: Internationally renowned journalist, novelist, and man-about-town who married Consuelo in December 1926 and suffered a fatal stroke eleven months later. Among his numerous books (an edition of his complete works published in 1923 filled twenty-six volumes) was a biography of the notorious World War I seductress and secret agent Mata Hari, in whose arrest he was rumored to have played a role, though he always denied it.

in a low, husky voice, "Is it true you belong to a very strict, secret order, even more severe than the Jesuits, a sect that requires you to devote yourself exclusively to art?"

"Of course," he replied. "Have you heard, as well, that we shave off half our mustaches on nights when the moon is full, and they grow back instantly?"

My other chaperone on that ocean liner was Benjamin Crémieux, who was going to Buenos Aires to deliver a series of lectures. He had the face of a rabbi, and there was fire in his gaze and warmth in his voice. His words, I felt, were charged with a secret power that reassured me.

"When you're not laughing, your hair grows sad," he told me. "Your hair tires out quicker than anything else about you. Your curls droop like sleepy children. It's curious: when you light up and start telling stories about magic and circuses and the volcanoes in El Salvador, your hair comes alive again, too. If you want to be beautiful, you must always laugh. Promise me that tonight you won't let your hair fall asleep."

He spoke to me as if I were a butterfly that he was asking to hold its wings open wide so he could have a better view of their colors. Despite the long, threadbare jacket he always wore and his beard, which made him look very serious, he was the youngest of my friends. His Jewish blood was pure and just. He seemed happy to be himself, to live his own life. He said he loved me because I knew how to transform myself into something new at every hour of the day. I didn't feel particularly flattered by this; I would have preferred to be like him, stable and contented with what God and nature had allowed me to be.

By the end of the voyage, Viñes, Crémieux, and I had become inseparable.

✦

ON THE NIGHT BEFORE our arrival in Buenos Aires, very late, Don Ricardo played a strange and brilliant prelude, then announced that it was titled "La niña del Massilia."

"That is you," he said, holding the sheets of music out to me. "You are *la niña*, the little girl, on this ship."

Rita immediately wanted to play the piece with him on her guitar, for only her guitar, she said, could reveal the true meaning of the music, and of what Viñes had sensed in me.

When we docked, caught up in the feverish activity of landing, we were like automatons, hardly speaking to one another except out of politeness. Then I heard someone shouting on the bridge: "Where is the widow of Gómez Carrillo? *¿Dónde está la viuda de Gómez Carrillo?*"

Only with an effort did I realize they were calling for me. "Señores, I am she," I murmured timidly.

"Oh! We thought you'd be an old lady!"

"I am what I can be," I said, as cameras flashed all around me. "Could you please direct me to a hotel?"

They thought I was joking. A government minister had come to the dock to welcome me. He announced that I was the guest of the Argentine government and that I would be staying at the Hotel España, the residence of of-

8

ficial guests. The president apologized for not receiving me at his home, but he was much occupied with a pending revolution.

"What? A revolution?"

"Yes, madame, and a real one. But he is wise, Don El Peludo, this is his third term in office. He knows how to handle this type of incident."

"Will it happen soon, your revolution? Do you often have revolutions in this country?"

"We haven't had one for quite some time now. They say this one will take place on Wednesday."

"Is there no way of preventing it?"

"No," the minister answered, "I don't think so. The president doesn't want to have anything to do with it. He's waiting calmly for the revolution to come to him. He refuses to take any measure against the students who are demonstrating in the street, shouting 'Down with El Peludo.' The situation is serious, but I'm happy that you still have several days ahead of you in which to pay a visit to the president. I would advise you to go and see him tomorrow morning. He was very fond of your husband and will be happy to talk about him with his widow."

The next day, therefore, I hired a car to take me to the Casa Rosada, the government residence. On the way, I passed the only New York–style skyscraper of which the Argentine capital could boast, after which the car plunged on past some vacant lots in the very heart of the city and a row of little houses that looked as if they had every intention of staying right there forever.

I found El Peludo, or "Shaggy-Head,"* as they called him, to be very wise and serene. He told me with a smile that he was getting on in years and ate hardly anything anymore except fresh eggs—he had managed to find some good hens, which he was raising on his property. He had always refused to live in the presidential palace, so he walked there every day from his own home.

Reluctant to mention the sudden death of our dear Gómez Carrillo, I asked the president what they could possibly be thinking of, all those people who were talking about a revolution happening on Wednesday. He grew serious but not somber. "They've decided to have their revolution," he said. "The students . . . they've been talking about it for several years now. Maybe they'll do it someday. If so, I hope it will be after I die. I've always given in to their demands. I sign, I sign, all day long, and I approve of all their positions."

"Perhaps you sign too much," I hazarded, "and that's the problem?"

"The death of Gómez Carrillo," he said, without answering me, "caused me great pain. As you know, he had promised to come to Buenos Aires for a while to take over the Ministry of Education, which I think is the most important of all the ministries. I followed all his advice and

*Hipólito Yrigoyen (1852–1933), president of Argentina from 1916 to 1922, reelected in 1928, and overthrown in a 1930 revolution led by General José Félix Uriburu.

replaced the old schoolmarms with young, pretty girls. I remember what a nightmare it was every morning when I was a boy to have to face my old-maid schoolteacher, with her false teeth, who had lost all her love for children. Now when a nice girl presents herself, even without a diploma, she's hired. . . . I think children must learn more easily from a beautiful woman . . ."

Smiling a little, I let him ramble on, imagining the complaints of parents whose children were being placed in the hands of ignorant, inexperienced beauty queens.

The minister, Señor G., invited me to a dinner with many other government officials that same evening. The revolution was still set for Wednesday. The women were very beautiful, and the food was superb. Meals in Buenos Aires are three times more abundant than in Europe. So far, I was enjoying my stay.

2

*B*ENJAMIN CRÉMIEUX had just given his first lecture at the Amigos del Arte. All of Buenos Aires society was there, and everyone was talking about the revolution.

"They're all very nice," Crémieux confided, "and I'd love to be able to stay on here for several weeks, but they're starting to scare me with their revolution. It seems to amuse them to speak of it. Maybe they think a revolution takes no victims. I was a soldier in the last war, and I don't like the sound of bullets. I'm a calm man by nature.

"Incidentally," he added, stroking his beard, "would you like to come by my hotel this afternoon? I want to introduce you to an interesting friend of mine, a Frenchman. Don't stand me up, whatever you do. I'll be waiting for you."

That afternoon at Crémieux's hotel, there was a cocktail party in his honor. People spoke of one thing or another, but conversation always returned to the revolution, which was beginning to get on my nerves. It occurred to me that this revolution was certainly taking its time in coming.

"And your revolution, when will it be?" someone would say jokingly.

"Mine's happening on Thursday, I'll wager anything you want," another would answer.

I glanced at the clock and decided to leave without saying good-bye to Crémieux, for fear he would try to stop me. As I was putting on my coat, a very tall, dark-haired man burst into the lobby. He came straight toward me and, tugging at the sleeves of my coat to keep me from putting it on, said, "You're leaving already, and I've barely just arrived! Stay a few minutes longer."

"But I've got to go," I said. "People are waiting for me."

Crémieux hurried over, his teeth gleaming against his black beard, and declared, "Yes, yes: stay. This is the man that I promised you would meet. I warned you on the boat that I was going to introduce you to an aviator you were certain to like because he's a man who loves Latin America as much as you do. He speaks Spanish—badly—but understands it very well."

Turning to face the dark-haired man, his hand on my arm, he said, tugging at his beard, "She's very Spanish, you know, and when a Spanish woman loses her temper, watch out!"

The dark-haired man was so tall, I had to raise my eyes to the sky in order to see him.

"Benjamin, you hadn't told me there would be such pretty women here. I'm very grateful."

Then, turning to me: "Don't leave. Here, have a seat in this armchair."

He pushed me so hard I lost my balance and found myself sitting down. He apologized, but I could no longer protest.

"Who are you, anyway?" I said at last, trying to reach the carpet with the tips of my toes, for I was literally a prisoner in the armchair, which was too deep and too high for me.

"I beg your pardon," Crémieux replied. "I forgot to introduce you. Antoine de Saint-Exupéry, pilot and aviator. He'll show you Buenos Aires from above, and the stars too. You see, he adores the stars."

"I don't like to fly," I said. "I don't like things that go fast. I don't like seeing too many faces at once. And I want to leave."

"But faces have nothing to do with stars!" the dark-haired man cried.

"You think our heads are so distant from the stars?"

"Oh!" he exclaimed in surprise. "You have stars in your head, do you?"

"I have yet to meet a man who has seen my true stars," I confessed with a touch of melancholy. "But we're talking nonsense. I told you I don't like to fly. Even walking too fast makes my head spin."

The dark-haired man had not released my arm and was crouching next to my armchair, examining me as if I were some indefinable object. I felt embarrassed and ridiculous, as if I were some kind of doll that could make a noise that resembled speech, or as if the words I spoke were losing their meaning. His hand pressed heavily on my arm, and in spite of myself I felt I was his prey, caged in the velvet armchair, unable to flee. He went on asking me questions and forcing me to answer. I wanted no further communication with him and felt utterly stupid, but something inside me made it impossible to leave. I began to rage against the female nature. I made one more attempt, like a firefly giving off its final burst of light, spirit, strength.

"I'm going," I said gently, struggling to extricate myself from the armchair.

His long arms blocked my way.

"But you know very well that you're coming with me in my plane to see the Rio de la Plata from beyond the clouds. It's fantastically beautiful, you'll see a sunset like no other in the world!"

Crémieux read the fear on my face, the fear of a bird caught in a trap. Wanting to come to my rescue, he declared firmly, "She has to go, Saint-Ex. A group of friends is waiting for her, and I must leave you as well. I have my guests to attend to."

But the dark-haired man was still blocking my way. He spoke in a serious voice now. "I'm sending my chauffeur to pick up your friends so that they can come with us and watch the sunset."

"That's impossible," I said. "There are twelve of them."

"So what? I have all the airplanes you could want. In this country I'm . . . well, let's say I'm the aviation boss. I'm in charge of the airmail service."

Resistance was futile. He was in command. He made a phone call to my friends; we were all in his hands.

The joy in Crémieux's expression helped me resign myself to my fate. I asked the dark-haired man to sit down and let me catch my breath. I pointed out that everyone was staring at us and that he was keeping me from breathing; I could barely speak.

He laughed wholeheartedly. Then, passing his hand over his cheeks, he swore loudly and said, "I haven't shaved! I'm just back from a flight that lasted two days and two nights."

He disappeared into the hotel barbershop and came back ten minutes later, smooth-cheeked and merry as a child. "Crémieux," he shouted, "next time you invite a pretty woman you must let me know in advance!"

"Oh really, no one let you know?" Crémieux asked pointedly.

"Let's have a drink, you and I, I'm thirsty," he said to

me. "And forgive me if I talk too much, I haven't seen a soul for almost a week. I'll tell you stories about Patagonia, about birds and monkeys smaller than my fist."

He took my hands in his. "How small they are!" he exclaimed. "You know, I can read palms."

He kept my hands for quite a while. I tried to pull away, but he didn't want to let go. "No, I'm studying them. The lines in your palm are parallel. You'll have a double life. I don't know how to explain it, but they're all parallel. No, I don't believe your character is entirely secret. But something has marked you. It was probably your country, the fact that you were transplanted from Central America to Europe."

Suddenly I was thrilled by his attention, but still I tried to resist. "I really don't like flying in planes," I said. "I don't like speed. I prefer to sit quietly in a corner. It must be because of my country. El Salvador is a land of earthquakes; between one minute and the next you can find yourself with the place Vendôme on your doorstep."

"Well, then," he said, laughing, "I'll go very slowly in my plane. I'm having a bus pick up your friends. They're staying at the Hotel Occidental; we're bringing them here for you. Look, the ones who agreed to join us are already here!"

EVERYTHING WAS ARRANGED, and twenty minutes later we were all jammed in a car en route to the airfield and the promised sunset. It took a good hour to drive from Buenos Aires to Pacheco, and in the crush of the car I listened to this dark-haired man tell me the story of his life, of his night flights. "You know, what you're telling me is so beautiful," I said to him, "you should write it down."

"Very well, I'll write, for you. I've already written a book, did you know? A memoir of my first airmail flights. I wrote it five years ago, when I was young."

"But five years is nothing!" I said.

"Five years is a long time. I was very young, in the Sahara Desert. . . . The book is called *Southern Mail.** We'll pass by my place on the way back, and I'll give you a copy. It was a complete flop. I sold three copies, one to my aunt, another to my sister, and another to a friend of my sister's. Three . . . People laughed at me, but if you say my stories are good, I'll write them down. I'll do it for you alone, a very long letter . . ."

I was the only woman in the car. Madame E., who was supposed to come with us, had begged off, claiming that the road out to the airfield was too dusty. Saint-Exupéry talked and talked with tremendous enthusiasm. His images had extraordinary charm, and there was a wild note of truth to even his most fantastical stories. Crémieux asked him questions, and he had an inexhaustible supply of answers. He said again that he hadn't spoken for a week and deluged us with a thousand tales of aviation.

We finally reached the airfield. A beautiful, silvery air-

---

*Saint-Exupéry's first book, *Courrier-Sud,* a barely fictionalized account of his experiences as a mail pilot, was published in France in 1928 and appeared in English in 1933.

plane was waiting for us. I wanted to ride in the passengers' cabin, but he insisted that I sit next to him in the copilot's seat. The cockpit was separated from the cabin by heavy curtains. I don't know how men could fly in those airplanes. He closed the curtains. I stole a glance at his hands: beautiful, intelligent, wiry hands, both delicate and strong; they were like the hands painted by Raphael, and his character was revealed in them. I was afraid, but I trusted him with my life.

When we took off, the muscles in his face relaxed. We were flying over plains and water. My stomach was queasy. I felt myself go pale and gave a deep sigh. The altitude plugged up my ears, and I wanted to yawn. Suddenly he cut off the throttle. "Have you flown many times before?"

"No. This is the first time," I said shyly.

"Do you like it?" he asked, looking at me in amusement.

"No, it's strange. Just strange."

He pulled the joystick down in order to speak into my ear. Then he pulled it back up again, then down again to talk to me some more. He teased and frightened us by doing loop-the-loops. I smiled.

He rested his hand on my knee and, leaning his cheek toward me, said, "Will you kiss me?"

"But Monsieur de Saint-Exupéry, you know that in my country we kiss people we love, and only when we know them very well. I'm a widow, a very recent widow. How can you ask me to kiss you?"

He nibbled at his lip to hold back a smile.

"Kiss me or I'll drown you," he said, making as if to plunge the plane into the ocean.

I bit my handkerchief in anger. Why did I have to kiss a man I'd only just met? The joke struck me as being in very bad taste.

"Is this how you persuade women to kiss you?" I asked. "It won't work with me. I've had enough of this flight. Land the plane, please; I'll be very glad when you do. I have just lost my husband, and I am sad."

"Oh no, we're falling!"

"I don't much care."

Then he gazed at me, cut off the power, and said, "I know what it is. You won't kiss me because I'm ugly."

I saw tears like pearls rolling from his eyes down onto his necktie, and my heart melted with tenderness. I leaned over as best I could and kissed him. He kissed me back violently, and we stayed like that for two or three minutes while the plane rose and fell as he cut the power off and revved it back up again. All the passengers were sick. We could hear them complaining and moaning behind us.

"No, you're not ugly," I said, "but you're too strong for me. You're hurting me. You don't kiss me; you bite me, you eat me. I want to land now."

"Forgive me," he said. "I don't know much about women. I love you because you're a child and you're scared."

"You're going to hurt me in the end. You're quite mad."

"I only seem to be. I always do whatever I want, even when it's bad for me."

"Listen, I can't shout like this any longer. Let's go back down to earth. I don't feel well, and I don't want to faint."

"That's not possible," he said. "Look, down there, the Rio de la Plata."

"Right, that's the Rio de la Plata, but I want to see the city."

"I hope you're not airsick . . ."

"A little."

"Here, take this pill. Stick out your tongue."

He put the pill in my mouth and squeezed my hands nervously. "What tiny hands! A child's hands. Give them to me forever!"

"But I don't want to have stumps at the end of my arms."

"What a silly fool you are! I'm asking you to marry me. I love your hands. I want to keep them all to myself."

"But you've known me only a few hours."

"You'll see," he said. "You will marry me."

We landed at last; all of our friends were sick. Crémieux had vomited all over his shirt, and Viñes felt completely unable to give his concert.

Saint-Exupéry carried me to the car. We were all three driven to his house. All my life I will remember that drive. We passed the windows of jewelers' shops, sparkling with precious stones—emeralds, immense diamonds, bracelets—and boutiques with feathers and tiny stuffed birds. It really was a Paris in miniature. . . . It reminded me of the rue de Rivoli.

We arrived and took an elevator up to Saint-Exupéry's bachelor quarters, where we had some coffee and then lay down wherever we could—Viñes and Crémieux on the same sofa, I in Saint-Exupéry's bed. My head was spinning, and my stomach was still upset. I no longer knew where I was. I curled up tight, and he read me a passage from *Southern Mail*. I could barely take in a word of it and finally blurted, "Please, would you leave me alone for a moment? I'm hot, I'd like to take a shower."

He went into the other room. I took a shower, and he gave me a bathrobe. I lay back down. He came and lay beside me, saying, "Don't be afraid, I won't rape you." Then he added, "I like to be liked. I don't like to steal things. I like to be given them."

I smiled. "Listen," I said. "I'll soon be back in Paris, and in spite of everything our flight will be a nice memory. It's just that right now my friends are all sick and I am too, a bit."

"Here," he said. "Have another pill."

I took the pill and fell asleep. I woke up during the night, and he gave me some hot broth. Then he had me watch a film he had made. "This is what I watch after my flights," he told me. The images were accompanied by a strange music, Indian songs. I was utterly worn out. This man was too overwhelming; his inner world was too rich. In some vague way I informed him that Viñes was giving a concert that evening and would have to be taken to the theater. He assured me that Viñes was fast asleep, that it was three o'clock in the morning, and that I should be a good girl and go back to sleep, too.

When I awoke, I was in his arms.

3

MEANWHILE, my friends had disappeared. When I saw them again several days later, they swore to me that they would never ride in an airplane again. Poor Crémieux! Just the word "airplane" made him feel queasy. "There are some kinds of nausea," he said, "that you never forget." The day of the revolution was approaching, so I proposed to Crémieux that we leave on the next boat, the following day.

"Don't worry," he said. "Let's give it another day. Why don't you come and have lunch with me at my hotel instead? Are you free?"

"Of course, darling. I'll see you tomorrow, then!"

I went back to my hotel, where everything was in a state of bubbling agitation. The chambermaids were coming and going and whispering endlessly behind the doors, but I was perfectly happy: the next day, I would have lunch with Crémieux, and then we would leave for Paris.

That evening, I had dinner with Minister G. at the hotel. He was an intelligent man, endowed with a singular liveliness of spirit and great tenderness. He had insisted on inviting me to dinner in memory of Gómez Carrillo. The atmosphere of the hotel contrasted with my state of mind, for I wanted to look lovely in his honor. I wore a white dress and sang as I walked through the corridors, with a veil of black lace over my hair.

I was aware of the political difficulties of the moment and found it very kind of the minister, under the circumstances, to devote his evening to me. He begged my pardon for choosing a table in a side room, as a precautionary measure.

"I've invited some friends of Gómez Carrillo," he said. "Their wives are lovely, and they're all eager to meet you. They want to see the woman who replaced 'La Violettera,' Raquel Meller, in the Master's heart!"

Gómez Carrillo's divorce and our subsequent marriage had fired their imagination. I didn't want to say another word about it and changed the subject to the president.

"But tell me about Don El Peludo. I think he's very nice. I spent an hour with him, and he talked to me about his hens. 'I'm getting old, I like fresh eggs,' he kept saying. I think he's grown tired of his responsibilities. He signs papers without looking at them."

Minister G. was a true friend of the president, but even he knew that the revolutionaries were preparing to throw him out of the Casa Rosada.

As we were being served a variety of wonderful dishes and Argentine wines, an urgent letter was delivered to our table, a letter from my pilot, who had just spent a day and a night in the sky. Still in the grip of the flight's emotions, he wrote about the storms he'd traveled through, the emergency landings. He spoke of flowers, squalls, dreams, and solid ground. He said he had returned to the land of men only in order to see me, to touch me, to take my hand. He begged me to wait for him quietly, like a good girl.

I laughed and read the letter aloud to the table. It began, "Madame, or darling, if you will allow me," and ended, "Your fiancé, if you will have me." We all thought the letter was marvelous and inspired.

That night I dreamed of his hands, which were signaling to me. The sky was an inferno. It was a night flight without hope, and I alone had the power to bring back the sun and set him on the right course once more. I awoke so agitated that I phoned Crémieux, good-hearted Crémieux, and woke him up. He reached the conclusion that I should accept Saint-Exupéry's proposal of marriage. After that dream, he said, I could not leave him on his own. "He has great talent as a writer; if you love him, he will write his book, and it will be magnificent." And Crémieux was right: *Night Flight* was born from that first love letter.

The next day, Crémieux, Viñes, Saint-Exupéry, and I were all sitting at a table in the Brasserie Munich together, laughing and talking merrily. "You'll write that great book of yours," Crémieux told Saint-Ex. "You'll see."

"If she is holding my hand," he answered. "If she will agree to be my wife."

⭐

At last I accepted him—I think I had run out of arguments. Mad with joy, he wanted to buy me the biggest diamond in all of Buenos Aires. Then he was called to the phone. "I have to go at once," he said. "Let's drive out to the airfield together; we'll celebrate our engagement there since that's where you first kissed me."

Crémieux did not want to accompany us on another expedition, so only Viñes came along, telling Saint-Exupéry, "Hurry up, or I'll start thinking I'm the one who's the fiancé of 'la niña del Massilia'! There's no piano here at your airfield," he complained once we were there. "You'll have to have one brought in."

"For you, I'll have one brought all the way from Paris," I laughed.

Tonio came over to us, his face serious. "I have to leave you," he said.

"But you can't leave me! We're supposed to be celebrating our engagement tonight." I was still laughing. I didn't understand the situation at all, but I was very happy.

"See that pilot over there, the one who's leaving? He's afraid. He already turned back once, out of fear. He claims he won't be able to get through."

"Get through what?" I asked.

"The night." Tonio snorted. "The weather forecast isn't very good. But it's always good enough for me. Daurat used to say, 'They must be saved from their own fear.' If he won't do it, I'm going to take his place. The mail has to go out this evening."

In the meantime, we ate oysters and drank white wine. I was beginning to feel afraid myself, afraid of the night. The telephones were all ringing at once; the telegraph, a couple of yards away, rasped out messages in Morse code.

The other pilots were asking for their orders. The halo of light over the radio operator gave him a sinister look.

After some time, we heard the loud roar of an engine. The space in front of my eyes was enveloped in a radiant, milky haze. Tonio rang a bell. An Argentine (the dresser, just like in the theater) arrived, and, quicker than words can say, slipped Tonio's boots on, wrapped him in a leather coat, and gave him his gloves. Outside, the other pilot clambered down from the plane. He'd turned back.

"Have him go to my office!" Tonio shouted as he gulped down the rest of the oysters, took a huge bite from the loaf of bread, and drank straight from the wine bottle. "I beg your pardon," he said to me, "I have to rush."

The frightened pilot came in, accompanied by a secretary. He stood there, ashamed, breathing heavily, no pride left in him. He took off his helmet.

Tonio dictated to the secretary: "Boulevard Haussmann, Paris. Pilot Albert has been dismissed; please send word to all the other aviation companies."

"If you send that message, I'll kill you!" Albert shouted. He moved toward Tonio, who was dashing to his plane.

"You, a man who is afraid of the night, you want to kill me?" Saint-Ex lashed out at him. "Wait until I get back!"

The pilot had a gun in his hand. He was weeping.

"You won't get through, you'll be crushed," he said, still weeping.

Viñes and I were paralyzed. A sip of white wine loosened the knots around our throats. *"Niña, niña, ¿nos vamos a casa?"* Viñes whispered to me, eager to leave.

"No, Ricardo. Tonight is my engagement party."

Ricardo smoothed his mustache. A shout rang across the hangar: "Ricardo Viñes!"

Viñes jumped. "What did I do wrong? I certainly have no wish to fly."

"A radiogram for you."

"For me?"

Ricardo was puzzled. He searched for his glasses, which refused to emerge from his pocket. Meanwhile, Pilot Albert was swearing as he headed off into the darkness, his head hanging low.

Ricardo finally read the message: "A thousand pardons for my absence. Go on with the engagement party at the airfield until I return. Clearer sky and better wind for my return. Around midnight, I hope. Your friend, Saint-Ex."

"A telegram, as fast as that? Bravo!" Viñes exclaimed, laughing from the quick sequence of conflicting emotions. "Well, after an engagement party like this one, the wedding promises to be *una boda magnífica, inesperada*— magnificent and unusual!"

That was the first of the night flights that would disturb my sleep from then on.

THE NEXT DAY we celebrated our engagement with a café au lait at the airfield. Tonio had flown the mail to the next station, where he found a replacement pilot. Someone announced that the revolution was going to break out that very day. I took the information calmly. Nothing could worry me, now that my pilot had come back.

Viñes and I returned to Buenos Aires to sleep. Tonio had to stay at the airfield, waiting for news about the mail delivery.

The telephone startled me out of my sleep. It was Crémieux. "Wake up! The revolution is here!" he shouted. "They're shooting in your street—can you hear it?"

"Oh, really?" I mumbled. "I got to bed very late last night . . . wait a second, I'm going over to the window. Yes, there are shots. I guess it is the revolution, but I'll come and have breakfast with you. Wait for me."

Hardly had I dressed when I realized that all the servants had disappeared. There was just one old man in a corner, who wanted nothing but handed me an urgent letter, which I tore out of his hands. Then Tonio suddenly appeared out of nowhere, like a devil, running into my room.

"Oh, there you are! I've been so afraid for you. The airfield is a long way from Buenos Aires. . . . The thought of getting here too late and losing you caused me more anguish than all my flights put together. Come!"

"But why? It's nothing, just a revolution. I saw revolutions in Mexico when I was fifteen, with my classmates. From time to time a bullet goes astray, but hardly anyone ever dies of it. Civilians don't know how to shoot. It takes years of practice for people to learn how to kill."

Tonio laughed. "Good, if you're not afraid, then I won't be either. Anyway, look, I've brought my camera. I want to film the revolution from down there, where the shooting is. My friends back in France will love it. You remember the short films I made that I showed you?"

"Yes," I said, "but first come with me to see Crémieux. He's waiting to have breakfast with us."

"He's waiting for you, not me."

"But we're engaged!"

"No one would think so," he said, staring into my eyes. "I have very little free time, but when I come to see you, you have other social engagements."

"Yes, if you can call a revolution a social engagement."

At this point we were walking slowly down the street and had started to argue. He didn't give me time to think. I wanted to protest. I told him I didn't want to spend my life at an airfield or sitting in a chair somewhere waiting for him. But the bullets whizzed past faster than my thoughts. He was squeezing my arm very hard.

"Hurry up!" he said. "We're going to get killed. Look, there are two, no, three men fallen in battle, right there."

"Maybe they're only wounded . . ."

"Walk, walk faster, *petite fille*! Or I'm going to have to carry you on my back." He gave the order very seriously, eyeing my high heels and the short steps I was taking.

"You must never run when crossing a street through gunfire," I told him. "The men on the opposite sidewalk, the revolutionaries, will be more likely to pick us out. Anyway, you don't look at all like an Argentine. The soldiers in the trucks aren't taking any notice of us, they're only shooting at armed men."

"If that's how you see it, why don't we dance down the middle of the street, little one?"

Some of the revolutionaries were forcing their way into private buildings; others were shooting from the rooftops.

A man armed with a rifle suddenly threatened us, but Tonio, in a strong, calm voice that resonated over the sound of gunfire, announced, "I am French. Look," he added, showing his Legion of Honor medal.

That gesture sufficed to resolve the situation, but I was still frightened. "Quick, let's run and hide behind that garage door."

We spent a good hour behind the door, watching the revolution. Men fell without a sound, they were quickly picked up and carried away, and others appeared from a tunnel to replace them. Then it became clear that we couldn't stay there any longer. We were growing nervous, so we walked to the corner. There was no revolution there, but the windows were shut and heads could be seen behind them, peering out: the agitation of an anthill in turmoil.

We finally reached Crémieux's hotel. He was glad to be able to discuss the morning's events with us. "El Peludo is your friend," he told me. "The people staying at this hotel are against him, so be careful what you say." He was laughing; it was his first revolution. A few planes were still threatening Buenos Aires, in case the government resisted. But at the Casa Rosada, El Peludo had surrendered unconditionally.

By late afternoon the revolutionaries had won. The insurgents began to throw the furniture of people who belonged to the president's party out into the streets. They tied a rope to his statue and dragged it along the ground, and set fire to all the ministries. Tonio and I ran back to my hotel to save my luggage and then went back to stay with Crémieux. Suddenly, a siren rang out. It belonged to a newspaper called *Crítica,* the government organ.

"Oh, no," I said. "What if that's the counterrevolution?"

"Where should we go?" Crémieux cried.

"I'm not going anywhere." I said firmly. "I'm appalled by all this upheaval. I came to Buenos Aires to relax!"

Tonio and Crémieux laughed. In the end we decided to go up to the roof, where Tonio could use his camera. "It would be such a pity not to film this," he said. We went from rooftop to rooftop. Tonio wanted to go down to the street. Crémieux advised me to keep my cool and let him take his pictures. "We'll stay tucked away in a little corner of the roof to keep an eye on the situation."

As it turned out, the offices of *Crítica,* located right next to the hotel, were engulfed in flames. The smoke choked us, forcing us to retreat.

That evening we drank cocktails at the hotel bar. Crémieux had definitely decided to leave the following Monday. No longer quite sure where I was or what I should do, I sat there in my torn dress, lost between the smoke from the burning newspaper offices and the flowers of the piano bar.

4

As I walked through the city, each step a new adventure, I wondered why it had befallen me to witness these strange things: the revolution, my visit to the president, his statue dragged through the street amid the nervous laughter of a young nation that believed itself to be free for the first time. The toppled statue was the symbol of that freedom. The marble had stood through fair weather and foul, but the storms in the students' hearts had done more damage than all the tempests of the pampas.

The real Don El Peludo would go to prison a few days later, on a boat that journeyed in darkness among islands where nothing could ever bring peace to his heart. He was old, and the plan was to have him "suicided" there, in the implacable winds that blow across the seas. Whole nights had been spent in discussion of where to send this dictator, whom the Argentine people themselves had engendered. No more lugubrious spot could be found for a man who, as even decent people said, was innocent but had neglected his duties as the father of his people.

I was afraid of the strange atmosphere hovering over Buenos Aires. No door offered any security, every window looked like a trap. It was all too much for a free citizen like me, arriving from Paris, where everything, even death, even misery and injustice, was so simple. Here everything had yet to be discovered or invented. I walked slowly. Why had I arrived at the exact moment when the anthill had exploded? Perhaps I was unlucky. I had come to find friends, to find peace to soothe my young widow's heart, and everywhere I found the discontent of this tropical race, which was boiling over for the first time.

In my pocket I could feel the love letter from my Flying Knight. I touched it with my fingertips and could sense it there with every step, every movement, every quiver of my hips. I told myself that it was a love letter. And love . . . love . . .

I went on' walking.

Too many emotions were sweeping through me. It was time for me to think, to grow up. I wanted to understand. I knew there was something in this whole story that I had yet to decipher. I didn't know if it was just me or if it was life in general that was making me listen so attentively to the rhythm of the new era that had come to meet me. I slowed down further, watching the gray sky that hung low over the mansard roofs of Buenos Aires: there was no shade in this landscape, no trees, only a few passersby. I dreamed of the beautiful chestnut trees of Paris, the Seine that curves through the city, the booksellers with their stalls along the quais who could always distract and calm me at times like these.

An Argentine friend once told me she owned five thousand trees. In Buenos Aires, the trees are numbered. All the trees you see there come from far away; they are brought to the city like prisoners, and promised that they will receive all kinds of love and care if they will only grow. In that country, men go out to find trees and ask them to come and grow back home, to give shelter and shade. I knew of some estates where the trees flourished under the constant care of gardeners. But the pampa is hard. It doesn't want to give anything away; it wants to be solitary, it wants to be the pampa. There's something quite magical about the effort the landowners expend to make anything green grow there. A harvest is a miracle. But the more obstacles man faces, the more worthy he becomes of bringing about miracles.

Tonio's letter was still rustling against my dress, against my hip, speaking to me even though I didn't want to listen. I was trying to understand what was happening to me in that hard and tender country. I felt alone, orphaned, far from the chestnut trees of avenue Henri-Martin in Paris, exiled from the Luxembourg Gardens. The haughtiness that arose from my solitude and my difficulty in seeing things clearly at least gave me the feeling that I really did exist.

I was being offered the role of the wife in a play. Was I right for the part? Did I really want to play it? I was starting to get a migraine from thinking so hard when, if only to relax a little, I finally yielded to the call of my love letter. I put my hand in my pocket and slowly drew it out. He, my Flying Knight, was offering me everything: his heart, his name, his life. He told me that his life was a flight and he wanted to sweep me off with him, that he found me light and delicate but believed that my youth

34

could withstand the surprises he promised me: sleepless nights, last-minute changes of plan, never any luggage, nothing at all except my life, suspended from his. He said again that he was sure of coming back to earth to find me, to snatch me up with dizzying speed, that I would be his garden, that he would give me light and I would give him solid ground on the earth, among men, the solid ground of a home, a cup of hot coffee made just for him, flowers always waiting for him on the table. I was afraid of reading these words; they made me want to look back, all the way back to my country, where the houses and people were safe.

The gloomy streets yielded up no sign to calm my fears. Suddenly I was overcome with exhaustion. I didn't even cry. I tore at my hair like an animal caught in a trap. Why should I accept this impossible union with a wild bird who would fly across skies that were too high for me? Why was my childlike soul allowing itself to be tempted by his promises of clouds and tomorrows full of rainbows? I closed my eyes, put the letter back in my pocket, and walked on toward a church to ask God for guidance. Only He could heal the wound that had opened in my heart. I remembered what my mother used to tell me: "God," she would say, "does not want us to be sad and confused. He wants us to be cheerful and strong." Then why do you perplex me like this, Lord? I shivered with fear. I was feverish, I couldn't go on thinking any longer, but my heart was whispering, "If Crémieux leaves without me, I'll be all alone, with no advice or protection. I'll be nothing more than a doll in the arms of the great aviator, the man who travels through the skies." The letter kept on murmuring with every step I took.

Finally I reached the church. It was Père Landhe's parish. He was there, as if he had been waiting for me. Immediately I told him about my lightning-fast engagement and took the letter from my pocket. He read it aloud, slowly, as if to inform me of its contents. Looking into my eyes, he said, "If you love him, I advise you to marry him. He is a force of nature, an honest man, a bachelor; with God's help you will found a happy home."

I took the letter from his hands and left him.

I found myself alone again, making my way through the sounds of Buenos Aires. By chance I happened to pass my former hotel, the Hotel España. Curious, I went in and asked to see my room. No one objected. The lobby and the stairways were a little chaotic, but the staff seemed calm and resigned. I pushed open the door of my room, where I had heard so much talk of the revolution. I found my trunk there, intact but too heavy for me to carry. A letter addressed to me lay on top. The envelope was stained, as if from drops of water. I opened it and began to read. It was another letter from my pilot, telling me once more that he wanted to marry me, that he refused to let me go back to France, that he knew very well I was a guest of the government and advised me not to get mixed up in the politics of the country, but to take the love he bore me seriously. Our friend Crémieux, he told me, was in favor of this marriage, which would be for life. He asked me to be a grown-up for him and to take care of his heart. I put this letter away in my pocket with the other one, and as the pages of the two letters slid against each other, they seemed to let out a soft lament.

Finally I left the hotel. In the street, I talked to myself. I saw his tender face again, his dark, round, piercing eyes. The last time I had seen him awake, after days and nights of flying, he had been as fresh as an angel who had passed through a stormy night but was ready to go dancing or take off and fly again. He could eat once a day or not at all; he could guzzle a barrel of liquid or go several days without swallowing a single drop. His only schedule was set by the storms in the sky and the tempests in his heart. Once, arriving at my hotel and watching me drink a glass of water, he said, "Oh! I know what I need. I haven't drunk anything since yesterday. Pour me a drink."

I handed him a glass of water and a bottle of cognac. He poured the whole bottle of cognac down his throat, and then the water, without thinking. He had forgotten that the other people who were there might also want a drink. He didn't even bother to excuse himself for this because he hated to lose the thread of the conversation. That really irritated him. If he was interrupted during one of his stories, he would sometimes remain silent for the rest of the evening. Or I should say for the whole night, since he never had any notion of what time it was. His visits would last until breakfast—he found such a pace entirely natural. Sometimes sleep caught up with him, and then he would sleep wherever he was and no one could wake him.

One day he was delivered from the airfield. He had given my address to his driver, who brought him to me fast asleep, as if dropping off a package. At the hotel, the staff said to me teasingly, "Your pilot is asleep, someone has just brought him for you. He sleeps! He sleeps!" What was I to do with this man? I stretched him out on a sofa, asked my chambermaid to take care of him when he awoke, and, to protect my reputation, left my room to him and took another one.

Tireless as he was, he could be annoyed at having to make the simplest gestures. For example, he hated to go to the trouble of tapping the ashes from his cigarette into an ashtray. Even if they were dropping into the folds of his pants, he would ignore them to keep from interrupting a conversation, seemingly oblivious to the fate of his clothing. So what if his pants caught fire!

I continued to walk alone through the streets, dreaming of my sleeping pilot. I must have looked like a fool, wandering around, bumping into passersby, not knowing where I was going. Suddenly a man took hold of my arm and shouted, "Get in! Get into the car."

"Is that you, Tonio?"

"Yes, it's me. I've been looking all over for you. You look wretched, you're all hunched over. What's wrong? Have you lost something?"

"I think I've lost my head."

He laughed exuberantly and said, "My driver was the one who recognized you. I wouldn't have known it was you. Why are you so sad? You look like an orphan."

"I look sad because I don't have the courage to escape from you," I said. "And I think I don't want to understand the truth: for you, I am nothing but a dream. You like to play with life, you're not afraid of anything, not even of me. But I want you to know that I am not an object or a doll: I don't change faces on command, I like to sit down every day in the same place, on my own chair, and I know that you, you like to leave, to go to a new place every day. If you tell me honestly that your letter and your declaration of love are nothing more than an essay on love, a fairy tale, a dream of love, I won't be angry. You're a great poet, a flying knight, a handsome fellow, strong and smart. Don't mock a poor girl like me who has no treasure other than her heart and her life."

"So what you're saying," he answered, "is that somehow you think I have too many good qualities to be your husband?"

"To make a good husband, perhaps," I said pensively.

"Oh, women are all alike! They love to hear about other people's love, but to live it, to love with their own hearts, that's something else entirely—something that is given only by the grace of God. Why don't you believe in love?" he asked, holding my hand very tightly. "Why, young as you are, are you so mistrustful of life? Why are you so bitter about the sweetness of living?"

"How many women have you wanted to marry, Tonio? How many fiancées have you had?"

"I'll tell you. Only one, when I was very young. I was engaged to a young girl who was paralyzed, in a body cast. The doctor said she might never again be able to walk, but I played with her and I loved her. She was the fiancée of my games and my dreams. Only her head could move, outside the plaster, to tell me her dreams. But she also told me lies. She was engaged to all my friends, and she made each one of them believe he was the one master of her heart. And in a sense we all were. But later the other fiancés married women who could walk, and I was the only one who stayed with her. So she loved me for my fidelity. Then the grown-ups started interfering in our engagement. The grown-ups found another, richer fiancé, and I wept. Yes, I wept. I was useless, but the time had come for me to do my military service. I chose aviation. I was just at the age limit, I had to work miracles. . . . In Morocco, a colonel wanted to take me under his wing. I came back as a commercial pilot and I've never left aviation, because I'm faithful. I haven't forgotten my first fiancée; this is the first time I've wanted another one."

"And your parents?"

"Oh, my mother is a very good woman. I'll ask her to come to our wedding. She'll understand."

"But my family is waiting for me in San Salvador. I was widowed a very short time ago, and we hardly know each other. What's more, I'm practically engaged to Lucien, a friend of my late husband's. You, you're always busy with your flights."

"No, no, I'm not always flying, I only fly when something goes wrong. I have several pilots who fly into the interior of South America. But if you want, I'll take you to visit each of the stops on the France–South America line: Paraguay, Patagonia, and farther still. . . . I've built airfields, seen little villages, but it's all starting to function on its own. I'll stay in Buenos Aires to supervise the lines. I'll write. I haven't written anything since *Southern Mail*. Except the forty-page letter I wrote for you. And to say that

I admire you, that I love you. Every day I'll ask you to be my companion for life. I need you. I swear to you, I know you are the woman for me."

"I'm overwhelmed," I said. "If I believed I could bring you something fine, something beautiful, I might be able to decide to remarry—but not so quickly. Tonio, are you sure you want a wife for your whole life?"

"Consuelo," he said, "I want you for all eternity. I've thought of everything. Here's the telegram I sent to my mother. It went out yesterday. I cannot leave you for a single day. Look at the letters I've sent you every day—I can't do anything now but love you. If you love me, I will strive to give you a famous name, a name as celebrated as your husband, Gómez Carrillo's. You will be far better off giving up a life as a great man's widow to become the wife of a living man who will protect you with all his strength. To convince you of this, I've just written you a letter a hundred pages long. Read it, please, I beg you. It is the storm in my heart, the storm in my life, which comes to you from far, far away. Believe me: before you, I was alone in the world, desperate. That was why I went to live in the desert as an airplane mechanic. I had no woman, no hope, no purpose. Then I was posted here, where I earn a handsome living. I have a bank account. I've been saving money for twenty-six years. I live in a little bachelor flat on the passage Geremez, a place where only birds live, and a few people from time to time. I took the flat for a week and stayed on. I will faithfully carry out my duty to those I love. And my life as a pilot—well, you know it has its risks, like all professions. I haven't even bought myself a winter coat yet, for fear I won't manage to make it through till winter."

I think I interested him because, like him, I could do things my own way if I wanted to. The two of us could form a new kind of union; we could be free together.

Crémieux approved of our plans. "You're going to live an intense life," he said to Tonio. "Don't let jealous people get to you, always keep moving ahead." And he confided to me, "He's a great fellow: make him write, and people will talk about the two of you." A few days later, Crémieux left.

At the Brasserie Munich, my big Tonio, in a white suit, pretended he couldn't sleep and that soon, in just a few days, we would be married. His mother was coming. A pretty house had been rented for us, in Tagle. And if I was good, he told me, I could live there right away, without hiding from Buenos Aires society, because he would be my life, my whole life.

So I went to Tagle. Some friends came for a house-warming party, and Ricardo, who was still giving concerts, came to our home and staggered us with his immense talent, which fired Tonio's imagination. Marriage would wait until my future mother-in-law had arrived.

The house in Tagle was small, but it had spacious terraces and an isolated study where I put a small cask of port with a golden tap. I also hung a guanaco's skin on the wall, along with some animal heads and a few of my own drawings. Our friends called it "the room of the *enfants terribles*."

I was happy. "When you look deep inside yourself for marvels, sometimes you find them. I could say, as a Christian, that when you seek the divine, you shall find it."

5

"WHERE DOES ALL THIS BELONG, Tonio?" I said, eying his suitcases and trunks full of papers in the entryway of our new house.

"It doesn't much matter. In the garage, so as not to clutter up the house. All ten trunks are made of wood and nailed shut, so the papers are safe. In any case, I don't remember what I can possibly have put in there. But this is all I have, darling. I take them from one place to the next. Every trunk is a stopover, a hotel I've stayed in since I became a pilot. But I haven't always been a pilot—I was also a mechanic on the Río de Oro once . . . I was young then!"

"When was that, Tonio?"

"Three years ago. Life goes fast, you know. I can still remember when Monsieur Daurat called me into his office one day. He doesn't say much as a rule. He acts, he thinks. He loves his work because it connects him to the forward surge of humanity. He always seems to set in motion whatever is best in a man. The pilots don't much like him, but they want to be like him. . . . And I do, too. I'd done a few flights on the line, here and there. Then one day in Toulouse, he wanted me in his office. 'You're going to leave for Port-Etienne, in Mauritania,' he tells me.

'Takeoff is at three-fifteen. You'll spend a few months there. The work is easy, but we often lose planes.' I say to Daurat, 'But I'll be far away from my family!' 'You'll write to them by airmail,' he snaps back. 'But my luggage?' I protested. 'Don't take much, we've got a lot of mail to carry on the plane. You can take your razor and your toothbrush. It's hot there: ninety degrees in the shade.' Then, very loudly, he says, 'Be there on time. Next!'

"And another pilot came in. I was floored. Should I go? I knew perfectly well that if I refused, I'd be fired. It would mean the end of my career as a pilot. I put all my plans and appointments out of my mind and asked my conscience: Refuse or accept? I had to accept: refusal would be too easy. I could always say no once I was there and come back. After all, it wasn't a jail. I wrote to my mother and my friends, and there I was, on time, at the airfield. Monsieur Daurat walked me to the plane without a word. Once I was in the air, he waved.

"The next evening we were in Port-Etienne. We drank coffee, ate some chocolate. The radioman had a good supply. As usual, I hadn't brought a thing. But I've kept you standing there, my darling. Let's sit on my trunks, just as we did in Port-Etienne. Monsieur Daurat sent them to me, one by one, and I had them nailed shut like that. Everything I had was inside them. But at Port-Etienne I didn't need anything. I'd wrap a towel around my head for long walks, but more often than not I was naked. I always had a rifle with me; it was dangerous to go too far from the hangar. The Maures were and still are the Christians' enemies, but they were the purest people I have ever known.

"We had to negotiate with them very adroitly in order to build a hangar. The talks were like the intrigues of the *Thousand and One Nights*. They asked for the hangar's weight in gold before they would let us set up a base there. Later I learned that the trick was always to say yes and to discuss the real price afterward. They demanded a thousand camels and a thousand slaves armed with nine thousand rifles, two thousand pounds of sugar and of tea—and we said yes to everything. Finally we met with the tribe's chief, who showed up to hear our response with his face covered, accompanied by two of his men bearing loaded guns. We offered them mint tea, which they never refused. We all had to squat down on our haunches, and that gave them confidence. In the end: a hundred pesetas, ten pounds of tea, and the same of sugar, and as for the slaves, we would buy them when we could find some, which wasn't easy. Do you know the proper way to make a slave?"

"No."

"You're not tired of this?"

"No," I said. "I love your stories, I feel as though there's no end to them."

"Well, then: the Maures send their most trusted men to buy tea, dried mint, sugar, and guns. These men reach the pasturelands full of flocks that belong to rich merchants who deal in rugs, honey, or copper, and they are very friendly. The herdsmen let themselves be charmed, even though they know that these Maures, disguised as Moroccans, are wolves. But an Arab loves to play. Then the Maure sets his trap: 'Come with me,' he says. 'You know the region well. I have a little flock in such and such a place, I'll trust you with it. You'll be my friend.'

"And the herdsman gathers up his provisions, says good-bye to his wife, and leaves. Once they're on rebel territory, the Maures run into other Maures, as if by chance. They say to the shepherd, 'Ah, we're going to make a good slave of you, you're solid, we like you.' They put him in a hole for several days, taking him out for one hour each day in order to put another slave in and to beat him with a stick. They give him a good thrashing. He receives a glass of water and is then returned to the hole to stand with a box over his head. After the full moon, there's a ceremony. He's taken out of the hole, and this time there are no beatings. He's dressed in new clothes, and he's allowed to sleep. A beautiful female slave massages him—she's his new wife—and everyone is his friend. It's up to him now to be a good and faithful slave. If he tries to escape, as they expect him to, he'll be caught by another tribe, where he can expect the same treatment. After three or four times, even the most hardened man will indeed become a good slave. If he's young, he'll become the lover of his master's wife; then he'll poison the water and escape with her to another tribe . . ."

"Yes," I said, "there are ways and ways of making slaves of all of us, even in the Bible. I would like to be your slave, but for love."

"Petite fille," Tonio said with a laugh, "you don't know what you're saying."

Standing among all those trunks he looked immense to me, a giant. He had the strength of a Maure. We decided that the trunks would go into his study, on the second floor. He carried them up effortlessly, as if each one were a single book. I was ashamed, I felt unworthy of him. I thought I should have moved them long before, to make him finally feel at home.

The next day, after he had left for the airfield at five in the morning, I started opening his trunks. It took three days of such hard work that I thought my head would explode. I forbade him to go up and see what I was doing, and then, on the third day, I announced, "Go to your study."

"If you want me to," he said, pensive.

He went in.

"Oh! No more trunks!" he cried, going red with anger. "But who has touched my things?"

"Me."

"You, my sweet?"

"Everything has been organized on this big worktable here. It wasn't easy. Look: the thickest files are over here, and these little papers are the radiotelegrams you've received on your flights. Each bundle is pinned to a page and then placed in a folder, numbered in red ink in the following order: (1) letters from Moroccan women; (2) letters from French women; (3) letters from your family; (4) business letters and old telegrams; (5) notes on flying;

(6) unfinished letters, handwritten manuscripts, rough drafts, notes on fear, family photos, photos of cities, photos of women, old newspaper clippings.

"And in here I put books, notebooks, flight logbooks, and some stacks of files—on music, on songs, on cameras and lenses. And in the bookshelf's compartments, an album of collages. And the little things, the souvenirs, are on the bookshelf. The trunks are all empty now. Nothing's been left out, I swear. All that remains are the envelopes from a few letters, with some old newspapers in one of them. I've done my best so that you'll have all your things here in our house."

"Yes, yes," he said. "But would you mind leaving me now? I need to be alone. I'm very grateful. I'll work night and day on your book."

"On your tempest," I said.

"No, the tempest is over, but I must tell its story, to make you happy. Give me some tea, I don't want any dinner. I want to stay up here with my papers."

So I shut my fiancé in his study. Only if he showed me five or six pages of work did he have the right to come into the future newlyweds' bedroom. Not before. He liked my little game.

Our Czech servants, Léon and his wife, often asked me about our marriage. There had been no word from Tonio's mother. We had learned from some friends at the consulate that his family was making inquiries about my origins. That bothered me, and for the first time sadness overcame us. I was beginning to feel stifled, but I didn't slow the pace of his mandated task. He buckled down to work and even thanked me for my severity.

My friends in Argentina kept asking, "So when is the wedding?" Two of my former husband's friends came to tell us that we were the scandal of Buenos Aires, that I owed it to the memory of Gómez Carrillo not to behave like this. I let Tonio answer them.

The date we had set for our wedding was not far off. When it arrived, we went to city hall together to put our names down in the register. I was glad. If his mother wasn't coming . . . well, we'd wait for her to arrive before having the church wedding. We were in agreement about this, and our diplomat friends agreed with us, too. After all, we were in charge of our own lives. I was wearing a new outfit that day, and so was he. When our business at city hall was over, we had decided to go to the Brasserie Munich, just the two of us.

"Name? Address? The woman first."

I gave my name and address, then it was his turn. He was shaking. He looked at me, crying like a child. I couldn't do it. No, it was too sad. "No, no," I blurted, "I don't want to marry a man who's weeping. No."

I tugged at his sleeve, and we careened down the steps of city hall as if we'd both lost our minds. It was over. I could feel my heart beating in my throat. He took both my hands and said, "Thank you, thank you, you are good, you are very good. I can't get married so far from my family. My mother will arrive soon."

"Yes, Tonio," I said quietly, "it will be better that way."

Neither of us was crying anymore.

"Come," he said, "let's have lunch."

In secret, I swore to myself that I would never go back up the stairs to city hall. I was still shaking. I was certain that I had come to the end of my adventure.

★

The house in Tagle, which had trilled and warbled with birds and with our dreams, became gloomy. I felt as if I could no longer breathe. Our friends stopped coming to visit as often, and I spent hours looking out across the plains in front of the house, my head empty, my heart shattered. I was in love with a boy who was afraid to get married. He had seduced me, and now he was growing more and more distant.

My Argentine friends no longer invited me to their homes. In their eyes I was shameless, a merry widow. My pilot went out alone. I prayed to God and decided never again to speak to Tonio about our botched plan to marry. After he thanked me outside city hall, he didn't bring the subject up again. I had lost my return ticket to France. As the widow of an Argentine diplomat, I should have been entitled to a pension, but I no longer dared ask Gómez Carrillo's friends for anything.

I shut myself up in the house in Tagle. Tonio often found reasons not to be there for meals. It was like an un-spoken agreement between us; even if he was staying in Buenos Aires, he no longer ate any of his meals at home. He would come home at night to change his shirt and shave, while I stayed in my little boudoir, pretending to read a newspaper or a book. He would say, "I'll see you soon, *chérie*," and give me a guilty kiss, then flee into the night, trembling.

He would come home very late and find me waiting for him, always wearing an evening gown, smiling as if I were on my way to a ball; I would have a literary anecdote at the ready, a story from former days. We would drink very cold champagne, he would relax a little, and though I was dying of sadness I pretended nothing had changed between us. I would say, "Only five pages of tempest this evening." And he would go to his study.

"Lead me by the hand," he would say. "I don't know my way up the stairs." He loved to act the child. I set him down in his armchair, kissed him, and repeated in his ear, "You must write, write. Crémieux said so: 'He must write.' So hurry!"

"Thank you, thank you," he would mumble. "I'll write, because you ask me to." And in the morning I would find a few illegible pages on the little desk in my boudoir.

He would leave early for work, and I would sleep away the whole morning. Around three or four in the afternoon I would emerge from my bed, exhausted. I wasn't eating, and Léon would say, "If Madame does not eat, my wife and I will not eat, either."

An invitation for tea at the home of one of our lady friends arrived one day, but it was for Tonio alone. He came home to change and shave, as usual. My heart couldn't bear it any longer. I asked him to stay home with me, but he refused.

"I have a dinner to go to as well," he said.

I dressed in black and went out into the street, mad with grief. I wandered about at random and insulted my reflection in the windows. Suddenly, a young man stopped in front of me. He was a great admirer of Gómez Carrillo.

"Consuelito, are you all alone?"

"Yes, Luisito," I replied forlornly.

"But come, come!"

"Where?"

"To a tea."

"I'm not invited."

"But it's being given by my aunt," he said. "Come, quickly!"

I was welcomed with open arms and a certain degree of malice. On my friend's arm, I recovered my courage. Suddenly I was fine, far from my Don Juan pilot who told his stories about the desert with such great success. I announced that I was leaving on the next boat, that urgent matters were calling me back to Paris.

After that flowers filled the house once more, and Enrique's friends, too. They showered me with their affection. Now it was my turn to receive invitations. As for my pilot, he stayed home alone in Tagle, waiting for his mother.

I finally reserved a cabin on the next ocean liner.

"When your mother arrives," I said to Tonio, "you can tell her I had something to do in Paris. Lucien is waiting for me, I am going to marry him. It's my destiny."

He didn't say a word.

The days rushed by. Friends came to visit; we went to

the movies and took endless, rambling walks. Finally I found myself on the boat that was taking me back to France, my heart in ruins. My cabin was full of flowers: my friends had understood my sadness.

I fell asleep before the boat had begun to move. When I woke up, we were out on the open sea. The steward brought me a telegram. It was from Saint-Exupéry. I was also told that he was flying his plane over the boat. He would surface on the horizon from time to time and signal me from the sky. I was frightened almost to death.

I didn't leave my cabin until Rio de Janeiro, where I saw my teacher and friend, the great Mexican writer Alfonso Reyes. I was told that Tonio's mother was on another boat anchored there in the bay for a few hours. I tried to ignore this.

After eighteen days, we arrived: Le Havre, customs, my apartment on rue de Castellane. I was back in Paris. When I asked for Lucien, my concierge said he had not arrived. Where was he? There was a knock at the door: it was Lucien. Then the telephone rang, and I picked it up before I'd even had time to greet him.

"*Allô?*"

"Buenos Aires calling, please stay on the line."

Then: "It's me, Tonio. *Chérie,* I'm coming on the next boat to join you, to marry you."

"Oh, really? Listen, I have a visitor."

"Lucien?"

"Yes."

"Well, send him away. I don't want you to see him. I'm bringing you a puma."

"What?"

"A puma. I'll disembark in Spain so I can see you sooner. Leave for Spain right away. The trains are bad, so have a rest in Madrid, then wait for me in Almería."

"Excuse me, I thought I told you I had a visitor."

After that it was the same conversation, night and day. Finally I gave in after he told me, "Since you left, Léon, the valet, is always drunk, the rice is undercooked, and my underwear is being stolen. I will come to get you and marry you in any country in the world and you'll arrange a lovely room for me, but without a cask with a golden spigot, because that's been stolen, too. I'm not writing anymore. I'm making my mother cry because I'm in despair. Our separation is driving me mad."

I loved him, but I also realized how calm my life was without him. I had a considerable income as the widow of Gómez Carrillo, but if I married anyone else I would lose it. I had a lot of work to do, putting things in order, and I needed time for serious reflection, but the phone calls from Buenos Aires, from the little house in Tagle, drove me out of my mind. So one day I yielded. "Yes," I said. "I'll meet you in Almería."

I left without telling Lucien, who was behaving very badly. My dog would stay with the secretary, who said she loved it fiercely, as much as she loved my car. Everything was as it had been before.

I have a very precise memory of the local train, the hot bricks and copper boxes filled with boiling water to warm us up. Someone in another compartment was playing the guitar. To the rhythm of the train's rocking movement, I heard the chorus *"Porque yo te quiero, porque yo te quiero,"* and I traveled toward my Tonio telling myself, "Because I love you . . . because I love you . . ."

Madrid, and then Almería, the day of his arrival. I managed to get a special permit and went out to meet the ocean liner in a little rowboat. The ocean liner had had a breakdown, a broken propeller, and wouldn't be able to dock for a few days. My presence was announced; someone shouted: "The wife of the aviator Saint-Exupéry." He heard that and left his mother on the boat with the puma to throw himself into my arms. He told me that the whole family was waiting for him and his mother in Marseille. But he didn't want to introduce us right away. We had so much to say to each other, he said. His mother had hinted that marriage to a foreigner would shock the elderly members of the family. She had concluded, "But everything always works out in the end, with patience."

She was very diplomatic with him. She knew he was a child at heart and if you handled him the wrong way he would run away forever.

"I don't want to rush things with my mother, *tu comprends?* I'll leave the ship secretly in Almería, we'll buy an old car, hire a driver, and cross Spain on our honeymoon."

I said yes to everything.

Valencia . . . the people in the little inns . . . the laughter of our young lives . . .

Part Two

The South of France, 1931

6

ANTOINE REALLY WAS UNLIKE any other man. I
told myself I was insane: I had a house in France
and a fortune, thanks to the generosity of my late husband
who had made me his heir. Why torment myself further?
Everything could be so simple . . . I had friends in Paris,
and if I gave up the idea of marrying Tonio I could keep
my fortune, for Gómez Carrillo had been rich, he had
published books in Spain, in Paris; everything would be
easy for me if only I kept his name.

But I always went back to Tonio. In my mind, I had already begun to organize our life together. We would go
and live in my house, the Mirador, in the south of France;
it had been Gómez Carrillo's final home. Tonio would
finish his book, and then we would travel to Italy, Africa,
China. He would be a pilot again, for the Compagnie
Aéro-Orient. Plans ran through my head . . .

We had said nothing to each other about our difficulties. In every village we passed through, he gave me presents. "I want you to lose everything you have," he said, "so
that every single thing you're wearing will have come from
my hands."

He was thin; he looked as if he had suffered. The first
evening we were together again, we couldn't leave Al-

mería. Our feelings were too strong, and mingled with them were shyness and pain.

"I have only one question to ask you," he murmured, pale and worried, trembling with tenderness. "I haven't slept for the last several nights, though you know I'm never bothered by a lack of sleep, but only by the hours that separate me from you. My puma was unhappy on the boat—I couldn't feed it very well, and it tried to bite one of the sailors—I'm sure they're going to put it to sleep. But I was even more unhappy than the puma. I couldn't think of anything but your face, your way of talking. Speak to me, speak to me! I beg you. You're not saying anything, why? Do you think I haven't suffered enough? The phone calls I made from Buenos Aires were torture, and you never wanted to speak loudly or distinctly. Why? Did you always have a visitor with you? But I'm mad, I have no more time for unhappiness, I'm with you again now and no one in the world will ever be able to separate us. Will they?"

"Yes, Tonio," I said quietly. "Love is like faith. I left because you didn't trust me. Your family, too, they were asking for information about me, which, you must understand, was very painful to me."

"Listen, little one, let me explain. Where my parents live, in Provence, the men marry women of their own background, whose parents know their parents and grandparents, and so on from generation to generation. Someone new, in our country, it's like an earthquake, and so they wanted more information, in order to know, to be reassured. In Paris it's less unusual, the young men from good families marry rich American girls. But in Provence, no—we've kept the old ways. My poor dear mother lost her head and made us wait a little while, that's all. Besides, I'm very happy with the way you've handled things. If you hadn't left, my mother would have married us off in Buenos Aires, and I would have been uncomfortable. I don't really understand what happened when we were at city hall. I said to myself: this is for life, but I'm not sure I'll make her happy. Then I thought, since she wants to go, let her go; she's the one who'll take responsibility for the break, and that's for the best right now. At the time I had some very complicated matters to settle at the office with the Argentine airmail service. I was signing checks without knowing what they were paying for and my sweet mother was taking her time in coming across the Atlantic. Then you left me, and I was glad. Yes, I was glad, because you proved to me that you could live your life on your own. I knew you were sad, and so strong, so beautiful, and I wanted to see where your strength would take you. Only I didn't think much about what it would actually mean. When you were really gone, I could have thrown myself into the ocean. My mother can tell you about the trip we took to Asunción Lake in Paraguay. I never once opened my mouth. I was counting the hours, waiting to take the boat to come and find you. I would have carried you off no matter what, even if you hadn't come to Almería, even if you had married Lucien. But speak to me! Tell me that you need me too."

"Ah, Tonio," I said. "The truth is that I'm here now but I've gone back to Lucien. I told him our whole story, all my grief, and he consoled me and promised he would make me forget it all. And yet here I am. I've vanished from Paris without saying a word to him. I sent him a telegram from Madrid in a moment of remorse—I don't know what I told him."

"Don't worry," he said. "Don't think about anything except us."

"But he's only human, and I'm making him suffer . . ."

"Don't be afraid, I'll go see him. I'll explain that we're mad, the two of us, dangerously mad, mad with love. And that he, my God, is an old friend of yours, a friend for life. I don't hold the fact that he loves you against him. The whole world should love you! And I'll get your dog back, and your car, and your papers. Promise me we won't ever talk about him again, never. You don't need to know anything about it, I'll arrange everything in a very friendly way."

"Very well, Tonio," I said. "I entrust myself to you forever, forever . . ."

After that we stayed at the hotel in Almería for several days. He decided to hire a taxi to make excursions in the city and then to cross Spain. He didn't want to drive; we would be too far from each other, he said. The Valencia oranges, the little villages perched on white rocks, the places he had visited in his youth, he wanted to show me everything. He laughed like an oversized child. Our constant chattering in French drove the Spanish driver crazy.

At last we had to go back to France, because of my dog or Lucien or his family, I don't remember. He wanted to stay a few days longer, but I was afraid of keeping him from his family for too long; they were waiting for him and didn't know where he was.

*

BACK IN THE SOUTH OF FRANCE, we were happy at the Mirador, not far from Nice. Nothing troubled us except the smell of the mimosas, which was sometimes too strong. We couldn't bring ourselves to burn the bouquets, so we were constantly sneezing. Oh, the mimosas and the handkerchiefs in all colors! I was a newly engaged woman, but this time I wasn't waiting for a wedding. We said we were going to break with tradition, that we wouldn't go the way of people who hate each other because they're forced to marry or who marry to please their families. "You are my freedom," he told me. "You are the land where I want to live for the rest of my life. We are the law."

Agay, the home of Tonio's brother-in-law where his sister Didi lived, was only an hour away from the Mirador. Didi came to see us. The two of them walked in the gardens for hours, and I stayed behind, sitting in an armchair, waiting for their conversation to end.

"I beg of you, young future bride," Tonio said, "you who read books, don't wait for us. There is no end to a conversation when it is about you. The end is your disappearance—so sing, read, work!"

One day his sister told us that one of their cousins was coming to see Tonio and his young fiancée. I was nervous. Who was this cousin, really?

"A duchess," Tonio told me.

"Oh no, Tonio, I won't come with you. You go and see her on your own."

"She's coming with André Gide, you know," he said.

"Really?"

"André Gide is a great friend of my cousin's. He wants to speak to me. Come along with me."

At the request of the old writer and the duchess cousin, I decided to go. I was sure the cousin wanted to introduce some rich woman to Tonio. My God, the things that I, a slight young woman from the land of volcanos, was experiencing and coming to understand! I didn't know what tactics duchesses used or what kinds of intrigues relatives might devise in order to arrange a suitable marriage.

Gide did indeed come to Agay with the famous cousin. His voice was sugary and sometimes saccharine, the voice of a female worn out by sorrow and unconsummated love. There was nothing extraordinary about the cousin; she was elegant in her beautiful car, nothing more. She made a great show of being kind, but only Tonio's mother was really nice to me, at once attentive and compassionate.

The examination was going well, but then, during the meal, I drank something the wrong way and choked. The hairdresser had made my hair too curly, I was sweating, and my digestion was sluggish—to top it all off, I spilled wine on Tonio's pants. I don't remember anything else after that; a powerful migraine erased the faces of friends and guests for two days, and I stayed in darkness at the Mirador. I could hear Tonio circling like a caged puma.

Still, he was beginning to feel at home at the Mirador; he would leave, come back, go out again.

He also took care of me. He had stayed clear of the doctors in Nice and was reading strange medical treatises written by Spanish scholars. Among Gómez Carrillo's books he had discovered some famous works on magic that my former husband had written, and he spent whole days and nights bent over those arcane recipes, laughing like a child at his new game. He repeated the strange stories I told him during my delirium, a peculiar delirium without fever.

I was trembling with weakness and fear. He reassured me as best he could. He wanted me to be confident in life, but I was terrified at the prospect of seeing his family and friends again. What love-stricken young woman wouldn't tremble before a whole tribe that thought it owned her fiancé? I was of a different stock—I came from another land, another tribe, I spoke another language, I ate differently, I lived in a different way. That was why I was afraid, but my fiancé would give me no hint as to how I should behave.

I did not understand why there had been, from the beginning, so many misunderstandings about this marriage. Money could easily be acquired through the books and goods of Gómez Carrillo—one trip to Spain, and pesetas would have rained down over the pinecones of Agay. There were titles of nobility, even a marquis, among the Carrillos, and the Sandovals were of the highest class. I had priests and even cardinals in my family. Through the

Suncins I had a good dose of Indian blood, Mayan blood (which was then fashionable in Paris), and had inherited legends about the volcanoes that would have amused Tonio's family. But something deeper held them back, something to do with mixed blood . . .

In vain, Tonio tried to make them accept me. I wasn't French. They didn't want to see or know me—they were blind to my existence. I often complained of this to Tonio. He said it gave him a headache. He was greatly tormented by the situation and decided not to write for a while. He couldn't. He tried, but in vain. These dissensions between the Mirador and Agay did not gladden his heart. I stopped speaking.

One day he confided in me that he would soon be given a job as a pilot. I was delighted. "Oh yes, I'll go to the end of the world with you. You are my tree, and I'll be the vine that clings to you," I said eagerly.

"No, you're my graft," he told me, "my oxygen, my dose of the unknown. Only death can separate us."

I asked him to tell me stories about the dangers of flying, the moments when death was inescapable, and we laughed at death.

✦

LATER, THE COUSIN AND THE WRITER WITH the womanly voice wrote to Tonio and gave him their opinion of me: negative. Gide, in his aversion to me, wrote this sentence in his *Journal*, which can still be read there: "Saint-Exupéry returned from Argentina with a new book and a new fiancée. Read the book, saw the girl. Congratulated him heartily, but principally on the book."

✦

TONIO ALWAYS HELD MY HAND very tightly in his gigantic fist. He loved me, but I was wounded to the quick by the injustice being done to me. Nothing troubled me more than injustice. I was beginning to find certain defects in my future in-laws. Still, I wanted to smooth over the difficulties; I tried to be forgiving. Simone, his older sister, was a highly cultivated, brilliant woman who for her erudition and imagination could have been a close friend. But there it was: I was going to be her sister-in-law. I had taken her brother and was therefore a thief, and she was the victim of my robbery. He was her only brother. Later she wrote a line about me that was both funny and cruel: "Consuelo, that countess of the silver screen . . ."* I decided to take up the gauntlet, but I wept all the same.

Tonio's mother alone, with her exceptional intelligence and Christian faith, thought only of her little boy's happiness. The fact that I hadn't been born in France was no crime in her eyes. I was the woman her son loved, that was

*However, in 1963, Simone de Saint-Exupéry wrote, evoking her brother, "Certain women marked his life deeply, first of all Consuelo Suncin, the wife he married at Agay in 1931. This charming and fantastical creature with her inexhaustible vitality was, amid the material worries that harried his existence, an unfailing source of poetry. *The Little Prince* embodied her in the character of the rose" ("Antoine, *mon frère*," in *Saint-Exupéry*, 1963). [Note by Alain Vircondelet.]

all. I had to be all right if Tonio loved me. She gave me all her sympathy, and I rested against her white hair. She laughed long and hard at my stories of the Pacific. And as a true Christian, she could not allow us to be nothing more than lovers for the rest of our lives. She didn't care in the least what her cousins thought. She had raised her children until they were grown, and no one but she had the right to prevent them from doing whatever they wanted. Tonio wanted Consuelo, so Tonio would have Consuelo, no matter what the family thought! Or, for that matter, André Gide!

7

I LOVED GOING to the flower market in Nice with Tonio trailing along behind me: it reminded him of planes taking off at dawn, into the wind, because it was very early in the morning—the smell of the sea, the heaps of violets, carnations, chrysanthemums, and mimosas, and the bouquets of Parma violets that were grown in the mountains an hour outside of Nice, where the snow sometimes stayed on the ground all summer.

My former friends, those I'd met through my first hus- band, began coming to the Mirador: the Pozzo di Borgos,

Dr. Camus. . . . We came back from the market, Julie Dutremblay and I, our arms loaded with flowers, with little Toutoune, my dog, in tow. Our days were like one long schoolgirls' outing. The Mirador smelled wonderful, but the very sweetness of this life made my fiancé brood. I wondered if he was already bored by my presence. "No," he said, "quite the opposite." He couldn't stand it when I was away, even for an hour. He didn't like it when I drove. "You could hurt yourself," he would say every time.

Deep down I wondered what he was afraid of. It was the two of us, no doubt, and the strange pair we made. I convinced myself that we were not safe, that we were out of step with society. Yes, we would have to find a way to live together in harmony, for eternity. But how would we find it?

One Sunday, at mass, Tonio, seeing me so pensive and morose that I didn't even take communion, burst out laughing. He said out loud, as if speaking to himself, in a prayer he seemed to have been muttering since the mass began: "But it's very simple, we'll just have a religious wedding!" People turned to look at him, but he had already disappeared. I found him sitting in the car in his shirtsleeves, reading a newspaper. "Consuelo, I would like us to be married by a priest," he said, "but without going to city hall as we did before. I want us to be married in church so that if we have children we'll be at peace and in order."

I laughed. "But Tonio, in France, you have to go to city hall first. It's in Andorra, or in Spain, I'm not sure which, that people can marry in church alone." A civil marriage would have meant forfeiting my income as Gómez Carrillo's widow.

"We'll go wherever we have to go," he said. "Agreed?"

"Yes, Tonio," I replied, "that would be wonderful. I wouldn't even have to change my name, so everything would be fine. And the day you stop loving me, you can leave with my heart in your hands, and it will be blessed."

"And you, if you ever love another man, you'll have proven yourself faithless—but I don't want you to leave!"

We kissed each other and swore we would never forget this promise.

His mother arrived one day, not long after that, dressed all in black. She told us, "My children, you are going to be married on April 22, at the city hall in Nice. It will take only a few minutes. I've arranged everything. Give me your papers, I want to register you today for the exact time."

"Consuelo, find our papers," Tonio ordered, "and give them to my mother."

And that was that, with no further discussion.

ON APRIL 22, at the preordained hour, we were at the city hall in Nice. A few minutes more, and we would be married. Tonio and I had not exchanged a word on the subject since his mother's visit.

It was about that time that he began to write again. He started with "Le ventilateur" ("The Fan"), a kind of poem that began like this: "A fan is turning on my forehead, image of fatality . . ." He had started it on the boat that had brought him back from Argentina, his young puma constantly disturbing him as he wrote. (He'd taken it into his bathroom to give it a rest from the cage in the hold where it was kept.) He threw himself back into the text and told me, "Consuelo, I've never walked away from anything I started. I want to finish 'The Fan.'" At the same time he wrote some other poems, "The Cry of America," "The Extinct Suns" . . . I'll try to gather them all together someday and publish them.

Pierre d'Agay offered to let us use his château for our religious wedding on April 23. That was the wedding we passionately wanted. And so we were married at the old fortress of Agay, tucked away in its tranquil bay. An ancient castle that had withstood all the caprices of history and the mistral, Agay was built in the shape of a great prow, like a ship jutting out into the sea. An immense terrace, full of rhododendrons and geraniums, made its deck more beautiful than anything I'd seen on any boat, overlooking the pure blue of the Mediterranean. The discretion of the d'Agays, who avoided society, had kept the fishing boats and motorboats half a mile away all around. The family had lived at the castle for generations, and various members also lived throughout the village. I've never really been able to distinguish between all the sisters-in-law and mothers-in-law of the d'Agay sisters. I do know, and am grateful, that they were all very kind and very good to the two of us. Antoine was a little like their own child. Pierre d'Agay, his brother-in-law, considered him a brother.

Inside, the château was very simple, with large rooms made of stone and flagstone floors that several lifetimes could not wear out. The day of the wedding, flowers and liqueurs from the d'Agay farm were distributed by my sister-in-law Didi among all the local families. We laughed and sang.

My mother-in-law had thought of everything. She had arranged a honeymoon for us on the nearby island of Porquerolles.

We left Agay, exhausted by the wedding party and all the photographs.

"Clear sky, good wind," Tonio said as he used to during his night flights for the Aéropostale, to give courage to the radio operator and the copilot as they flew along the great stretches of the Río de Oro where, if their plane had broken down, they'd have been chopped into little pieces.

He was sleepy—he didn't like all the kissing and exuberant manifestations of joy he'd had to endure all day. We left the car to go up onto the pier. The sea was choppy. My aviator, who could usually do hand-to-hand combat with dragons, was seasick, and that only worsened his mood.

Other young couples like us were staying at the hotel, where everything catered to the needs of newlyweds. We found the atmosphere stifling. Tonio went to sleep fully clothed, on a sofa. He woke up the next morning at daybreak and begged me to go back to the Mirador with him. He had only one desire, he said, to finish "The Fan." It hurt me a little that he didn't know how to play the bridegroom.

"Forgive me, but I find all of this idiotic," he said,

thinking of all the young married couples exchanging polite remarks over breakfast after their first night of intimacy.

And without a word to the family, we went back to our Mirador.

✦

So THERE WE WERE AT LAST, in order and at peace. My name would be different from then on, but I wasn't used to it yet and continued to sign "the Widow Gómez Carrillo." Tonio scolded me and asked me to forget Gómez Carrillo because he was dead. I was never again to have anything to do with him or his books, or to travel to Spain to see his editors. Even today, fifteen years later, I've never written a single letter to collect the smallest portion of the handsome inheritance he so graciously left me. I'm a little ashamed to admit it, but I was young—that's my only excuse. My young husband wanted to write; he didn't want another writer in our home, and I understood.

I thought Tonio was a little isolated in Nice, a little melancholy. I had the idea that a character like the famous writer Maeterlinck,* a great friend of my first husband, would do him some good. Maeterlinck had always felt a strong bond with Gómez Carrillo. How would he receive the young aviator who was replacing him at the Mirador?

*Maurice Maeterlinck (1862–1949): Belgian playwright and essayist who won the Nobel Prize in 1911. His drama *Pelléas et Mélisande* (1892) was reworked into an opera by Claude Debussy.

Buzzing around like a little bee, I called and wrote to Sélysette Maeterlinck, a delightful woman who, while Gómez Carrillo was alive, had been a true friend to me. Immediately, she invited us to Orlamonde, their new residence. I was on tenterhooks—you're always nervous with people who know you—as I took my Tonio to see the Maeterlincks.

One minute after introducing him, I was reassured: Tonio had been examined and approved as a worthy successor to my late husband. Maeterlinck offered him a drink and even went down to his cellar to get a bottle of old brandy. Tonio talked to him about everything and nothing, about life. I can still see them there in the palace of Orlamonde, in that marble-and-crystal drawing room. Tonio had the beauty of a Roman; he was almost six and a half feet tall, towering straight into the sky, but light as a bird. He raised his hand, holding an enormous crystal goblet, and drank joyfully as he discussed the quality of different kinds of paper and of books, for a book printed on good Holland paper had just fallen to the ground. The brandy gave color and heat to the conversation. Maeterlinck was won over, even charmed. I felt I had been saved, reinvigorated.

"I'm writing a book right now, just some personal experiences," Tonio said. "I'm not a professional writer. I can't write about anything I haven't experienced. The whole of my being has to be involved in order for me to express myself—or, I'd even say, in order for me to grant myself the right to think."

8

WITH THE FINISHED MANUSCRIPT of *Night Flight* in hand, we left for Paris, for the little apartment at 10 rue de Castellane that my first husband had left me. It was a strange place, far too small for two people, but we loved each other madly. The entryway was full of books, and the living room was hung with old tapestries. Verlaine and Oscar Wilde* had both lived there during bad times, and a woman we called "Our Lady of the Green Eyes" had tried to commit suicide there; her portrait still hung on the wall. A man had thrown himself out the second-floor window, which was conveniently situated for that kind of thing, but he had succeeded only in breaking his legs. Another woman had shot herself with a revolver; the blood could never be completely removed from the rug. She hadn't died, either. Only Maître Gómez Carrillo had died there, in my arms.

*In his memoirs, Gómez Carrillo wrote of having flirted with Oscar Wilde, and claimed that Wilde once sent him a bouquet of flowers. As for the great French poet Paul Verlaine, Consuelo's late husband had often helped him out financially by buying small things from him—articles of clothing and even his cane—all of which Consuelo kept until her death.

In fact, it was his little pied-à-terre, his hideaway for gray and rainy days. He'd also owned a lovely country house at Nelle-la-Vallée, only an hour away from Paris.

So I brought my gigantic bird of a new husband to this apartment, a little vexed that I couldn't offer him a better home in Paris. But he thought it was perfect; he liked working in small rooms and assured me that if I didn't want to live anywhere else we would never move.

Gide had offered to write a preface for *Night Flight*. Despite his stubborn hostility toward me, I forced myself to be extremely pleasant and polite with him. Too bad if he didn't like me and preferred the company of men and old women.

Tonio was delighted with the preface, and so was I. I thought he fully deserved the admiration of Gide, Crémieux, and Paul Valéry. When you follow a work of literature day by day, page by page, and the fruit is finally ripe for other people to savor, you tend to think of it as a marvelous gift you've given the world. The warm welcome my husband's manuscript received seemed to me entirely natural and fitting. We knew *Night Flight* by heart, while the rest of them, the friends, relatives, and admirers, had barely seen the manuscript.

The congratulations and exclamations of enthusiasm, whether feigned or real, began to grow tedious after a while. However, when they came from the beauteous women of Paris whose great admiration made them "overflow," my husband almost blushed; encounters like these thrilled him. My heart began to rage with jealousy; my Spanish blood began to boil.

"Do you know what I dreamed last night?" he asked me one morning when he woke up. "No? Well I dreamed that God had met me on a path; I knew it was God because of a strange candle He was carrying in his hand. It's idiotic, this dream, but that's how it is. And I ran after Him to ask Him something about mankind, only the candle was shining, and I was afraid."

This happened during the period when the *N.R.F.** was in the throes of its great passion for my husband. He came home with his handkerchiefs covered in lipstick; I didn't want to be jealous, but it was starting to depress me. People would tell me, "We ran into Tonio in a car with two women." "Yes," he explained, "two secretaries from the *N.R.F.* who invited me to stop off and have some port at their place on my way home."

Paris worried me; all I could think of anymore was the pretty women who were constantly pestering him.

Oh, it's a profession, a religious vocation to be the companion of a great creator. It's a profession you learn only after years of practice—for it can be learned. I was a fool. I thought that I, too, had a right to be admired for his work. I thought it belonged to both of us. What a mistake! In fact, nothing belongs more fully to an artist than his creation—even if you give him your youth, your money, your love, your courage, nothing belongs to you.

*The *Nouvelle Revue Française:* France's most influential literary magazine, which was cofounded by André Gide.

It's pure childishness to say, "Oh yes, I helped my husband, I did." First of all, no one ever knows if the opposite isn't true. Perhaps with another wife, the writer would have been able to write something else. Certainly a woman always helps a man to live, but she can also make it more difficult for him to work. Every woman in an audience, after an hour of listening to him speak, dreamed of being Tonio's intimate friend, the only faithful and understanding admirer of her favorite author. To be the driving force behind the pilot of *Night Flight*, the great writer! And then, right at that moment, I had to put on a wifely face and say, "Come along, husband, it's late. Let's go home."

That was all it took. What a wife! What a shrew! How tactless! Just when she, the admirer, invited or introduced by chance, was going to have a private talk with her pilot, the legitimate wife appears! That, believe me, is unforgivable. And yet how could I never feel sleepy, never speak to him during those endless evenings? I would have had to be made of stone! Little by little I began to understand that it was best to let him go by himself, since I had faith in him. Like a child, I thought, let's trust in fate. There must be a God, for children and for wives!

But Tonio often grew bored during the long evenings when he went out without me, so he asked me to phone him wherever he was going. "Call me, I beg you," he told me. "I hate the endless chitchat, the lectures, the dinners. I've already said everything I have to say. Believe me, *ma femme*, I'd rather waste my time than my breath. It doesn't matter if the hostess is angry because you want me to come home right away. You know how I am; I'm very polite, and if you don't call, I can't come home!"

I'd gotten into the habit of going to the movies when he left and then passing by to pick him up at his friends' homes. Oh, I thought I was very clever! I told myself he was tired of going out so much, he was invited against his will, he felt obliged to accept, without knowing why.

He was unsociable and solitary, but he also loved company. When the phone rang, it frightened him. His friends would talk to him for hours on end, and then he would want to go on with a conversation that had lasted until three in the morning the night before and would still be talking on the phone at two in the afternoon. We had breakfast with the telephone on the table. I felt completely powerless around him; I lost all common sense, like a little girl.

9

THE ARGENTINE AIRMAIL SERVICE was disbanded, and Tonio lost his post as its director in Buenos Aires. "You're unemployed, my love—relax!"

"No, Consuelo, we have to pay the rent, and for the drinks and the nights out."

He was constantly assailed by friends who invited him

out to restaurants, where he loved to pick up the check for the whole table. When he found himself short of money, he was crushed. In Buenos Aires he had earned twenty thousand francs a month, a handsome salary. And now here he was in Paris without a penny.

"I want to accept a position with Renault," he told me, speaking slowly, "at a fixed salary. It's more secure. I'll go to the office every day. It's a good job, I think. Some friends have found it for me."

It upset me a great deal to see him submit so meekly to the imprisonment of an office. "I'll start next month, if you want, darling."

"No, Tonio," I said. "I don't want you to take this job. Your path lies across the stars."

"Yes, you're right, Consuelo," he said. "Across the stars. You're the only one who understands."

That line about the stars, which was all I ever said to him on the subject, did the trick. He quickly changed his mind about the job with Renault. It was as if I had galvanized him, given him new hope.

He began to dream again, and to sing his "war song," as I used to call it in Buenos Aires—for every time he set off on a trip, whether by car or by plane, he would sing

Un poteau lugubre et sombre devant moi toujours se tient
Et je vois la route d'ombre dont nul homme ne revient.

(A dark and mournful finish line stands always in my
path

And I see the shadowy road from which no man ever
comes back.)

Ever since then, I hear those words every time I start off
on a journey.

✦

ONE BEAUTIFUL SUMMER DAY, Tonio announced that
he had to leave for Toulouse to meet with Didier Daurat.

"I want to go back to work as a simple mail pilot," he
told Daurat. "Assign me a taxi, quick!" (In pilot slang, an
airplane was a taxi.) "I'm bored in Paris. I'll go anywhere,
I'll fly wherever you send me. My wife will come with me.
I'm ready to go. Tomorrow, if you want. I await your orders."

He had great respect for Didier Daurat and had based
the character of Rivière, in *Night Flight,* on him.

Back in Paris, he started opening drawers and cup-
boards, sniffing his leather flying gear, his coat, helmet,
and straps, his safety lamps, his compasses, spreading
them out tenderly on the rug. The phone rang all the
time. His Parisian friends wanted to invite him out, but he
turned them all down.

"I'm busy," he would say. "I'm going back to work as a
mail pilot. I've had enough of getting fat in the cafés and
brasseries of Paris. Good-bye, I don't have another
minute, I'm packing my bags. My wife will tell you." That
meant he was completely out of their reach.

He pulled on his stiff leather coat, hardened by lack of use, the old comrade of many flights. From its pockets, he took little slips of paper. One day as he was reading them, he burst into uproarious laughter.

"But why are you laughing like that?" I asked. "What's so funny? Why are you laughing like a madman?

"I can't tell you, it's idiotic," he said, laughing harder and harder.

"Come on, please . . . tell me!"

"Well, it has to do with a noise, and with my radio operator a long time ago, flying over Patagonia."

"But I don't see anything funny about that."

"Because I was afraid of the noise, I didn't understand."

"What?"

"Yes, I was afraid, until my radioman handed me a note about the noise. Read it for yourself. I've just found it again, here it is."

I took the piece of paper and read: "The noise isn't coming from the plane. Don't be afraid. It is a fart. I'm very ill, monsieur."

It was my turn to laugh out loud. He took me in his arms. "Oh darling," I told him, "I'm so happy. I can't imagine you anywhere except in the sky. Am I wrong?"

"Why are you crying?" he asked me.

"I don't know. I've never liked your life in Paris. It's less frightening for me to have you up among the stars than down among Parisian women."

He lay me on the ground, right in the middle of all his things, and tickled me madly.

"Ow, ow, Tonio, stop! You're hurting me—seriously," I said.

"Where?"

"Here, in my stomach."

"Ah, the appendix," he said sagely. "It will be removed this very night. Dr. Martell, I hold him in the highest esteem. . . . Let's go to the hospital. Tomorrow your appendix will be far away. We won't be taking it with us to Morocco!"

It was all childishly simple. I felt I had nothing to fear when I was with him.

MONSIEUR DAURAT had already called Tonio back in to give him his orders: for the time being, he would be piloting the Toulouse–Casablanca line.

As soon as a pilot accepted a job, he no longer knew where he would be spending the next night. If the night went well, he would arrive somewhere in the world— Barcelona, Casablanca, Port-Etienne, Cap-Juby, Buenos Aires . . . and then there were the routes to the Orient, including the legendary Paris–Saigon . . .

Everything happened just as Tonio had said it would: I saw his doctor, and the operation was performed. His mother took loving care of me while I spent a few days in Saint-Maurice-de-Rémens, convalescing. Then she sent me to Toulouse to join her son at the Hôtel Lafayette. There I had the pleasure of meeting Daurat and seeing him up close. He was a very serious man; what most impressed me about him was his iron will.

Toulouse was a dead city—it didn't exist for me at all. I devoted myself entirely to my friendship with the pilots, who risked their lives every day and were oblivious to the dangers they faced and the importance of their task, which gave other men an example of heroism. To them it was just a job, and I admired them even more for that.

These pilots had traveled across nights and strong winds, and it bored them to hear their own praises sung. They wanted to drink beer, to play dice or poker. I was a quick study at poker; from time to time, timidly, I would ask what the names of the other pilots were. At the end of the first evening, I risked one small request for information about my husband. I learned to be guarded and to act tough around the pilots. I had been alone in Toulouse for a week while my husband was in the skies. I was living in his room and waiting for news of him.

"Ah, *oui*, Saint-Ex, they had him take a 'taxi' all the way to Dakar. He'll replace a pilot there."

"Why?" I asked.

"Because the pilot was killed. Look, Madame de Saint-Ex, that's three times now that I've taken three spades from you."

"Really, is that what you heard?" My heart felt as if it were skipping rope in my chest, it was pounding so madly. Where was my angel?

The next day when I awoke, my husband at last appeared in our room, but only in order to empty out all the drawers. We were leaving for Casablanca, with a stop in

Spain. We always lived at this bohemian pace, in a perpetual state of urgency.

"Maybe you'd like to have a swim in Almería," he said; "it's summer down there."

"Yes, Tonio darling," I said. "I'd love to."

"Uh-oh, look—the suitcase is full. You can't bring all these things. Choose two dresses, that's enough. Your nightgowns are of no use; it's too hot in Morocco."

A few hours later, we were in Alicante. We went to the beach. He swam very quickly and I wanted to catch up, but the scar from my appendix operation kept me from showing off my talents as a water nymph. It still hurt.

❦

We were here today, gone tomorrow. At times I felt like a fugitive. He didn't know what his destiny was, and neither did I, but I certainly had no regrets about his not taking the job with Renault.

In the middle of the night he would hold me very tenderly, as if I were a small, beloved animal. One night, begging my forgiveness, he said, "I don't yet know how to be your husband. Please forgive me. I get all tangled up in your ribbons. I'm still surprised to have a little girl like you beside me." I was half asleep, and he lifted me up in his strong arms.

"Ninety pounds," he said. "I weigh three times more. My cherished little dwarf, tomorrow you'll arrive in a beautiful country. You will love it, if you really love me. A friend has already rented a nice apartment for us in the palace of Glaoui. You'll often be alone—you'll have time to enjoy yourself, take walks, maybe even think of me."

I slept very little that night. I imagined the palace of Glaoui surrounded by desert sands. I was already following him to his destiny.

⭐

AT LAST the much-talked-of palace was revealed to me. The stairway was made of marble, the rooms were very large, and the furniture was almost nonexistent, in keeping with Arab sobriety. There were huge carpets on the floor and walls, large copper trays used as tables in all the rooms, divans, blue and white tiles, and very low beds.

The wives of the other pilots took me to the marketplace and instructed me in the ways of the provincial city of Casa, where the sun is eternal. The Roi de la Bière café, at cocktail hour, reunited us with the other pilots. Poker . . . Pernod . . . eggs in aspic . . . racy stories. I heard such a collection of them that I could put together an anthology. But life gave us much more than other people's stories.

I spent my time reading at a bookstore owned by Madame Allard, dreaming about my life, strolling around the Arab city. A pilot named Guerrero came in one day while I was chatting with the bookseller. "Bonsoir, Madame de Saint-Ex," he said. "Would you like to have dinner with me this evening? Here, this is from your husband; he bought you some fresh spiny lobsters in Port-Etienne and asked me to bring them to you."

"Yes, Guerrero," I said. "Come over to my place, and we'll cook; Madame Allard will come, too."

"I'm flying the same route as your husband," Guerrero explained. "By chance I had a problem with my leg, so I stayed over in Cisneros to rest up. Saint-Ex was looking very careworn to me. 'Well, old man,' I said to myself, 'for a young newlywed, you look positively papal.' But we don't actually say anything to each other. Suddenly, Saint-Ex shouts, 'Fantastic! Eggs in aspic are fantastic, don't you think, Guerrero?'

" 'What about eggs in aspic?' I asked. 'Would you please explain?'

" 'All right,' he said. 'I had my first fight with my wife over eggs in aspic. We were eating out, at the Roi de la Bière. I come home dead on my feet after a night of flying and she wants me, nonetheless, to have dinner at the Roi de la Bière. I don't say much at home, you know, I don't open my mouth. . . . At the café, the waiter asks me what I'll have, and my wife looks at me, worried. I answer, "Eggs in aspic"; there was a dish of them right there in front of us. I hadn't thought about ordering a full meal. "Are you sick? Are you upset?" she asks me.

" 'I don't answer. They bring me two eggs in aspic.

" ' "And then, Monsieur, what will you have as a main course?" the waiter asks.

" ' "Two eggs in aspic."

" 'My wife didn't say a thing. I wanted to laugh. But for the second time, they brought me eggs in aspic. And for dessert, the same story.

" 'I didn't want to say anything. Or think. It was all the

87

same to me if I ate six eggs in aspic or anything else. But it irritated Consuelo. She was sitting there on the banquette, and then, right there in the middle of all the other customers, she stood up and shouted, "Look at them, your eggs in aspic . . . I like eggs in aspic, too!"

" 'She took all the eggs that were on the table and crushed them between her fingers right there in front of everyone, made a purée of them, and then ran home crying.

" 'I couldn't keep a straight face. I burst out laughing. The waiter and the woman at the cash register looked so funny, watching Consuelo attacking the eggs. After a few minutes I left, too. Go tell her that the scene is forgotten, Guerrero. Tell her I'm not angry and I'm coming home tomorrow for my birthday. I'm sending her these lobsters to make her happy. And most of all, tell her she shouldn't mistake their claws for eggs in aspic.' "

THE PILOTS' LIVES were simple and orderly, like those of all men of action. My husband flew the mail route between Casablanca and Port-Etienne.* A few years earlier a single pilot had been responsible for the entire route from Casa to Dakar, but Monsieur Daurat had persuaded the government to make some improvements. The pilots had changed, and the planes had been partially modernized.

*Port-Etienne: A town on the Mauritanian coast, at the border of Western Sahara, now known as Nouadhibou.

Staying over in Port-Etienne was no fun: there were hardly more than a dozen men there, including the Arab laborers who were slaves of the Maures. My husband often told me, "One day I'll take you to see Madame la Capitaine. She's French, and she has a garden there, in that country where nothing green grows. She gets freshwater in by boat from Bordeaux and soil from the Canary Islands. In a little wooden box, she's growing three lettuces and two tomato plants. She washes her hair in freshwater from Bordeaux, then waters her garden with the same water. To shelter her little vegetable patch from the desert sands, she has the box lowered to the bottom of a well. . . . When we stop over on our way through, she invites us to dinner; we always have canned food to eat, but she has her garden pulled up out of the well and displays it on the table. Her two miserable tomato plants, her three lettuces . . . It's touching!"

When he came back, Saint-Ex told me, "You can understand that after spending time out in the desert sands like that, I come home a little wild. Down there, I think crudely; I'm a big bear, as you call me. It makes life easier. . . . I'm a bear, I tell myself, and I retreat into my silence. I'm like a different man there, I have a different skin, I need rest, calm, peace. So you make conversation for me all by yourself, giving me details about the letters we've received from France, about our friends in Casablanca, you talk to me about your life, about life in general. I admire you, you forget nothing, you keep me informed about this country. The doctor in Casa did this, the colonel said that . . . The latest news from the papers.

But when I see you exhausted because I'm a bear who devours your words, your tender gestures, I'd like to dance for you alone, the way a bear dances, to entertain you, to tell you that I'm your bear, yours, for life.

"Listen, some funny things happen to us during the stopovers. The other day, a Christian association for the protection of women, near Dakar, sent us some fifteen-year-old girls to keep the pilots company during their night off!

"They sell those poor creatures in the market as slaves, you know. The association let us know its schedule of fees. We were to pay these virgin girls four French francs for the evening. To them, it's a lot of money, in their far corner of the desert. We often ask them to sweep out the shack, wash a glass for us, clean a gasoline lamp. One day, Mermoz,* who was coming back quite late from a café in Dakar, found a little girl of about fourteen at his door. He had drunk a lot, and he told her to leave. But the little girl grew upset and started to cry; it was the only way she had of showing her despair since she didn't speak French. So Mermoz told her, 'Come in, you can sleep with me.' He starts taking her clothes off, taking off her burnous, but she weeps all the harder. He gives her the four francs, not wanting to pay any more than the official rate, for the sake

*Jean Mermoz (1901–1936): One of the most famous French aviators of the day and the first to fly from France to South America. A longtime friend of Saint-Exupéry, he disappeared during a flight over the South Atlantic; his book *Mes vols* (My Flights) was published posthumously in 1937.

of the other men. He puts her burnous back on. The tears don't stop. He takes the burnous off again and gives her a second fistful of money. 'To hell with the official rates, you're nice, you're going to sleep.' But the little girl, almost naked in the darkness, doesn't want to leave and goes on sobbing. He no longer knows what to do. He gives her presents: his watch, which fills her with wonder, his eau de Cologne. She calms down for a moment, then plunges back into her despair. Mermoz becomes enraged. He shouts, 'I've had enough! Leave, I want to sleep; go home.' The little girl just stands there, looking lost, immobile, like someone who hasn't yet done what she came to do. Her deep eyes gleam with an anguished light. Her mouth half open, she can't say anything in the language of this white man who flies, who comes down out of the sky. Sounds emerge from her throat softly, as if she were speaking to herself. In the face of her immense sorrow, the pilot takes pity on her; once again he takes off the white cloth that covers her and looks her over attentively. She wasn't like the other Bedouin women, who come submissively, their eyes lowered before wickedness. . . . The pilot finds her beautiful, even more beautiful with her strange expression. He tries to soothe the look of a hunted animal out of her eyes. 'That's how several of my fellow pilots have married Arab girls,' he says to himself. At dawn, he pushes the girl out of bed. 'Go away.' She feels the order in the pilot's muscles. She leaves the bed. She understands that she must go. But she sits down on the ground again, to show him she will not leave. This is more than Mermoz can bear. 'Oh, right, you want to follow me like a slave, a dog . . .' And he says the word in Arabic. She screams in indignation. An airplane comes rumbling down the runway. Mermoz looks at her, then shuts his eyes. Maybe, he thinks, if I pretend I'm asleep, she'll leave. He still has long hours of flying ahead of him. He must sleep. If he falls asleep in the middle of a flight, it will be this stubborn girl's fault. She's stronger than he is. The pilot sighs. The two of them sneak quick glances at each other. He laughs nervously; the girl does, too. The door of the shack opens, and the pilot who just landed comes in. 'Hello, old man!' 'Is that you, Tonio?' 'Yes.'

" 'I haven't slept all night, look,' Mermoz says, pointing to the little Arab girl sitting on the ground. 'I'm exhausted, she doesn't want to go. I've given her everything already, my money, even my pocketknife!'

"The little Arab girl gets quickly to her feet. 'Perhaps you speak Arabic, monsieur?' she says. 'You see, I am the laundress. I can't leave here without the dirty sheets. As for the rest of it, I'm perfectly satisfied; he's generous, your friend!' "

Tonio translates the little Arab girl's desires. Mermoz lets out a curse, then loads her up with all the dirty laundry. She's finally happy and leaves.

Mermoz claimed that this story happened to Tonio, but Tonio swore that it was Mermoz who had lived through it.

I loved listening to him tell stories like this. I'm only sorry that I repeat them awkwardly because I have no way of reproducing his laugh, his voice. He was spellbinding when he told stories about the desert.

ITS NAME was the only palatial thing about the palace of Glaoui. In fact, it was a large and luxurious block of flats—the rental apartments of Glaoui, really. The architecture and décor were in the modern Arab style, influenced by our French civilization. What hard work it was to give a personal touch to those square rooms with their hard, unforgiving light! I understood the wisdom of the Arab sheiks: the only thing that can stand up to light like this is light itself: space. You cover the mosaics with white rugs and the walls with Arab weavings that give off a warm glow, and you set large gilded copper trays opposite each other as tabletops. You have to find the largest ones possible. They're sold by weight; some are silver-plated, it's rare to find any in gold. Tonio loved one great, gloomy tray, which was grayish, almost black, with timeworn designs. The more you looked at it, the less you understood the images engraved on it. We tried to read them, and it became a pastime, an obsession.

My first weeks in that apartment gave me an education in how to create a harmonious décor. Like all men, my husband wasn't fond of having the furniture moved around. When he was there, I couldn't shift even one small table; he thought it was a waste of time. I suffered over this. After studying and understanding the angles of the windows and checking on the location of the electrical switches to make sure the rooms would be as comfortable as possible for reading and writing, I made my plan.

One day, Tonio had to leave from the airfield at three

o'clock; this time I had decided not to go with him to see him off, which took me two whole hours. I claimed I had a headache, a letter to write to my relatives. But Tonio understood human nature too well; something told me he was suspicious. First of all, he wouldn't accept my refusal to accompany him. I couldn't bring myself to tell him offhandedly, "I don't like going to the airfield with you to see you off." Anyway, it would have been a lie. Every time he left, I trembled. On one occasion I was very fearful for him because we had recently buried a pilot who had crashed. Tonio circled once over the runway, just to get a closer look at me and give me a wave good-bye. He had hardly committed this imprudent act when his radio operator announced the arrival of a telegram, punishing him with a fine. We had to do as we were told and ended up paying dearly for his little spin over my head.

So I went to the airfield to keep from upsetting him, very quiet and well behaved, but withdrawn. He was adorable.

"Au revoir, chéri," I told him. "Don't forget, I put some vegetables in your provision basket, some tomatoes. They're well wrapped up but delicate, and you'll have to take them out as soon as you arrive or the heat will cook them. The lettuce, the cucumbers, the radishes—put them in water as soon as you arrive. You have enough to last all week, even for your fellow pilots. They'll be glad to have something besides canned food to eat."

I was the only wife who went to the market and packed oddly shaped bundles into empty gasoline containers. He didn't like fresh milk, but I would fill thermoses with ice cream, fresh meat packed in ice chips, and chicken soup, all of them labeled. My husband was happy as he handed out his provisions; he himself ate bread and cheese. These preparations took time. To me, that was life: I was providing him with the energy he would use during his nights of flying. And coffee: it had to be very strong. I stuffed his pockets with chocolates and mints. He always protested, "But, *chérie*, I don't need anything, believe me." But then, when he came back, he brought me presents from the other pilots who had eaten my soups and vegetables. They were the ones who worried about Tonio's eating habits. "Otherwise," they said, "Madame de Saint-Ex will stop sending the supplies that make our meals a little better . . ."

That day, when I didn't want to go with him to the airfield, Tonio was watching me out of the corner of his eye. I tried to leave before the plane took off. "Darling, I'm a little out of sorts from all the noise and the smell of gasoline," I said. "It's hot, I'd like to take a cool bath. I'll go to the hairdresser. Then I'll pay a visit to Madame C."

"One favor, please," he said. "Whenever you're doing something you want to hide from me, don't give so many pretexts. A single one is sufficient, otherwise it makes me suspicious."

I went home, calm: he was gone. Now I could get started on what I had to do. I worked all day. When nightfall surprised me, I hadn't yet finished. I sent my Ahmed and my Fatimas home and lay down in the enormous bathroom on the divan used for massages, collapsing with exhaustion.

In the middle of the night, there were footsteps on the mosaic tiles, agile footsteps, a thief's footsteps . . . I was terrified. How rash I had been to send all my people away. Only the cook was there, sleeping across from the kitchen. I held my breath as the footsteps moved away and returned. Someone was there in my house, making himself at home. The visitor switched on a light. I was shaking. My jewels . . . I tore the rings off my fingers and crawled into the laundry basket. The thief wouldn't look in there. I was scared; there was no revolver in this room. The thief, emboldened at not seeing anyone there, continued to walk through rooms that were empty because I had moved everything into a maid's room in order to wash and repaint the walls and rearrange the furniture. That was my plan. Finally, the thief, flashlight in hand, came into the bathroom and calmly used my toilet. I caught a glimpse of his head from my hiding place in the basket. It was my husband! I started to move, and the laundry I'd taken cover under began erupting like a volcano. Tonio was truly afraid. I shouted, "Help! Help me, I can't breathe!"

He stood there motionless, petrified. He had found all the rooms empty, but now he heard me crying out and saw me battling against some shirts that were wrapped around my neck. He thought he could see two people in the movements of his shirts. Finally I managed to struggle out of the laundry basket on my own. He was pale, breathing hard. I was enraged.

"You terrify me in the middle of the night and then you can't even help me out of my hiding place! I could have suffocated in there . . . I thought there was a thief. I put my rings in the basket. My watch must have been crushed. You're horrible."

"Listen, my crazy, crazy little girl, don't you see that I'm having even more trouble breathing than you are? I turned back in midflight. I came home. I thought, 'Consuelo doesn't love me anymore. And she's right: she's always alone. When I'm there, I'm thinking, I'm writing—I'm not a good companion. But it's better to say everything, know everything, settle everything. I don't want to hurt her. She must be with the man she loves. I can't leave her like that,' and so I didn't go. I asked Guerrero, who's on vacation but was at the airfield by chance, to fly the taxi for me and spent the day wandering aimlessly around the city. I wanted to write to you, instead of coming here. But I thought, 'I haven't noticed her acting remote or distant.' And I prayed. Finally I decided, 'All right, I'll go and tell her everything.' That's why I'm here. When I didn't see any furniture in our bedroom, in the salon, anywhere, I was terrified. You were really, definitively, gone, even the furniture was gone. I decided I would run away to China tomorrow. I looked for a letter, some trace of you: nothing. And there you were in the laundry basket! But what are you doing there?"

"Oh, Tonio, and you claim you're not jealous? Idiot!"

"But answer me: Where is the furniture?"

"You imbecile, you didn't see the buckets of paint next

to the front door? The painters are coming tomorrow. I wanted to surprise you, and instead you've given me a terrible fright . . ."

I couldn't get over my fear. I wept, I searched for my rings and my bracelet. Tonio found a mattress and lay down on the ground, fully dressed, clinging to one of my ankles as his only consolation for my tears and my love.

Later, in answer to my tears, my bracelet, my broken watch, the most beautiful words anyone ever spoke to me told me that I wasn't crying over my lost bracelet that night—I was already crying over death, which would separate me, "dear and ephemeral little girl" that I was, from everything.

10

I COULD NO LONGER SLEEP. The anguish of the night flights, which Tonio set off on twice a week, kept me awake. When he spent a few days with me between two mail flights, I thought of ways to please him, to take care of him. He isn't like other men, I said to myself. Such a child, such an angel fallen from the sky. I could have gone out like the other women, taken walks, gone to parties, but the mail flights were the only thing that mattered to me. They were my despair.

One day he took off around three in the afternoon. If all went well, he would land at his three stops, Cisneros, Port-Etienne, and Cap-Juby.* I asked the radioman for information about my husband's flight. The other pilots were also asking him for information. He had to guide them through the sky. And then there was Madame de Saint-Ex, who was always phoning: "Has my husband landed at his first stop?" "Yes" or "no" would be the reply, nothing more.

I had to wait a whole hour before I dared ask the same question again. "You are too nervous, Madame. Why don't you go and have a swim, it's a beautiful day. I'll take care of your husband's flight. The other pilots' wives aren't nearly as anxious."

The next day, I would start making phone calls again. "Your husband arrived safely" or "Your husband's had a breakdown. We're trying to get the plane fixed." And that was all. I had moved heaven and earth in order to live near the radio office, and if I didn't phone, I went by the office and stuck my head inside, smiling and waving my handkerchief to the other pilots who were there. They were superstitious and didn't like to see women around the office, but I was different, I was their neighbor. I would ask them to come up to my place, where I had freshwater, anchovies sent from Paris, and sugared almonds, and I would promise them that the prettiest of my women friends in

*Cisneros: A town to the north of Port-Etienne on the coast of Western Sahara, now known as Dakhla. Cap-Juby: A town to the north of Cisneros on the Moroccan coast, just above the border of Western Sahara, also known as Tarfaya.

Casablanca would join us for cocktails. I always managed to collect one or two pilots. I waited on them as if they were gods; they were my messenger angels. They would come and go, and finally, without my asking them anything, they would tell me, "Don't worry, your husband skipped a stop. The wind and the fog pushed him into the desert or out to sea. He thinks he'll arrive in Cisneros soon." And the hours would go by. They would take their leave of me with many a glass of Pernod under their belts. "Well, then, Madame de Saint-Ex, come to the restaurant, *chez l'Arabe,* yes . . . see you soon."

At the restaurant later that night, I would learn if he had reached Cisneros. Sometimes there was not another word, just tenderness, sweetness. The pilots were becoming my brothers. "But Madame de Saint-Ex, don't worry about it so much. Tonight we're going to paint the town red."

Dear God, it was no fun: the bars, the women, the smell of tobacco and kif* that permeated even the more or less decent places. If no one took me home at midnight, I knew my angel was in danger. One day, my good-hearted, kind Guerrero "took me to the country." The other pilots wanted to sleep. "Going to the country," in our lingo, meant "going to see the radioman."

Ah, the pilots' wives! It wasn't easy for the men or their wives. They felt sorry for us, and they loved us. Our husbands needed to win out against the night, to reach the next stop, because we were waiting for them. The rest of

*Kif or kef: Hashish.

it—the exhaustion, the hours of struggle against the un-foreseeable weather, the fog, the stupid orders from the head office in Paris that several liters of gasoline be re-moved in order to lighten the load—none of it mattered. "If we could land in fifteen more minutes, we'd be saved," wrote a pilot before falling into the sea and drowning. But orders had to be followed. They climbed aboard their machines like robots setting off to make war. War against the night.

Their homecoming was simple. We didn't talk about anything; we were all alive. They'd be off again in five days. For now, we would eat and drink. But Tonio, no: he wanted to read, he wanted to write. And so I had to make myself very small and scarce, had to live inside his pockets. I made sketches that bore no resemblance to any-thing. If that bothered him, I embroidered. Heaps of embroidered pillows piled up on the sofa. He liked for me to be in the same room with him when he was writing, and when he was out of ideas, he would ask me to listen and would read back one, two, or three pages, waiting for my reaction.

"So what are you thinking about? That doesn't evoke anything from you? Not interesting? I'm going to tear them up. It's ridiculous, they mean nothing!"

And then I would invent God knows what, I would dig down into my fund of stories and talk for an hour about a page he had just written.

Once this ordeal was behind us, he would look at me, very happy. "I'm sleepy," he would say. "Let's go to bed."

Or he would decide "I'd like to take a fast walk. Put on

your walking shoes, we're going to the beach. Let's go have some oysters and play some songs on the player piano at L'Oiseau Bleu, that little open-air dance hall by the sea!"

L'Oiseau Bleu had a bad reputation, but it was the only comfortable place, with no pretensions, in town. You felt right at home as soon as you walked in; you'd put a few coins in the piano and the music played. Food and drink would arrive at our table, and there was always a different waitress. Whichever one was free attended to the pilots who came with their "ladies," the others would keep the sailors company. You could almost say it had become the fashionable meeting place for all of Casablanca. There were hardly more than twenty families in the whole city who knew how to read and write correctly and had been baptized and married. There were two or three couples from our social milieu; though they had been in business, we shared a few topics of conversation with them. We were happy together.

★

WHEN TONIO LEFT on one of his mail runs, I practically had to be hospitalized. Anxiety would not let me sleep. I started back in on the same old dance around the radio operators, the same steps, the same anguish.

One day, two pilots who were standing in front of me said, "I've just come from the radio office. Everything's in a mess. Antoine has crashed. They've just sent another plane out to look for his body, and for the mail if it can be saved."

My ears were ringing. I made the sign of the cross and dashed to the radio office like a crazed gazelle. I was suffocating in the noonday heat. I had just run across the city, instead of taking a taxi; my legs had to fly—I hadn't stopped to think. At the doorway of the office I found a woman weeping with loud sobs; it was my friend Madame Antoine. So the pilot Jacques Antoine was the one who had gone down and not my husband, Antoine de Saint-Exupéry. I laughed like a madwoman. "Oh, Madame Antoine, what an idiot I am, it's your husband who's crashed." And I laughed, I couldn't stop laughing. The doctor arrived, and Madame Antoine and I both slept a whole day under the effects of a dose of morphine.

★

PINOT WAS SUPPOSED TO be getting married. Pinot was our friend; he liked to spend time with us. He had decided to leave the desert sands because he was engaged. His mother had arranged everything back in France: the trousseau, the house, all of it. Tonio told him, "We'll get all the pals together in my big apartment and say goodbye to your life as a pilot and a bachelor." Pinot accepted. Tonio spent half his monthly salary on champagne for the party.

Pinot was leaving Dakar forever. On his last mail flight, another pilot was supposed to replace him. But

Pinot insisted, "Come on. Let me fly the plane one last time." The pilot let him take over. He had a bad takeoff, the engine misfired several times, and he crashed on the runway. Good-bye, family, fiancée, party that was ready and waiting for him . . .

The sight of our banquet made Tonio melancholy. With his customary generosity, he had ruined himself to celebrate his friend, who was leaving the line forever. Yet we were no richer than the other pilots. Quite the contrary: we both had to live on just four thousand francs a month and a few other resources. The rent had to be paid for the Paris apartment on rue de Castellane and for the apartment in the Glaoui, which was considered insanely luxurious by the other pilots, who lived in little rooms with their wives, without ever having guests.

But Tonio needed space; he liked beautiful parquet floors, walls that weren't closing in on him, and nothing to encumber his footsteps. All he had to do was touch something in order for it to break. Even a piano he leaned against one day at a friend's house collapsed. He had no concept of his own weight, or his height. He often hit his head against the doors of cars or houses. He forgot he was as tall as a tree. This man who could fly over the desert and the sea didn't know how to strike a match without hurting himself. Safety matches were a terrible affliction to me. He struck them very hard, against anything, in order to light his cigarettes (he always lost lighters or destroyed the wick). Once, striking a match against a window, he made a deep cut in his thumb. I wept; he laughed. I couldn't get over the loss of the little piece of finger and nail that his beautiful hand would lack from then on. He thought he was invincible, for he constantly made use of all his forces, both physical and moral. He would grow irate if anyone was unjust to him or anyone else. One day, in a bistro, a man insulted us because of a little Pekinese I had that I loved dearly: Youti was part of our life. As he drank his Pernod, Tonio listened to this individual's insults. When the man fell silent, Tonio grabbed the chair the man was sitting on and set it down, with the man still on it, right in the middle of the street. The man stayed there on his chair for a few seconds, stunned; the people in the café laughed, and we left, giggling all the way home.

Youti was always a problem on our excursions: he was so small that we often forgot him. Several times, when we were already well on our way home, I cried, "Tonio, we left Youti at the restaurant." He made a U-turn and went back to get him. Once he had to go all the way to the home of an Arab who had already adopted him and given him a new name. The whole thing took him more than an hour, but he bore Youti triumphantly back to me.

As soon as I took my eyes off of him, Youti would dash off on errands of his own. Once in Casablanca he ran away from the apartment. For hours I looked for my beloved dog, crying like a baby. When Tonio came back from his flight, he said, "Darling, why didn't you come to meet me at the airfield?"

"Youti has left me," I sobbed. "The service entrance was left open and he ran away. The servants have been scouring the city for him in vain since three o'clock."

"All right, don't cry. Give me a kiss instead, and I'll bring you back your Youti."

He had a quick bath and then went out to look for the dog. People in Casa are still talking about the ruses he used to find him. "He cost us almost three hundred francs," he told me with a pensive air, "but I can't stand to see you cry. Here he is, your *toutou*."

Our walks through the city were our greatest indulgence. We didn't buy anything. We ate on the ground with the Arabs, meats seasoned with roasted herbs, fresh mutton. Tonio conversed with the legionnaires, men who had lost all their fortune in Paris and had gone to Morocco to rebuild their lives. And it could be done. A close friend traded his coat for a horse in the marketplace, then traded the horse for some goats, the goats for sheep, the sheep for slaves. He ended up having his own stable of horses, along with herds of animals that brought him considerable income. He married the daughter of a local *cadi*. He had a harem, children; he owned a house and land.

One day, on one of our walks through the hot streets among the snake charmers, I caught a strange microbe that began to eat into my foot, making a little hole half an inch wide that smelled awful and seemed to be rotting. My dog caught it after I did. He cried even harder than his mistress. I couldn't wear shoes. My foot was wrapped in bandages. The doctors held a lengthy conference about me, at which Tonio was present. He came out of the meeting a changed man. He said, "I won't go on my mail flight tomorrow."

"Why, Tonio?"

"Because I want to take care of you, to look after you. You won't heal if you're alone for long nights. I don't want to fly anymore."

"Then how will we live, Tonio?"

"Oh, we'll always find a way to eat. I know how to drive a truck."

"But no, Tonio, I'd rather you be a pilot. I want you to leave tomorrow on your mail flight. The vegetables have already been bought and packed up, I've made all the soups, everything is ready. Take this cake to Madame la Capitaine, please . . ."

"As you command, my wife. And when I come back we will leave for the islands." I thought he was joking.

Youti was moaning all the time. I sang songs to him. My Fatima and Ahmed took us to a veterinary sorcerer, and I gave him fifty francs for an ointment that smelled very good. My dog healed in three days. The hole he had had for a month went away, and the skin grew back; there was no more pus. I was delighted, but my own foot wasn't healing at the same rate. It smelled worse and worse. A second hole had appeared, on my calf. I was shaking, and I prayed to God to heal me. I became very melancholy and stayed home all day. To distract myself, I reread some pages my husband had just written, which he had left scattered across the table. As I was putting away his papers, I saw a word written in larger letters than the others: "Leprosy." I read it again: yes, "Leprosy." It was a letter to God, no less, in which he pleaded with the Lord not to abandon me because the doctor didn't want me to have any further contact with other people. He would, he wrote, go away with me to the islands where lepers live.

I understood why my friends were no longer visiting as often. I was afraid. Youti gave me a kiss. I cried.

We had come to this country to work, full of hope, full of energy. I never complained about anything. I had no money to buy new dresses or perfumes, but it didn't matter; the flowers smelled wonderful, and in my white summer dresses I was as elegant as my friends in Casa who wore the latest styles from Paris. My husband loved me. Could I destroy his life because of my leprosy? Had I infected him already? I should run away with an Arab who would accept me with my foot like that. In any case, I could go and beg in Fez, but what if I gave my disease to everyone? No, I had to leave for the islands all alone, to wait and see if Tonio had been infected.

I looked at my little hole as if I were looking at my coffin. It was time to take care of Youti—I had his bandages ready—and I decided to use the same ointment on myself. What did it matter? Things couldn't possibly get any worse. During the night, I couldn't breathe. I was purple, feverish. I put on more of the ointment, then took a hot bath, leaving my foot dangling outside the tub. Morning found me there, my body covered in red spots. The next day, same treatment. But my hole was clean. The itching was gone. The day Tonio came back from his mail flight, I was at the airfield, wearing my walking shoes, without a cane. And with Youti. He saw that the dog had recovered and understood at once.

"You used the same medicine as Youti?"

"Yes," I said. "It's over, but my whole body aches."

My husband took me in his arms and carried me off the airfield to the car. "Where is the sorcerer who saw to Youti?"

"Near Bousber."

We found him in a brothel; the girls served us tea. The Arab was very calm. "What your wife and your dog were suffering from is going to be cured," he said. "You must bathe your wife's body in milk. And then it will be over."

Tonio took baths in boiling milk with me. The remedy was a little costly, so we mixed some goat's milk in with the cow's milk. But I was well again.

Tonio told me, "I would have gone with you to the islands, *ma femme*. You are my reason for living. I love you as much as life itself."

Part Three

Paris–Côte d'Azur, 1932–1937

11

W<small>E WERE STILL LIVING</small> in Casablanca when
Night Flight finally went on sale in the Paris
bookstores.* We were worried about how it would be received. Every day, I bought the most important newspapers—*Comœdia, Le Figaro, Les Nouvelles Littéraires.* I cut
out all the good reviews and pasted them in a notebook—
sometimes two copies of them, because it tickled me to
see so many photos of Tonio. When he came back, he
laughed to see the same photos, the same articles. Then
Night Flight won an important literary prize, the Prix
Fémina, and became a favorite for the Prix Goncourt.
Gringoire printed a funny cartoon that showed a winged
aviator being ravished by the female judges of the Prix
Fémina. They had changed the date of their meeting
for him. In general, they awarded their prize after the
Goncourt, but that year they met before the Goncourt
was announced. Tonio and I were very pleased by this dis-
tinction.

Tonio's publisher called him back to Paris again. Tonio
was beginning to find all the traveling back and forth

Vol de nuit was published in France in October 1931 and came out in
English as *Night Flight* the following year.

quite an impediment to his sense of freedom. What was more, he couldn't get the company to give him more leave every month. So he decided, without telling me, to be a pilot no more. One day out of the blue he announced that we were leaving. And I followed . . .

★

THIS TIME WE WERE SETTLING in Paris for good. The apartment on rue de Castellane was far too small, but it was impossible to find a place to rent at that time—the prices were unbelievable. You had to bribe the concierges, pay key money, and run all over Paris, only to find nothing.

By chance we stumbled on a lovely apartment not far from where André Gide lived that was available, though many people were eager to rent it. But my husband was the man who had won the Prix Fémina, and the owner gave us his preference. The street was pleasant, and the apartment overlooked a garden, but we had to wait several months before moving in.

Tonio was overextended, forever busy with appointments, visits to the ladies of the Prix Fémina, photo sessions, invitations, and admirers, male and female. His success grew greater by the day. Distant cousins who had never before noticed that they were related to him were suddenly laying claim to the succesful writer. They even came to wish him a happy birthday, which they had never done before. Importunate lady admirers besieged us from all sides. I could no longer keep track of all the names, and we missed half our appointments. Tonio wasn't writing anymore; we spent our life in other people's houses; we didn't even have lunch alone together anymore.

Finally, one of his cousins took us off to her château, six hours out of Paris. At last, some green, some peace! Little old ladies sat by the fireside in the château's large, chilly rooms; I was delighted. But our stay ended all too quickly and our return to Paris was a nightmare once more. My husband was constantly on the telephone, even in the bathtub. My nerves could no longer take it. In the evening, we had to travel to Deauville, Honfleur, or Bagatelle, a constant coming and going that made no sense. There was talk of seizing the moment to make films of *Southern Mail* in France and of *Night Flight* in America. Editors, journalists, and agents were all sitting on his bed. We no longer had a single minute alone. At three in the morning, when the telephone finally quieted down, Tonio would fall into a dead sleep, and then, very early, the telephone would start in again. He had no secretary, there were only he and I, doing our best. After the calm of the white villas of Morocco and my anguish over his night flights, I was becoming almost hysterical. He would often ask me, "What can we do?"

He couldn't walk ten yards down the street without meeting up with some intellectual who spent his life in a café, such as Léon-Paul Fargue* and countless others.

*Léon-Paul Fargue (1876–1947): A French poet best known for his 1939 book *Le Piéton de Paris* (A Pedestrian in Paris), a collection of incidents, memories, and visions happened upon while strolling idly through Paris.

And then they would go off drinking and talking. It was hellish. No more home life, no more time spent thinking; we lived as if we were on public display in a shopwindow.

But Tonio loved the sky too much. He knew how the clouds changed, how the winds could be treacherous. He saw himself at the apogee of his career, but he also knew that everyone was waiting, watching, always hoping for the vertiginous fall of the current man of the hour. That was why he decided one day to run away from Paris. But it was harder now than it had been before. Rivière, the great Rivière of *Night Flight*, who was none other than Didier Daurat, director of the French airmail service, the Aéropostale, had been threatened with the worst: imprisonment based on false evidence, false testimony. He was accused of having stolen some mail, he had been dismissed from his position as head of the airmail service in Toulouse, and he was being called a forger. Chaumié, the head of civil aviation at the Ministry of Aviation, had been charged as well. Daurat and Chaumié: two men whose honesty could withstand any ordeal. The newspapers were full of the latest news of their trials. My husband stood firmly behind them; his confidence in the two accused men never wavered. He was right. It was like something from a Sherlock Holmes mystery: the real forger was finally discovered, and Daurat and Chaumié were acquitted. But the company had changed hands and would now belong to the state. Those who wanted to fly for it would have to meet special, very exacting requirements. Tonio did not persist. An airplane manufacturer had asked him to come to Saint-Laurent-de-La-Salanque, near Toulouse, to help perfect the prototype of a new plane. He accepted. He told me he had found work again, somewhat difficult work. The prototype had already drowned several of its crews. The manufacturer had tinkered with the motor a little and wanted to take the plane through some new tests with new pilots. Tonio left for Saint-Laurent. He gave me as his address the Hôtel Lafayette in Toulouse and begged me to stay in Paris. It was winter, but the apartment was heated only by two fireplaces. I was too weak to bear the chill, so he put me up in a room in a charming hotel on the Left Bank, the Hôtel du Pont-Royal.

I had asthma. I didn't know much about the disease and thought Morocco had given me its last gift: sand in my lungs. I couldn't breathe; I thought I was dying. My husband had disappeared to Toulouse a week before. I was going mad. I heard nothing from him. I asked my sister in Central America to come and help me, and fifteen days later she disembarked in Le Havre. On the telephone, my husband's voice was always half asleep and absent; by night he wrote or did whatever he wanted, and by day he was working in Toulouse. He very rarely flew the plane, which had endless mechanical problems.

"Little sister?" I asked.

"Yes," she said.

I was shaking.

"Lie down," she told me.

"Little sister, do you love me?"

"Yes, I love you. Now lie down. The doctor said you have to sleep."

"Little sister, I want to speak to my husband."

"If you're a good girl, I'll get him on the phone for you."

I could hear the distant voice of my husband saying, "Yes, Consuelo, I know, you're ill. Your sister is taking care of you. I'm not worried."

"Little sister, how long have I been sick? Three weeks? Four? Oh, little sister, why doesn't my husband come to see me?"

"Because he's working," she said.

"Little sister, I don't have any letters from my husband. He left a long time ago. Little sister, I know: he has nothing more to say to me."

"Don't think like that. I'm tempted to be angry with you. You are ill. You must not think of anything, anything . . ."

"Little sister, I feel better. For four days now, I haven't had asthma. Why do you keep me lying in bed with the shutters closed?"

"It's the doctor's orders."

"Little sister, ask him if I can get up."

The next day, I went to see the doctor.

"Madame, I do not invite all my patients to my home," the doctor told me. "But you are so alone. I've asked a very intelligent friend to dinner tonight. Promise me that you will not refuse to join us."

"I feel so unhappy, Doctor," I whispered. "I'm miserable."

"These things can happen to the happiest couples: distances, misunderstandings. Two people sometimes grow tired of each other. *C'est la fatigue à deux.*"

That evening, at dinner, the doctor's friend was there.

"May I introduce my patient, Madame de Saint-Exupéry, wife of the famous writer and pilot," he said with a flourish. "She thinks she is very sick, in other words, no longer loved by her husband. I've allowed her to get out of bed, and she's begun taking flying lessons. She wants to run away into the sky."

After dinner, the doctor's friend, André, a poet, took me back to my hotel. All the lights in the generally lackluster lobby were glowing. I asked him to join me in the bar for a moment, and he was happy to do so. We talked for a long time. Both of us had been despondent before we met, but by the end of the evening we found ourselves comforted and increasingly cheerful.

André came with me to my flying lessons, which he found absurd. He gave me poems to read, wonderful stories, and soon I was well again. I wanted to live, to play, to read more and more poems, more and more stories, ever more marvelous. With him I had found magic. I began to dream again. Through him I found the strength to go back to the apartment on rue de Castellane.

One evening after dinner, when I was back home, he told me the story of his last love. She was a married woman. He swore to me that never again did he want to love a married woman. I was in despair: I knew what he was driving at. He told me that he loved me, that I must go and see my husband in Saint-Laurent, or wherever he was, and tell him good-bye, tell him that I loved another man. That day, André believed I was free.

I was young, and André's wonderful nature ruled my heart. I left for Toulouse on a third-class ticket. My husband did not come to the train station, where I was expecting him to meet me. I went to his hotel. He asked me to let him sleep until one o'clock. I waited in his room, which smelled strongly of smoke, stale air, and leather flying gear. I shivered at the thought of the speech I would have to give him when he woke up. In my head, I repeated André's words. I wanted to carry my mission through to its end. But suddenly there was our friend Dubordier, another pilot, coming into the room.

"Do you want to have lunch?" he asked Tonio.

"No, but take my wife," Tonio yawned. "It's Sunday. I don't like taking my wife to restaurants on Sunday. You're granting me some time to sleep—thank you. She has to go back after that, take her to the train station. I've got to leave for Saint-Laurent in an hour. Good-bye, Consuelo. Kiss me, dear wife, and give your sister a kiss for me, too."

"But Tonio, I didn't come all the way here for this," I said. "I want to speak to you."

"I understand. You probably need money. Take all you want, *chérie*. I live on café au lait and croissants."

I went back to Paris.

"Oh, André, I couldn't tell him anything," I said miserably.

"Why?"

"He was asleep."

"You don't love me, but if you tell me that you do, I'll believe it. So write him, then."

"Yes," I said with new determination. "I can do that."

And the letter went off. When it reached Tonio, he hopped on a plane at once and came back to me.

"Yes, yes," I told him. "I'm leaving you for André."

"I'll die if you leave. Stay with me, I beg you. You are my wife!"

"But I love André, Tonio. I'm sorry if I've caused you any pain. I had no news of you from Saint-Laurent. I thought I was nothing more than a thing to you. A thing that you leave parked in a hotel. And André loves me. He's waiting for me."

"Then tell him to come and get you."

"Yes, I'll ask him to come."

I called him, and a few minutes later, André was at my house. He came with some of his friends. We talked, we drank. Tonio received them bare-chested. He looked very strong with his hairy chest, and he was also very cheerful. He served them Pernod on a silver tray. We all drank together, and I stayed with my husband for life.

We never mentioned it again.

THE NEXT DAY we flew to the south of France, where he wanted finally to fly in his great monster of a hydroplane. We arrived in Saint-Raphaël while my little sister, her role as nurse at an end, sailed back to her volcano in San Salvador.

"Tonio, I'm afraid of that plane of yours; it doesn't want to swim," I told him.

"I'm not," he said. "Every day, I fly a few minutes longer over the water. It groans, it cracks. You see how my arm is swollen, almost black and blue; well, that's because I had to hold the door shut—it was coming open. It needs a certain number of hours in flight; after that it's the manufacturer's business."

"But this whole comedy with the little boat that tracks your flights, the deep-sea diver, the nurse, the respirator, and you up in the air, it drives me crazy. You know, I would like to see you open up a shoe repair shop on some street corner."

"But today I know many things," he said. "I'm no longer afraid to go far away from you. You love me as if I were your father, you take better care of me than a wife your age should know how to. And it's a bald man you're mothering. Look at me: I really am bald. Darling, today I'm going to finish testing our monstrous creature. Come and see it; tell it to behave itself."

"That's all fine, Tonio," I said, "but where will we go then?"

"We'll fly somewhere else, wherever there's work for me to do. I prefer stormy nights to the café chatter of Paris, and airplanes are my only way of saving myself. You mustn't hate them; if I do the long-distance flight I'm thinking of and win the prize, I'll buy you a little plane, a Simoun. What color would you like it to be? You can have a bar installed inside, throw in some colored pillows, flowers, and we'll fly it around the world."

"Oh yes, Tonio, I love to dream, but on the ground. In the air, I grow fainthearted thinking of the long flights when you are alone. If you were to hurt yourself very badly someday and I couldn't come to help you, I would go mad."

"You can always help someone you love just by loving them very much, with all that you are."

"Yes, I know, Tonio . . ."

"All right, it's time to go. Forgive me, I have to be in the air in ten minutes. Tomorrow I'll be paid for the flight. It's a stroke of luck for us, we'll be rich, rich. Think about what present you'll want to give me once I've tamed the monster."

This was the time of the Great Depression in America; the Côte d'Azur was deserted, abandoned by its faithful visitors. The hotels stayed open nevertheless. The staff had to be paid and fed, and from time to time a French clientele would take advantage of their presence. But for the most part the great palaces were empty. My husband put me up at the Hôtel Continental. His entire family lived on the Côte, and for the price of a room we had a whole floor with full service and fires burning in the rooms. What luxury! My husband's friends, military pilots all of them, gathered at our place in the evening for cocktails, and we sang old French songs.

During Tonio's absence, I looked at the empty rooms, their unbelievable luxury. My dog chased itself through the suites. What peace, I thought to myself, what calm . . .

Suddenly I heard a violently loud noise that echoed through the city. Everyone ran to their windows, and so did I. I saw nothing but the sea, which had risen into the air like a cloud and then fell quickly back down, as if cannon balls were being thrown into it. As I watched the surface of the water, my dog took off and I ran to get him—the rascal had discovered another Pekinese. I carried Youti back angrily, and from my window, looking out at the sea, I slowly understood, as night fell on the icy water, that the cloud of water that had alarmed the population of Saint-Raphaël was my husband's monstrous hydroplane. It had slammed into the sea so fast that the water had risen several yards, only to fall back down with the terrible sound that had startled the whole city. As night fell, the sea was smooth again, smooth as the Dead Sea. I didn't move from my window. I don't know how long I stayed there, immobile. Someone knocked at the door, but so softly that my dog didn't even bark. It was strange. I hesitated to move from where I was, and I let them knock harder. After a few minutes, I went to the door. My husband was carried in on a stretcher, like a wounded man. We laid him down on the bed. He'd been given all kinds of medicines, artificial respiration, oxygen, and so forth. They left me alone with him.

"Ah, Tonio," I said, "you crashed into the sea. You're freezing. Your pants are all wet, they're getting the bed all wet. My little one, I'm here, let me give you a rub-down . . ."

In my great haste, I picked up the first bottle that came to hand. It was pure ammonia, which I used to bleach my dog's fur.

"Yes, that will warm your chest up, because you're so cold!"

His furry chest absorbed the ammonia until I was choking from it. It worked much better than eau de Cologne. The ammonia entered Tonio's lungs when he was already on the other side and made his bronchia react. He began breathing again, he stirred; water was coming out of his nose.

Stricken with fear, I shouted, "Help, my husband is dying, I'm all alone!" But by a miracle Tonio came back to himself. I pulled him into the bathroom by the head, like a huge doll, in the process banging his skull, which bled into the bathtub. A bellboy came to help me. We plunged him into boiling water. I wanted to cook him. He cried out, "Ow, it's too hot! Do you want me to die?"

"But darling, it's very good for you," I said.

"My clothes are still on."

"Yes, but what does it matter?"

"Help me take off my pants, I'm all stiff."

"Here, let me do it. You fell into the water."

"Ah, now I remember. Let me tell you what happened. My hydroplane didn't want to land on the water. I'm cold."

"But *chéri*, you're sitting in boiling water."

Captain Marville came up with the bellboy to see me, then the journalists arrived. The telephone began its frenetic ringing again—everyone wanted an interview.

A few hours later, we had a party in the Air Force barracks. We laughed and danced on the tables. But after that day, Tonio no longer wanted to sleep at night. He would press his nose against the window as I stood behind him in my nightgown, pulling him by his hand toward the bed. He would get up again and again. I would go and bring him back. It lasted a month, maybe two.

He had been as if dead. He had passed through death itself. Now he knew it.

12

"IT'S EASY TO DIE," he told me. "To drown. Let me tell you. You have very little time to get used to the idea that you can no longer breathe oxygen. You have to breathe water into your lungs. You must not cough, the water must not go in through your nose. You are, as I was, relieved to breathe in the first mouthful of water. It's cool, and everything is fine afterward. I realized that I had gone into the water with my plane. Water was already inside the cabin. If I didn't get out of there immediately, I was going to drown, to die. If I managed to find an open door and get back up to the surface, I would escape from death. I wasn't far from the coast, and even as tired as I was, I could swim. The rescue boat would see me. I groped, stretching my hand out to the right, then to the left. What an effort! I felt a great emptiness. My hand touched nothing. It was so dark, I had no notion of what position I was in. My plane had fallen backwards, I had my head down and my feet up. I thought of the turkey you had bought for me from some peasants the day before, which I had driven back to the Mirador. You wanted to celebrate Christmas in our home. The turkey was waiting for me; I couldn't drown. I wanted to go through an opening that my hand could feel, but my foot was caught in something metallic, like a chain around my ankle. I had a knife, but by the time I had cut off my leg or cut through the metal, I would have suffocated. I resigned myself to death, but I wanted to be in a more comfortable position. I didn't know that my head was down. I said to myself, "I want to die lying flat: let's go!" I pulled my legs out abruptly and decided to swallow my second mouthful of water once I was in the right position. I forced my legs to move. The leg that was stuck came loose. With a superhuman effort, I threw myself into the hole my hand had felt. It was the door leading into the passengers' cabin. I was swimming, suffocating, and I felt myself struggling to rotate into an upright position. My body reacted on its own until my head was upright again. I was able to stand up, and my head bumped against the ceiling. I was bleeding. But there was still a pocket of air up there. I took a good long breath. Then I took stock of my situation.

"The plane I was in had an upper section like a convertible car where the engineer had been sitting, along with the mechanic who had been looking after the plane's last flight. In the fall, the two men were thrown free of the plane, into the sea. The little boat that 'baby-sat' my flights saw them fall and went immediately to their rescue. The mechanic had a very thorough acquaintance with this prototype, which had already drowned several of its crews. The last time, near Marseille, they had died because they couldn't get out of the plane. It was close to the coast, but the metal had been twisted in the fall, the doors were stuck, and the men had died because they were unable to open them.

"Immediately after he was rescued, the mechanic dove down with all his strength and courage to the bottom of the sea. Perhaps it was because he was used to working on the ill-fated flights of this particular prototype, perhaps it was chance or simply the will of God, I don't know: on his very first dive he came upon the wing of the submerged plane. He tore up his hand trying to open the door. He needed air and went back to the surface. That was all he could do. The others rushed to his rescue. As for me, down in the bottom of the sea, I had heard a vague sound. Through the door, which he had managed to pry open a little way, a dim greenish light entered the passengers' cabin where I was, and I tried to think. The water was already up to my mouth. I tried to win a few more seconds by putting my nose against the ceiling to get the last of the oxygen left in the plane. The blood flowing from my head wound refreshed my palate a little. I understood that my only chance of saving myself was to throw myself towards that greenish light, which couldn't be anything but the bottom of the sea, the open sea.

"If I could manage it, I would find myself back outside this steel prison, and return to the surface. I gathered the last of my strength, checked my knees and feet, which were hurting, clenched and unclenched my hands, and after a great yawn against the ceiling of the plane, which made me smile because it was like a kiss good-bye to this machine that had wanted to drown me, I threw myself toward the green light and quickly found the limpid water of the Mediterranean. I rose to the surface. My hands were seen by the rescue boat, and they fished me out of the high seas, senseless, stiff, as if dead. The nurse, the diver, and the mechanic gave me first aid. They had forgotten the respirator. My heart wasn't beating. It was a little too late. That was why they took me to you at the hotel, where the ammonia rub you gave me woke up my sleeping bronchia.

"Life, my little wife, oh, Consuelo—I owe you my life."

13

ONE DAY MY MOTHER-IN-LAW, Marie de Saint-Exupéry, took us to the château where Tonio grew up and which he had so beautifully described in *Southern Mail*. It was an old provincial château. The parquet floors in its vast salons gleamed as only the French know how to make them gleam. Made of small pieces of inlaid wood, they had become, with the caress of many footsteps and the famous French method of waxing, as smooth as a vast platter. The library of Saint-Maurice, with its red felt and baronial furniture, seemed like something from a fairy tale, and the stairway was so long it looked as if it went up to Heaven. The shadows cast by the trees in the region's famous light made the sunsets magical.

All the neighbors came to see us, kiss us, and wish us all kinds of wonderful happiness once again.

However, Tonio had to think about his career as a pilot. Our vacation under the tall branches of Saint-Maurice was soon over, and one morning we had to go back to Paris, to our new apartment on the rue de Chanaleilles.

Our new home was flooded with light, and the rooms were well proportioned. The walls were painted green, the green of a forest in early spring, and I hung curtains of pale green tulle at the windows, one at a time, for we were quite poor then. But we were together, and we were happy. Tonio rested. He would walk through the apartment for hours without doing anything, looking at me, talking to me. I played the lady of the house, serious and diligent.

Creating intimacy in three small rooms on the ground floor, with simple furniture and a telephone that never stopped ringing, required a great deal of energy and imagination and all the courage of a young, devoted, and loving wife.

After a week of work, I was very tired. Our maid came back to us, but she stole; Tonio caught her at it. A man, an Arab, replaced her. He adored Tonio. Life was easier that way. Tonio was happy as a child with his big Arab servant. It reminded us of our life in Morocco. We gave parties; the servant prepared enormous platters of couscous that we ate sitting on the floor, and we had as many as twenty people over at a time. We read, we sang. . . . But we were seriously in need of money. Tonio was hard at work developing an idea for a film, but it didn't bring in any income.

"Consuelo," he told me, "you know very well that I can't stay here between these four walls waiting for the good Lord to rain fistfuls of gold down upon me."

"It could happen, Tonio. Your book is selling very well. Your screenplays are in the hands of good agents. You'll see, they'll come to find you here with pots of gold."

"I'm tired of doing nothing. It's very nice of you to play a record for me on the gramophone every day when I wake up, and I do love Bach, it's true, but I'm starting to get bored. Though I'd love to have been a composer, like him, to be able to say things without words, in that secret language that is given only to the elect, the initiates, to poets . . . I often wonder if there are different breeds of men."

"Yes, Tonio, I believe we're all very different from one another. A flower, a white tablecloth, and the sound of your footsteps are enough for me. I like to hear them as much as the music of your Bach. They speak to me, they explain life to me. You are my key of sol, my key of fa. Through you, I come to God more quickly."

"And for me you are my child, even when I am far from you, even for a day. When I fly away forever, I will be holding your hand. But you mustn't act like a frail child who weeps and gazes at its guardian with sobs and tears. I have to leave, leave, leave . . ."

One day a lady presented herself at our house and offered to be Tonio's agent. She told him she would teach him to write screenplays. He asked me to let him go out alone with her. I didn't understand why I had to be absent in order for him to learn, but I trusted my husband. They went out together all the time, to cafés and other places, and spent long hours talking. But Tonio still wasn't writing. I suffered, all alone between my green walls.

A friend of ours asked him for some articles for the magazine *Marianne*. Tonio said he didn't know how to write for magazines and refused. But we had to pay our rent—we were already two months late. So Tonio went through his papers and found a short story, "Prince of Argentina." His text was accepted, and he was paid for it. He gave them another one. For my part, little by little, by making myself small, simple, and tender, I was able to get him to sit down at his table and write his screenplay. He quickly became involved in what he was doing. He liked his characters, and when his admirers came knocking at our door, he was annoyed. He was traveling, flying, dying with his characters, and those were sunny days in our home. Alas, I knew it couldn't last long.

He was offered a chance to go to Moscow to write an article. The idea thrilled him.

"I'm leaving, Consuelo, I'm leaving tomorrow for Moscow. I need to see men and nations as they evolve. I feel like a eunuch tied down at home by your ribbons."

My poor ribbons! He asked me for the one I was wearing in my hair, to carry with him in his wallet. His face was already distant, as if carved out of wood or steel. He was already in Moscow, sharing in the rigors of the five-year plan being developed there. From time to time, he muttered a few thoughts. "I know the Russians have very good planes," he said once. "They're doing advanced research. They're very strong."

"Yes, Tonio, the Russians are strong," I said skeptically. "They've forgotten their songs, they've forgotten love. I hear that they no longer have families there. The children are placed in nurseries from the moment they're born."

"That may be true for now. They need all their strength. They're preparing for a great struggle, they no longer have time to sing or to love. But one day they'll go back to their music, their songs, their women, their lives as men. I'm sorry I'm not taking you with me. I'll tell you everything. The phone lines between Paris and Russia are very good and not expensive. Every evening I'll tell you what I've seen. Pack my bags."

Before leaving, Tonio gave me some money. This time his absence didn't make me sad. I would work on the house a little and have some surprises ready for him when he returned.

I also decided to take some sculpting classes at the Académie Ranson. The sculptor Maillol encouraged me to do it. The Académie was my Russia. One day, at sunset, drinking a glass of Pernod with my studio friends, I heard the cries of a newspaper vendor: "Fatal accident! The *Maxime-Gorki,* the giant Russian airplane, crashes!

All passengers dead!" Saint-Ex was supposed to fly on the *Maxime-Gorki*. It had been planned as part of the article he was writing. Everything around me dissolved into a haze of huge newspaper headlines shouted out by vendors who jumbled together all the day's stories to tempt prospective buyers.

As it turned out, my husband had flown in the giant airplane the day before. It was another of the miracles of his life, for he was supposed to have made the flight on the day of the crash. During that period, the Russians guarded all their airports closely; they were already making ready for their fierce war against the Germans. But they had found Tonio to be a true devotee of aviation, and the head of the airport hadn't been able to wait until the next day to show him the enormous plaything they had invented. Thanks to him, Tonio had flown alone with the crew of the *Maxime-Gorki* one day before the catastrophe. I held the newspaper on my knees. One of my classmates read me the article. Little by little, I read in his expression that my husband had not been on board the plane when it crashed.

I went back to rue de Chanaleilles, where I stayed glued to the telephone, waiting to hear my strolling minstrel's voice. The phone call came exactly on time, as it did every evening. And I was able to fall asleep that night, still dreaming about the new horizons he was discovering.

In the morning, the concierge woke me up. In her sourest voice, she demanded that I get dressed immediately. My apartment was being seized. The furniture and all the little possessions I cherished would be sold at auction on the spot. I persuaded them to give me a few hours, to refrain from piling the furniture up in the street, and to let me stay in the apartment waiting for my husband's call.

It came at the expected time. When I told him about the events of the day, he laughed and begged my pardon for not having warned me.

"I have a letter in my pocket that will explain the whole story to you," he added. "In any case, our furniture is worthless. The proceeds from this seizure will satisfy the government, and it will save us from having to pay huge taxes on the money I earned during the years in Buenos Aires."

He added, "After this I'll have a clean slate and we'll be very careful to pay our taxes every year. Please rent a small apartment at the Hôtel du Pont-Royal, where I'll come to join you soon."

Of course, at the hotel our life was more public. His article about Russia, which was published in a Parisian daily paper, once again enlarged our circle of admirers and flatterers. Our brief life of intimacy was beginning to unravel.

14

"Consuelo, Consuelo, I'm bored! I'm bored to death. I can't sit in an armchair all day, or in a café. I have legs, I need to walk, to walk . . ."

"I know, Tonio, cities make you sick to your stomach. You love your fellowmen for their work. You don't understood what we call the sweetness of life, those exquisite moments of sharing nothing more than good or bad weather. Unfortunately for me, and for you too sometimes, you're the kind of man who is constantly in need of struggle, conquest. Leave, then. Leave."

I sensed that Tonio was suffering for all mankind, that in some way he wanted to make them better. He was a man who chose his own destiny, but he had to pay a high price for his freedom, and he knew it. There were no more long dinners now, no more evenings of dancing, no more losing ourselves in parties. Not one spare second was granted him, for something almost divine had made him a kind of seed, destined to sow a better race of men on the earth. He had to be helped in his struggles, in the painful process of giving birth to himself and to his books, amid all the everyday cares that harried him and among all those who had not yet perceived that something in his heart was speaking with God.

I was still very young then, and I didn't fully under-stand all these things. I observed my husband the way one watches a great tree grow, without ever being conscious of its transformation. I touched him as if I were touching a tree in his garden, a tree in whose shadow I would have liked, much later, to fall into my final sleep. I was used to my tree's miracles. His detachment from material things had almost become natural to me. And we lived in expec-tation of discovering a better world that would not be un-attainable.

Every evening in our modest rooms in the Hôtel du Pont-Royal, he unfolded and refolded his maps. He spoke to me of Baghdad, of strange cities still undiscovered, and of the white Indians who are supposed to exist somewhere along the course of the Amazon.

"Consuelo, don't you think that in the water, in the ocean, there are pathways, and beings moving about who think as we do but simply do not breathe as we do, and whose proportions are probably elastic—I mean, who en-large and shrink in a minute?"

"Certainly, Tonio," I would say, carried away with the notion of letting my imagination fly. "I think that the whales, the giant fish that we see, may be no more than pebbles in the ocean, or earthworms. I believe that these characters you're imagining move through the water more easily than we do on land. Perhaps, at this very moment, a woman like me, her body covered with eyes and endowed with greater sensitivity than I have, is thinking exactly what we've just said to each other. Maybe she's dreaming, 'On earth, the existence of thinking beings must be difficult. It's so green there, there are so many plants, stones, minerals, things that are so hard! The trees are so large they can't possibly leave any space where living beings can be born and live!' "

"Little Consuelo, listen to me, I want to leave. I'll go from Paris to Saigon, very fast, and there I will find you a little house so you can come and tell me stories."

"Saigon is very far from Paris, Tonio."

"*Oui, ma femme,* but the planes are safer now, they fly very fast. I'm longing to go to China."

"Because you like Chinese women?"

"Oh Consuelo, I like women who are small and quiet. I will surround you like a queen with a dozen of those small people so that you can play with them and you will never be alone."

★

ONE EVENING IN JANUARY 1936 I made enough very strong black coffee to fill several thermoses.* It would keep him from sleeping during the long flight from Paris to Saigon.

"Perhaps you could take some oranges along," I said. "Promise me, Tonio, that you won't fly over water or even anything that looks like water. It's silly of me to bother you with my superstitions, but I don't believe water likes you."

---

*In fact, Saint-Exupéry set off on his Paris–Saigon flight on December 29, 1935; Consuelo's memory is a few days off the mark here.

"On the contrary, maybe it does like me; the Mediterranean let me swim like a fish, remember? You're unfair to water, my darling. Don't give me any oranges, I have a lot more fuel in my plane this time. I won't even take an overcoat."

"Oh Tonio, I wish it were spring already and that we were both in Saigon, in a house full of flowers!"

"When it is, you'll be able to feed me all the oranges you want, and the little Chinese women will pick them the way young girls pick cherries in France."

Then the mechanic and Lucas, an aviator friend, came in without knocking. They spoke in serious tones, in the voices of men who had been awake all night preparing with all possible care the route that the pilot would follow for several days and nights. They both felt responsible for their older brother, who, like a bird, was singing "Le temps des cerises" ("Cherry Blossom Time"), kissing me, and demanding another piece of chocolate, as if he were simply leaving for a drive to the suburbs.

We crossed Paris laughing and singing. I told him I didn't want to spend the whole spring in Saigon or China. He would have to bring me back quickly to Agay, where I had promised to meet his mother and sisters. I thought the water in the Orient might be too salty to swim in.

Reporters from *L'Intransigeant, Paris-Soir,* and the other daily papers studied his every word and gesture on the runway. My husband was a true giant, and it was hard for me to stay close to him. The journalists did their job, taking pictures when we kissed and when he waved goodbye. The engine roared, and then there was nothing.

THE WAITING HAD BEGUN. I no longer sang or laughed. I was free of my wifely duties, my woman's heart seemed useless.

Paris was still asleep. I asked my friends to let me walk by myself for a while on the Champs-Elysées. I circled around the Arc de Triomphe, and for the first time, full of emotion, I stopped to gaze at the flame that burns in memory of the Unknown Soldier. I meditated and prayed for the men who had been missing since the war. I prayed for myself, too, and watched the city slowly awakening to go about its life. First there were only a few passersby, then the last of the night owls who hadn't yet gone home, then the laborers in the train stations and the great marketplaces of Les Halles. And there were the unmistakable middle-aged women who were on their way to help other people with their housekeeping. The rhythms of their footsteps and their gazes were all alike. At eight o'clock, the waiters began to open the terraces of the cafés. I watched them and felt like having a café au lait.

How could I be of use? What was my role, really? What was my immediate duty? To wait, wait, and wait some more . . .

The faces of the office workers who stopped to have a coffee on their way to work passed before me and distracted me from the anxiousness in my heart, which remained fixed on Tonio's absence and the danger he could be in.

But he, he was ensconced in his sky, bound for the Orient.

15

M<small>Y HUSBAND WOULD BE FLYING</small> for several days over sands and strange cities that loomed ever larger in my childish imagination, like the Bible's endless deserts. I thought nostagically of my home in El Salvador, where I used to watch sorcerers pawing the dry earth in search of water like animals on the scent of a female. The wait for rain was a very tense time; the pastures were dry and the herds were dying for lack of water, which had disappeared because of the earthquakes. The peasants were worried; all their hopes lay in the sorcerers' hands. The answer their divining rods received was a matter of life and death for the whole country. The riverbed was dry. The river had gone off on a journey through the bowels of the earth, or somewhere else for all I know. I saw whole flocks lie down on the earth to die and heard their choruses of dying moans. Yet the sky was pure blue; tropical sunlight bathed the country, flouting the hopes of men and beasts. During those agonizing days, the land-owners would gather together under the full moon, light huge bonfires that blazed red in their courtyards, make coffee, and chant prayers to make the rain come. Often the miracle took place, and rain—longed-for, cherished rain— would put thousands of sheep back on their feet. Among the men who chanted for rain that way, no one could say who would be rich or poor the next day. Equality was determined by fate. On one stretch of land, there might be dew that very night; on another, drought, thirst, and death.

I too had to pray, chant, wait, wait, and hope. I tried to remember the dignity of the peasants in the driest regions of my country. I was in an arid land, a land of tribulation. Would he succeed or wouldn't he?

The complicated numbers the engineer reported meant nothing to me. I couldn't have cared less about any of that. My only hope lay in our youth, which to me seemed eternal, and in our love, which was so pure that it had to have touched God. My hope lay in his strong hands, which knew how to throw all of his bodily weight, all of his energy and vitality, into the air currents flowing through an unknown sky. Only he knew how to fly like that toward the marvelous Orient.

I made my way to the atelier of one of my painter friends, André Derain. He was waiting for dawn and the first colors of the day to create a miracle of light on the hair, lips, and dresses of his models. I knew his habits well and slipped in without making a sound. I breathed in the smell of the coffee he was making on a large coal-burning stove while a very young girl, completely naked, her breasts just beginning to bloom, let her hair down, making herself look all the more naked. I sat down in the atelier's old red armchair. I don't think even my heartbeat made a sound that day. The great painter came and went, blowing on his big cup of coffee, eyeing the first gleams of sunlight, touching his model's long hair with one finger.

In the middle of his little promenade, he finally discovered me.

"You, Consuelo, here so early?"

"Yes," I said. "My husband has left on a long flight and I didn't know where to go so early in the morning, so I came to sit here with you, if I won't disturb you."

"But I want to paint you just as you are: don't move."

"Oh no, that's too much for me to bear. You know, my husband is going to be in the air for whole days and nights and, who knows, perhaps for the rest of his life!"

He understood the gravity of the situation, for he loved his friend Antoine, and asked the model to serve me a cup of coffee.

He didn't work at all that day. We talked about pilots, their simplicity, their way of risking their lives, how they chose to forget their companions who were killed. For them, it was natural to meet a monster-wind, a dragon-wind, a conquering wind. It was so simple. That day, Derain and his model saw me as something more alive than a woman. I contained in myself the whole life of another person, the religion of another being concentrated in the love that lay within me. They consecrated their entire day to me.

Toward evening we received the first news of our pilot: all was well. "Clear sky. No wind. Making headway." That was the telegram Tonio sent me!

The second day of waiting was devoid of news. No hope. I kept a vigil. The telephone lay mute and motionless near my pillow. Toward evening, some friends came over—the silence was growing troubling. No news. Catastrophe could be read on every face. The silence expanded around us.

On the third day, the headlines of all the newspapers read, "Saint-Exupéry Disappears on Paris–Saigon Flight."*

Despair. Grief. I was wrenched with anguish and pain. I had a presentiment of great misfortune. I hadn't wanted him to go, yet everything in me had encouraged him to do it.

Then a message arrived, enormous, lifesaving: "It's me, Saint-Exupéry, I'm alive."

I left at once with his mother for Marseille, where he was to dock on his return from his epic journey. We both stood on the Vieux-Port waiting for the boat, amid friends, curious onlookers, and journalists who had come to capture his first smile, his first emotion, for a front-page photo.

His boat was delayed for several hours. His mother and I had nothing more to say to each other. A great weariness overcame us both, we could feel it in our arms, our whole bodies. And then the siren announced that our dear Tonio was finally going to be returned to us.

At that moment I cried out, "No, it's not possible. I will never see him again!"

I ran away, swift as a gazelle, but one of my friends caught me and held me back with all his force, saying, "But you're mad!"

*On December 30, 1935, Saint-Exupéry's plane crashed in the Libyan desert, 125 miles west of Cairo. He and his mechanic, André Prévot, walked through the desert for four days until they were picked up by Bedouins and returned to civilization.

"Yes, I'm mad from waiting, I'm afraid. I want nothing more, nothing in the world. He is alive, he is alive, that was all I wanted to know, and now I can go, I can go to a place where no one ever waits again, for anything."

A fit of weeping calmed me down. Soon my husband was holding me in his arms. "But you look like a clown with these tears flowing on all sides. Messieurs, take a picture of my wife," he added, turning toward the journalists. "She is none too lovely to look at today, she's in the midst of a great tempest, so leave me alone with her. I'm the only one who can save her." And he whispered in my ear, "Let's go to the hotel, the two of us. Don't be afraid. I'm with you. I have so many stories to tell you. Is it true that you tried to flee when the boat came in? Is it true that you wanted to run away? Is it true that you wanted me to go from door to door asking where you were? I would have walked all my life to find you, just as I walked on and on, despite my thirst, to see you again. Why did you want to run away?"

"Do I really look like a clown?" I asked him, huddling very tightly against him.

"Yes, you have a big banana nose, but soon you'll be beautiful, very beautiful. You'll sleep in my arms, nice and calm, and I'll take you to see the desert that spared my life. I won't leave you again, ever."

My mother-in-law announced that some friends were giving a magnificent dinner for us and that we should get dressed for it.

"It's wartime, *ma petite maman*," Tonio answered. "My wife and I are going just as we are."

With his big hands, he gestured toward his casual clothes and my tousled head.

My mother-in-law resigned herself to it, but she wasn't entirely pleased.

I don't know how we got back to Paris and then to a clinic in Divonne-les-Bains. I do remember a doctor who made me take a bath in very hot water, which calmed my nerves.

I was finally able to sleep again, and to smile, and I wrote to my husband to come and pick me up. I was cured; I no longer wanted to run away, I wanted only to be in his arms. I was no longer a fruit that falls from the tree but a seed that wanted to be sowed, planted in the ground for all eternity. I wanted to live in my husband's heart. He was my star, my destiny, my faith, my end. I was small, but I had within me an immense power for living. I had gathered all the starlight in the universe into my eyes in order to bathe him in its glow.

A love like that was a serious illness, an illness from which you never entirely recover.

Soon I was unfair, jealous, belligerent, impossible to live with. I would not give so much as a smile to all the women whose names were noted down in his book every day for cocktails, lunches, meetings in Paris. I missed the clear sky God had given me when he made me Tonio's wife. I was very bad—I couldn't endure the feigned shyness of the young girls, the high school girls who asked him to give them his autograph on a book or a photo, to say nothing of my conduct toward the women who dared to intrude further on our intimacy.

In spite of everything, I lost the battle. Tonio needed more gentle landscapes, tenderer things, lighter baggage that could be left anywhere.

16

$\mathcal{I}$ WAS UNHAPPY, horribly unhappy. I confided in everyone: my dressmaker, my doctor, my lawyer, my best friend. I told all of Paris. I thought, justifiably, that all of Paris would take pity on me, would protect and console me in my romantic sorrows. I was young and naïve. Today I understand what Napoleon meant when he said, "For the pain of love, the only remedy is flight."

I had reached that point. One of my friends loaned me the keys to his pied-à-terre so I could go there and cry as much as I wanted. I was no longer loved. That was the kind of woman I had become: an unloved woman. I had just enough strength left to keep from crying in front of my servants or those who rejoiced in my despair. I took refuge in the pied-à-terre when I couldn't hold out any longer and wept to my heart's content; the moment I got there I took my clothes off and started crying, and went on crying until the clock struck the time when I had to return to my home and my duties as the lady of the house. My unhappiness made me forget what it was to rest. Tonio heard about a clinic in Switzerland where I could undergo a sleeping treatment. Soon I was shipped off there.

The clinic in Bern was a kind of penal colony: I had an empty room with only a bed, not even a table, and there were nightly walks to tire out the patients. When I had trouble relaxing, two ogresses came in the middle of the night and, each holding me firmly by one arm, made me pace up and down the garden paths. I decided I would be the one to wear them out. I had learned to walk in the desert! When they reached the limits of their strength, they took me back to my bed and suggested I wake them up if I wanted to go for another turn around the garden. I stretched out on my bed just long enough to rest a little and then called to them that I wanted to go back outside and walk!

I already knew the garden pathways by heart. I talked to them about the trees and all the journeys I had made in my life.

"Why can't we go for a walk in the city for a change of scene?" I proposed.

By seven A.M., they were the ones leaning on me.

The next day a different woman was assigned to me, along with a thickset man, and those two were tireless. After three weeks of forced marches, I still couldn't fall asleep.

ONE DAY, AT LUNCHTIME, my husband appeared. He was led into the dining room, where each table had a number. I didn't have the strength to eat even the lone potato I had been allotted. A familiar and somewhat brusque voice called, "Consuelo!"

For three weeks he had forgotten me, or else his letters had not been delivered.

All my bitterness suddenly rose up in my heart. His hand rested on my shoulder. "They told me: it's number seven. Forgive me, I didn't recognize you."

"What do *you* want?"

I was pale and thin. He took me in his arms.

"Come with me right now. I'll take you away from here."

"They're killing me. I've written you several times. I've begged you to come at once, and you haven't answered me a single time!"

I wept in his arms. The attendants had pushed us into a small side room. "Tell me that you're feeling fine," he whispered in my ear. "I'm going to ask them to put your clothes on." But the nurse was already pulling me out of his arms, saying it was time to take a shower.

I saw nothing more of Tonio after that. I no longer wrote to him. I had lost all hope of ever leaving that hellish place. His brief visit had been like a dream. I wasn't even sure that he had actually been there. I was hungry, very hungry. The smell of food reached me from far away, from the other building, through the window. I began filching bits of bread from the neighboring room, which was occupied by a man with a goiter who never ate a thing. I mustered up a little energy, and with the help of a priest who came on Saturdays to administer confession to the patients I managed to send a long telegram to a woman friend in Paris, describing my situation.

My husband was busy at that time writing the script for his film *Anne-Marie*. My friend had a hard time finagling an invitation from his group, which was staying in a little city on the outskirts of Paris.

She finally got there and cried to Tonio, "Consuelo has to steal bread just to stay alive. If you're too busy to rescue her, I'll have to be the one to do it."

My husband knew I wasn't allowed to have any correspondence. He told the story to his companions. "What a magnificent subject for a film," they said. "But your wife is dying, Saint-Ex!"

Tonio explained that the doctor had assured him I was making progress and was in good enough condition to undergo his infallible treatment. It was extremely important that he refrain from spoiling me or writing to me.

The actors and the director protested and persuaded him that after the anguish I had endured during his disappearance in Libya, this was enough to drive me mad. They bundled him aboard a train bound for Switzerland, and he arrived at the clinic once more.

His first gesture was to show me two tickets for Paris. I didn't understand, I couldn't hear very well, he had to repeat everything. He was weeping like a child and begging me to forgive him. I had lost about thirty pounds, and he had to use a piece of string to hold my skirt up around my waist.

We spent three days in a hotel in Bern. He made me drink milk, eat; he gave me some peanuts I barely touched.

In the train that took us back to Paris, he reproached me for not having given him a clear description of how severe the clinic's regime was and swore to me that he had known nothing about it. I wasn't well enough to bear the idea of going back to Paris, into the maelstrom that always surrounded him. I told him I wanted to go to El Salvador and stay there until my skirt would stay up around my waist again.

"I'll follow you to the end of the world," he swore.

In the end he followed me only to Thonon-les-Bains; he knew a doctor there who could help me regain my strength.

His Parisian friends, the women, the movie people, found this inadmissible: he was becoming my nursemaid. One day I read the draft of a letter in which he said to one of his Egerias that she was beautiful but her way of thinking was not and that he didn't spend his days at the foot of his wife's bed, caring for her like a nanny. He was writing, and when he had written a page, he read it to his wife, which gave her the strength to eat a meal with him and gave him the courage to work.

Around Thonon there were a number of spots where will-o'-the-wisps sometimes appeared. That was Tonio's favorite pastime. He was constantly going out to watch them, for he believed in the fantastic. He would spend whole nights with a pharmacist who was staying at our hotel, pursuing and studying those tremulous flames that flare up from the belly of the earth. I was beginning to come back to life, and I felt like laughing with him again.

When he decided I was well, he took me back to Paris, to the Hôtel Lutétia. I couldn't conceal my distress at being in that hotel again, with all the memories. "Will we always live in a hotel?" I asked him.

He asked me to stay inside all afternoon and relax. And meekly I obeyed; I was beginning to breathe freely again, through sunny days of love.

It was the beginning of a new era. Parisian life, the decorators and their silks, the overstuffed armchairs, the Baccarat crystal champagne flutes, the rare perfumes, the refinements of the salons were nothing but the playthings of degenerates. Death was already in them. Life would soon prove me right on that point. The women who organized opium smoking parties and all the rest of the *dolce far niente* were obscene. I knew Tonio was not like those people.

I realized I was not cut out to be the wife of a fashionable writer. Sharing our laughter and our intimacy with others was always catastrophic for me. I wanted to stand beside my husband like a fierce sentinel, intensely jealous of anything that could rob him of his power, his invulnerability. I knew intuitively that he was made to die, but I wanted him to arrive at his own end, the one God was leading him to.

So I waited for him as usual, but this time with the strength our reunion had given me. Around five o'clock he came back, a piece of paper in his hand. "There's your present!"

I took it and read: it was a receipt for a duplex apartment at the top of a building on place Vauban. I looked at the floor plan: two terraces, ten rooms. I was overwhelmed! I was crying, but I wanted to move in that very night.

He took an interest in every curtain, every detail of the decor. What color did I want the walls to be?

"The color of water in a bathtub," I answered.

He had some painter friends come over to find exactly the right color. Only Marcel Duchamp found the secret, one gray day.

It was the first real home we had had since our marriage. Our friends, who had been waiting a long time, made up for lost time. The doors of our home were always open. They would say to Boris, our Russian butler, "I'm not invited, but here I am. I'm a friend of Madame."

Every woman said, "I'm not invited, but I know Monsieur very well."

Boris fed borscht to the whole company.

TONIO WAS DOING LESS PILOTING, but his love of aviation only grew. Generous and unthinking by nature, he brought home all his friends from the boulevards and the cafés, and they came back to visit more often than he would have liked. He would go out to dream on the terrace, which overlooked the dome of the Invalides, while the Paris International Exposition flooded the night with sound and light.

The sounds and lights of our intimacy, meanwhile, were beginning to wane. There was too much coming and going at home. I still hadn't completely recovered from my stay in Bern. At night I wandered down the long hallways of our apartment, sometimes dreaming of a little village on the African coast where I could live serenely with Tonio, immersed in the manuscripts that would be the only thing to separate us.

The evenings, full of guitars, were also full of pitfalls. The faces of Picasso, Max Ernst, Duchamp, other Surrealists, and so many other writers, painters, and filmmakers weren't what I needed to put my mind at rest: I needed intimacy, a silence shared by two. Tonio understood and suggested we take a trip around the Mediterranean in our plane, a Simoun.

IN MOROCCO, the French army, accompanied by drums, trumpets, and vivid cavalrymen mounted on Arab horses, paraded in front of Lyautey's coffin.* This was our first

---

*Marshal of France Louis Hubert Lyautey (1854–1934) organized the French protectorate of Morocco and kept that country under French control during World War I.

stop. We took our place among our military friends, draped in their capes of black, light blue, bright red, and white, with embroidery and golden tassels. The luxury of all the rippling fabic was like a kind of music. The natives, in their immaculate, starched capes, covered kilometers of hot sunny ground with a layer of white snow.

A colonel who looked like a handsome parakeet in his splendid uniform came to kiss my husband familiarly on both cheeks.

"You're my prisoner, and your wife is, too," he told us. "I know you're on a lecture tour, and I have to find time to see you as best I can, and the only way is for you to leave with me right now: I'm off for Cairo."

After lunch, my husband suddenly decided to go and leave me there. The trip, he claimed, would be too long, too fatiguing, I had visits to pay to our old friends in Casablanca, the plane from Casa to Athens was comfortable, and so on. In short, he said he would meet me in Athens in two weeks. Before I had a chance to protest, the two of them had dashed off into the crowd, which hadn't yet dispersed, and I was left alone among the Arabs and the camels.

Once again the waiting began.

I took the plane two weeks later, as agreed, arriving in Athens just in time for the coronation of King George. Everyone was in a state of great excitement. My husband was delivering his lecture in a theater. I took a seat in the first row, after having promised him to take off my hat if he was speaking too softly, and to pull it down over my eyes if everything was going well. When he spoke in public, Tonio's voice tended to be faint, timid, and subdued. That night he began to speak calmly and with great composure, explaining that he had lost his voice but would do his best to recount his experiences as an aviator anyway. In fact, he was speaking in a high-pitched voice, like a little boy repeating his lesson with absolute confidence. I had always seen him with his hands shaking whenever he found himself behind a podium, and when I saw him suddenly so much at ease, so sure of himself, I fainted. My Tonio had been transformed.

I came to with the help of some smelling salts, very confused. He continued his lecture, undisturbed. It was an unqualified success.

⭑

THE NEXT DAY we left for Rome. M. de Chambrun, the ambassador, recommended, in light of the diplomatic situation, that Tonio not give his lecture. We were delighted by the chance to escape from a visit to Il Duce and went home. The trip in the Simoun, which for me had been only somewhat enjoyable, nevertheless provoked the jealousy of all his women friends in Paris, each of whom believed she was destined to play the role of the ideal companion for Tonio, a role for which they all found me extremely unsuited. Back on place Vauban, he told our friends about the storm we had ridden out over the Adriatic, between Athens and Rome, when I'd been gnawing on my handkerchief. He added that in Rome I had disguised his mechanic, forcing him to put on a habit in order to go and see the pope.

At the other end of the table, a few yards away from my husband, I continued to preside over dinner parties with guests I did not know. At home I kept silent, but at other people's houses I became actively unpleasant. Around midnight, Tonio always brought home a few very pretty women with compliant husbands, and everyone settled into our place until dawn. The songs, the card tricks, the stories about the African desert, everything Tonio talked about, all of which I knew by heart, was replayed every evening. Around one in the morning, Boris would ask my permission to go to bed. And I would be the only one left to make sure everyone had something to eat and drink.

Soon I was unable to cope with the innumerable phone calls that succeeded one another all morning, and a secretary had to be hired, though we were already short on money because of the plane, the apartment, and Tonio, who was no longer writing. Despite that, the secretary settled in and manifested a fervent devotion to her boss. She had the face of an umbrella and was no longer very young, but she rendered us a thousand services, including some that no one had asked her to render. She was like a bell that rings all by itself. She did all she could to keep me away from everything. She had decided that I should ignore all phone calls for my husband. There were unexpected visits at the most extraordinary hours. The secretary would say, "Monsieur made that appointment." And I had the right only to remain silent.

Tonio was never free to go with me to the circus, which I adored, or to the movies. I no longer understood what was happening in my home. I wondered if I still had his permission to be there. On weekends he asked me to accept invitations to places outside the city, where I went against my will, convinced that on place Vauban, meanwhile, a very good time was being had without me. In vain I sought the reason for the distance that was growing between us, though there had been no quarrel or any clear reason for it. Sleep abandoned me once more. But where he was concerned, my patience had no limits.

Everyone complained of my irritability. "How can you stand a woman like that?" his friends asked in perfidious amazement.

Amid all the evenings of guitar music and card tricks, the only thing left of our intimacy was worries about money, for those parties cost a lot—liquor, flowers, services, all the rest—and the laughter that I forced myself to draw from somewhere, I don't know where, from a country that all of us carry inside ourselves for times of agony. My husband asked me why I was so pale, why I wasn't having any fun. A friend of mine, a poet, declared one day, "Forced labor would be easier than what your wife is going through. This is your sixtieth night of merrymaking. You're killing her! If you're out to destroy her, at least tell her so. Are you enjoying this? When are you ever going to let her sleep?"

After that, the guitars went somewhere else for a few days and Tonio stayed home. He plunged into the blackest kind of work: his bank accounts. There was nothing left.

He became edgy and unfair. Only the dog found grace in his arms. From time to time he came to my room to look in on me. Fortunately, I had gone back to sculpting.

"Are you there, Consuelo?"

"Yes, Tonio, I'm still here . . ."

The secretary had broken a finger, and we had a short stretch of peace. Things weren't going well with Tonio, but I could do nothing for him.

He had prepared his Simoun for a Paris–Timbuktu flight: he had to write an article for *Paris-Soir*. He'd been paid in advance for the article, but all the money had gone to pay his debts. He was irritable and taciturn and paced whole miles through the house. He was as agitated as a windmill, grinding out blackness. Finally I made up my mind to speak to him; the look of indifference he put on as soon as I went in augured badly for what was to follow.

"You're unhappy," I began. "Tell me what is tormenting you. With all my heart I want to help you. It isn't curiosity that moves me. But I feel that you are far from me. Be my friend and tell me about your troubles."

"For more than two weeks I've been running all over Paris doing all I can to find the money I need for my flight. Fuel and insurance alone already cost more than sixty thousand francs. I hardly have enough to keep the household fed. And of course that doesn't include the rent, the secretary, the servants who haven't been paid . . ."

He had never confided in me at all about his finances.

"I think *Paris-Soir* could advance you that much, no?"

"They've refused."

"And your publisher?"

"He also refused. He doesn't care about my flights, only my books, which is natural."

"Will you let me try?"

"Do whatever you want," he concluded petulantly. "All I know is that I have to leave in ten days."

I went into the sitting room and asked my dear friend Suzanne Werth to accompany me on my mission. But when I left the office of Prouvost, the editor of *Paris-Soir*, I was not only disappointed at having been turned down, but anguished. Prouvost had complained emphatically that my husband hadn't lived up to his commitments to the magazine.

I rested for an hour at Suzanne's place on rue d'Assas, and then, drawing all my courage from my love for Tonio, I went to see his publisher. He received me immediately with the utmost courtesy but explained that it was his brother who handled all financial matters.

"I know," I told him, "that you have advanced Tonio a certain amount of money for his forthcoming books, and I want to be loyal to you. A movie studio would like to buy a screenplay by Tonio titled *Igor* for five hundred thousand francs. He's also going to make it into a book, probably a novel. You know very well that he doesn't want to hear anything more about the movies after his first two films. Since your brother is involved in the movies, he may be able to negotiate a better deal than I can. Tonio told me to come to an agreement at any price because he needs sixty thousand francs immediately, for his flight. What should I do?"

"Tonio must come and see me. He will have his money."

I threw myself at him and kissed him. I ran to do the same to Tonio. But I didn't receive as warm a welcome as I had expected.

"You've undoubtedly misunderstood something."

"No, Suzanne can attest."

"Is it true?"

He passed up the chance to thank me in order to go and pick up his check.

Since his accident in Libya, his liver had been bothering him. He couldn't sleep. One of my women friends, who was my confidante at that time, gave me a bed that allowed me to sleep in another room, on another floor. The bed was much too large to fit into our bedroom. She also suggested I have my own telephone line installed so that I would be disturbed less often.

CHRISTMAS WAS COMING. I thought a visit to his mother would bring my husband a little calm. His sister insisted that I bring him to Agay to celebrate the anniversary of the miracle that had saved him from the Libyan desert. Tonio instructed me to pack my bags. It was December 22. That evening, he drove me to the Train Bleu. He was held back in Paris by business matters, and the

Simoun was being repaired; he promised to join me the next day.

I arrived at a house where he was the one they were waiting for, not me; I was used to this, but now, for the first time, I took it badly. I told his mother and sister, "Instead of Tonio, it's me. He's not coming."

He had promised to come, but I was sure he wouldn't. I could feel it in the way he had sipped his drink, the way he had spoken to me.

"I don't know what's happened. He's changed, that's all. I'm worn out. I'm very sorry about this. He forced me to come. Accept me, but believe me, I'm not happy about it."

"*Mais non*, Consuelo, he'll arrive tomorrow, you'll see. Go and rest," my mother-in-law reassured me.

Christmas. The château was in a festive mood. All the village children were invited to come and receive their toys. Everyone was laughing, singing, the children were dressed as angels, the stuffed turkeys smelled of golden chestnuts, and everyone rejoiced as midnight approached. Still no Tonio. The telephone rang a few minutes before that solemn hour. He was calling his mother. He barely said a word to her and wanted to speak to me. I refused.

"Tell him from me that he is supposed to be here at midnight; he promised."

"But he's asking for your help, he needs you in Paris. If I had a husband like him," his mother added, "I would follow him to the ends of the earth."

She won.

"It's very late," I conceded. "I can't go back to Paris by myself tonight."

For the first time, I asked someone to go with me.

"All right," Tonio's sister Didi said. "We'll leave after midnight."

At Saulieu, in Burgundy, our car crashed. Luckily, I was not at the steering wheel.

My sister-in-law was in the hospital when Tonio came to get me. A fine Christmas that was! There was some risk that she would be permanently disfigured. We took her back with us to Paris, where I gave her my room and moved into the living room. She smiled at my husband, her head covered with bandages. Finally the specialists calmed our fears: there was no longer any question of surgery. With rest, they promised, everything would be fine and her face would be back to normal. I took tender care of her, surrounding her with my knickknacks, offering her my radio. Tonio spent long hours at the foot of her bed. One thing was strange: she begged me to leave whenever she was with Tonio or E.* The three of them spent long hours together in my room. When I went in, silence fell. Once I went in to ask my sister-in-law what she wanted for lunch. I was friendly, I said laughingly: "You look as if you're conspiring. What's up?"

They all adopted an absent air. I was afraid to go into my own bedroom. I didn't understand what was going on, but Didi was doing better. She was laughing again; the

*The woman Consuelo refers to as "E." is almost certainly Nelly de Vogüé, who for many years was Antoine de Saint-Exupéry's mistress. In 1949, under the pseudonym Pierre Chevrier, de Vogüé published a biography of Saint-Exupéry that was long considered the definitive work on his life.

radio was doing the trick. I tried to make sure that Tonio was getting enough sleep: his Paris–Timbuktu flight was only a few days away. But the evenings with my sister-in-law stretched very late into the night. I felt as though I were surrounded with pitfalls, there in my own home. Tonio seemed like an actor who had never read his lines but found himself suddenly pushed onto a stage to act out an interminable play in which everyone knew their part except him, and he had to improvise.

One night, very late, I asked Tonio to join me. He hadn't once come to see me since Christmas Day. I was living on the upper floor. I shouted down the stairs, "Tonio, will you bring me the thermometer, I think I have a fever."

He arrived with the deck of cards he always had with him, either to help himself concentrate or to delay his responses at problematic moments. I gripped his wrists hard, my eyes full of tears. "Let's end this game, Tonio. Nothing, nothing is right anymore. You know that perfectly well."

"What?" he repeated.

His voice, however, expressed a desire to know what I meant.

"You don't love me anymore. I bother you. I bother your sister. You try not to look at me. Even when we're eating together. Right now, the touch of my hands on yours is distasteful to you. But I won't let you go, you're going to have to listen to me."

The telephone in his part of the apartment rang. Tonio tried to extricate himself from me.

"You won't answer. Every evening, I listen to you talking on the phone for hours. You lower your voice as if you were afraid of being heard when I go to the kitchen to get a glass of milk to help me sleep."

At that moment my telephone rang, though it must have been at least four o'clock in the morning. I answered. It was E., who asked me some question, I don't remember what, and excused herself for having called at that hour; she knew, she said, that Tonio wasn't sleeping.

"No, you must excuse me," I replied. "I'm talking to him right now."

Tonio was sitting on my bed, silent and immobile.

"Since you don't want to talk," I went on, "I will. Do you understand this? Someone pursues me into my own bedroom because there's no answer on your line? Yes, I am jealous! Though I have no reason to be, because you don't love me. You hate me right now, God knows why. Yet you know that nothing ugly, nothing bad has ever happened to you because of me. Could it be the opposite that you love? You have never lied to me, even now when you're silent as a tomb. I would so like to know what you're thinking! I have the right to know and to stop feeling constantly threatened. You're doing card tricks to distract me, but your face is growing sad. I know it well. I'm not a saint or a healer. I'm sure I can do nothing for you because you've stripped me of my power to help you with my love. What's more, I don't believe there's anything you can do at this point to set my mind at ease. Sleep. Forget my voice, if it's unpleasant to you. But don't forget what I'm going to say to you: the most terrible dramas are those veiled in mystery."

His telephone rang again. This time I told him to answer it.

★

HIS PUBLISHER gave a big party to celebrate Didi's recovery. Morand, Pourtalès, and many other writers were there. Didi, thrilled, never left her brother's side, and he never left the side of E., who was at her most beautiful that evening, as long as she didn't show her teeth.

Around one in the morning, I reproached my husband for not having spoken a single word to me all evening. He answered, "I've known my sister for thirty-five years, and I've only known you for seven!"

I felt as if I'd been banished from the planet. I took the key to our apartment from my purse and gave it to him.

"Here's the key. I do not want to stay with a husband who repudiates me."

I had spoken very loudly. The conversation around us stopped. Everyone thought I was a horrible woman. A shrew. I felt that my life was over. The lady of the house gave me my coat without a word. I felt as if I were falling into a void.

I woke up in a bed in Vaugirard hospital, in a ward with people who had no papers. I'd been picked up during the night, on the sidewalk. The cries of my fellow patients had awoken me. I raised my head. One man had had a knife stuck in his belly. A woman was gesticulating, standing on her bed, held back by two nurses who struggled to calm her down while a male nurse sprayed her with cold water.

An injection finally quieted her down; then it was my turn.

"Thanks," I told them, "I'm sleeping very well."

After my stay in the clinic in Bern, I knew how to act with nurses and their stern treatment. I pretended to sleep. My ruse succeeded, and they moved to another bed. I tried to piece together my memories.

I repeated to myself, "There is, in Paris, a man who is my husband. He will come to get me." I finally fell asleep with that thought. But very soon I began shaking with fever. The next morning, the man who brought the patients their food appeared. He was coughing. In my most angelic voice, I advised him to take some pills. "They're too expensive," he answered.

"Here, take my pearl. I don't need rings in the hospital."

I took off a ring and handed it to him.

"If I can do anything for you, tell me, but quickly."

As he was biting the pearl to see if it was fake, I sighed. "Oh, it's difficult. You won't be able to."

"Tell me anyway."

"You'll have to get me out of here. I've kept my dress on under the nightgown."

"Can you walk?"

"Yes, of course. Run, even!"

"I'll leave the door at the end of the garden open for a minute. Go slowly, don't run; if anyone sees you, tell them you came to visit a patient."

That was how I made my escape and went home to place Vauban. Humiliated, in despair. I had been locked up!

It was very hard for me to walk past my concierges in an evening gown, shivering with cold—I'd lost my coat during my late-night blackout—my hair in a mess. I later found out that they knew all about my night's misadventures; in fact, they'd been the first to know, as was always the case in Paris.

The police had gone to the apartment twice to confirm that my husband had no intention of collecting his wife from that ward full of derelicts, but they hadn't been able to see him or speak to him over the phone. It was therefore difficult for them to make a decision about my case. Tonio's door had remained shut, and my sister-in-law's voice had answered that her brother was sleeping and they were sending a friend to see the patient. The police had had to fall back on the concierge, who had gone to the hospital while I was sleeping to identify me.

I went into my room and found a woman sleeping in my bed, fully dressed.

Tonio was leaving at four o'clock on the Paris–Toulouse train. For the first time, I hadn't taken the trouble to pack his bags. That nagging thought prevented me from getting any sleep, and I finally got out of bed to see to that little task, which I had never failed to carry out.

Part Four

Paris–Guatemala–El Salvador–
Paris, 1938–1940

Antoine de Saint-Exupéry (third from left) with fellow aviators Henri Guillaumet, Léon Antoine, and Marcel Reine at Cap Juby in Morocco in 1926.

Saint-Exupéry (center, in flight gear) with his plane in Rio in 1928.

Consuelo Suncin Sandoval de Gómez in 1930.

Consuelo and Antoine de Saint-Exupéry's wedding, April 23, 1931, at Agay, his brother-in-law's chateau on the Côte d'Azur. Already twice widowed at thirty, Consuelo wore black.

Consuelo and Tonio at El Mirador, their home in Nice, just after their marriage.

Together in Paris in the early 1930s.

Radio broadcast from aboard ship in 1936, after Saint-Exupéry's terrible crash and disappearance in the Libyan desert while attempting to fly from Paris to Saigon. Consuelo is almost sick with anxiety.

Consuelo and Tonio in Paris in early 1938, boarding a train for Le Havre. From there they embarked on different boats—she bound for Central America and he for New York, for his epic flight to Tierra del Fuego.

Consuelo with her dog at La Feuilleraie in 1939, just before the German invasion.

Captain Antoine de Saint-Exupéry at the wheel of his car in the early years of the war.

Saint-Exupéry kept this photo of Consuelo, taken at Greta Garbo's house in New York, on him at all times. On the back, Consuelo had written, "Don't lose yourself, don't lose me."

Consuelo's favorite photo of her husband in uniform. She said he looked as if he were dancing.

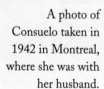

A photo of Consuelo taken in 1942 in Montreal, where she was with her husband.

A note and drawing left for Consuelo by Tonio one night when he waited up for her and she didn't come home: "Consuelo, Consuelo my love," it says. "Hurry back home..."

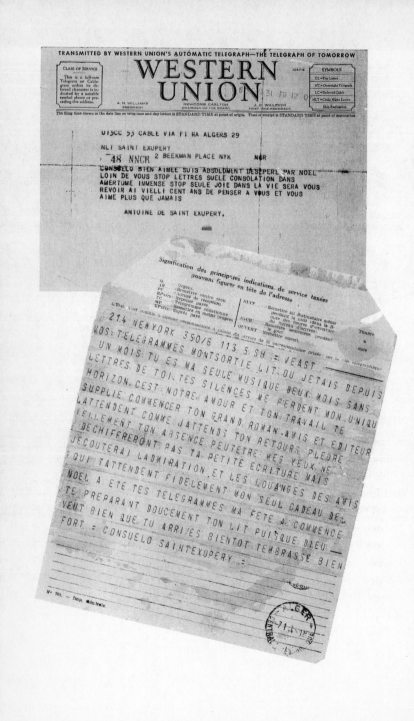

TRANSMITTED BY WESTERN UNION'S AUTOMATIC TELEGRAPH—THE TELEGRAPH OF TOMORROW

WESTERN UNION

CLASS OF SERVICE

This is a full-rate
Telegram or Cable-
gram unless its de-
ferred character is in-
dicated by a suitable
symbol above or pre-
ceding the address.

SYMBOLS

DL = Day Letter
NT = Overnight Telegram
LC = Deferred Cable
NLT = Cable Night Letter
Ship Radiogram

A. N. WILLIAMS   NEWCOMB CARLTON   J. C. WILLEVER
PRESIDENT   CHAIRMAN OF THE BOARD   FIRST VICE-PRESIDENT

The filing time shown in the date line on telegrams and day letters is STANDARD TIME at point of origin. Time of receipt is STANDARD TIME at point of destination

UISCC 55 CABLE VIA FI RA ALGERS 29

NLT SAINT EXUPERY

48 NNCR 2 BEEKMAN PLACE NYK   NCR

CONSUELO BIEN AIMEE SUIS ABSOLUMENT DESEPERE PAR NOEL
LOIN DE VOUS STOP LETTRES SUELE CONSOLATION DANS
AMERTUME IMMENSE STOP SEULE JOIE DANS LA VIE SERA VOUS
REVOIR AI VIELLI CENT ANS DE PENSER A VOUS ET VOUS
AIME PLUS QUE JAMAIS

ANTOINE DE SAINT EXUPERY.

Signification des principales indications de service taxées
pouvant figurer en tête de l'adresse

D. ...... Urgent.
CR. ...... Remettre contre reçu.
PC. ...... Accusé de réception.
RPx= ...... Réponse payée.
re ...... Télégramme collationné.
MP ...... Remettre en mains propres.
XPx= ...... Exprès payé.

NUIT ...... Remettre au destinataire même
pendant la nuit (dans la mi-
nute des heures d'ouverture
des bureaux d'arrivée).
JOUR ...... Remettre seulement pendant
le jour
OUVERT ...... Remettre ouvert.

L'Etat n'est soumis à aucune responsabilité à raison du service de la correspondance privée

Timbre
à
date

214 NEWYORK 350/6 113 5 SH 18 VEAST
MOS TELEGRAMMES MONTSORTIE LIT OU JETAIS DEPUIS
UN MOIS TU ES MA SEULE MUSIQUE DEUX MOIS SANS
LETTRES DE TOI TES SILENCES ME PERDENT MON UNIQU
HORIZON CEST NOTRE AMOUR ET TON TRAVAIL TE
SUPPLIE COMMENCER TON GRAND ROMAN AMIS ET EDITEUR
LATTENDENT COMME JATTENDS TON RETOURS PLEDRE
TELLEMENT TON ABSENCE PEUTETRE MES YEUX NE
DECHIFFRERONT PAS TA PETITE ECRITURE MAIS
JECOUTERAI LADMIRATION ET LES LOUANGES DES AMIS
QUI TATTENDENT FIDELEMENT MON SEUL CADEAU DE
NOEL A ETE TES TELEGRAMMES MA FETE A COMMENCE
TE PREPARANT DOUCEMENT TON LIT PUISQUE DIEU
VEUT BIEN QUE TU ARRIVES BIENTOT TEMBRASSE BIEN
FORT = CONSUELO SAINTEXUPERY =

Drawing done by Consuelo after her husband's disappearance (probably in the 1950s).

(OPPOSITE) Telegram sent by Saint-Exupéry on December 31, 1943, just before his disappearance: "Consuelo my love am plunged into despair by Christmas far from you. Letters only consolation in immense sorrow. Only joy in life would be to see you again. Have aged a hundred years thinking of you and love you more than ever, Antoine de Saint Exupéry." Consuelo wrote back: "Your telegrams got me out of bed where I've been for a month. You are my only music. Two months without letters from you—your silences—make me lose my horizon, our love and your work. Beg you to start your big novel. Friends and editor await it as I await your return. Weep so much my eyes may not decipher your tiny script, but will listen to the admiration and praise of friends who await you faithfully. My only Christmas present was your telegrams. My celebration began quietly preparing your bed, since God is willing for you to come soon. I kiss you with all my heart, Consuelo Saint-Exupéry."

Consuelo at the ceremony to name the Saint-Exupéry rose, on June 24, 1960. In the background is a bust of the aviator sculpted by Consuelo, which she called *Night Flight*.

17

T HERE WERE THREE OF US at lunch the next day; my sister-in-law was looking radiantly happy. No mention was made of my night. My husband sat down at the piano; he hadn't said a word to me since the day before. I looked awful and didn't dare budge from my chair. He gestured for me to come over to the piano and sit down on the bench next to him. He wanted to ask my forgiveness for not having gone to the hospital that night.

"I told Gaston to bring you back here," he said. "It would have been too painful for me to go myself. It took him two hours to find you. Since he didn't have a note signed by me, they didn't want to let him take you away. But I waited up in anguish, drained by the quarrel, imagining the worst. I was given some pills to take, and I fell asleep."

He went on plunking at the piano keys with one hand while the other caressed my hair, which was hanging down piteously in my face.

"You are not being good, little girl," he sang to the rhythm of his notes.

"Maybe you aren't, either!"

"You think?"

"I'm never sick when you are well."

"Maybe so," he answered, melancholy.

And he stopped playing. "I'm leaving for Toulouse at four o'clock."

"I'll talk to you on the train."

I kissed him, then ran to lock myself in my room.

"All aboard, all aboard . . ." Quick handshakes all around, then he hurried on board the train ahead of me. My sister-in-law took me by the shoulders and announced, "I'm the one who's going with him."

The train was starting to move. He stretched out his hand to Didi, to help her up.

That evening, around midnight, he called me. He spoke to me for more than an hour. He begged me to take the first train and come join him; his departure for Timbuktu* had been postponed for two or three days. But I no longer had the strength or the courage.

✦

WE SAW EACH OTHER once more when he came back to Marseille. The mere thought of the meeting made me shake, I didn't know whether from fear or from love. I was surrounded by good friends. I hadn't received any message

*On January 29, 1937, Saint-Ex and his faithful mechanic, André Prévot, set off on a 5,500-mile flight from Paris to the town of Timbuktu in central Mali, east of Mauritania and south of Algeria. They flew without a radio over trackless desert but arrived safely. After spending some time in Algeria, the two flew back to Paris in late March.

from him except the one laconically announcing his return.

Between his descent from the plane and dinnertime, everything was easy; all conversation was put off until later, and our true reunion was delayed. At the hotel, in front of his two closed suitcases, he stood immobile, staring fixedly at the floor. I began opening the latch of one of the suitcases. He jumped like a man startled out of sleep. "What do you want?"

"A pair of pajamas for you. Which suitcase are they in?"

Both of us rummaged in the suitcases, or rather in the jumble of clothes, until at last we found both a top and a bottom.

"I know, I know—you're going to tell me I mixed the dirty laundry in with the clean clothes. . . . But it's late. Let's go to sleep."

He needed to give an impression of composure.

Hotels in Marseille are not heated. In theory, the sun reigns unfailingly over the South. No native of Marseille will ever admit to being cold, even during the gray days iced over by the cold wind known as the mistral, which, in combination with the odors of the port and the salty sea air, has given the locals their low, husky voices. Through the window I watched the docks, which were always teeming with activity. As the night grew darker, the port's wealthy pimps became more active.

I couldn't think. I had waited for my husband to come back so eagerly, and there he was before me, cold as a marble statue, distant as the stars. I no longer felt any pain. I told myself that I had, once more, to wait for his return.

Making an effort to open my mouth, I asked him, "Are you sleepy?"

"*Oui, oui.* I'm very tired. Let's go and lie down."

I lowered my head and my whole body and plunged into the chaos of his suitcases to try to establish a little order. I had hardly picked up a pair of socks and some dirty handkerchiefs when he snatched them away, shouting, "Don't touch my things. I beg you not to touch my things. I am an adult, and I am entitled to fold my shirts and put them away by myself!"

I had always carefully packed and unpacked his suitcases. I was the only one who knew how his clothes had to be arranged. I felt a chill in the small of my back at his sudden change in attitude.

I thought he was ill or in a foul mood. Maybe he was worried about money. Half dressed, I slipped into bed. My heart was colder than his arms, colder than the blankets, which were frozen by the mistral. He closed the windows tightly, put out the lights, and gently sat down on the edge of the bed. He too could feel the fear that had filled my whole body.

Our return trip in the train took place in the same silence: we treated each other so formally that it was as if we were strangers forced to travel in the same compartment. We reached home, but that evening was just like the previous one. He fell asleep, but my female nerves kept me awake. Wary as a cat, I started across our big apartment. I went to the farthest room, where the sound of my anxious insomnia was least likely to be heard. Never before had I seen him so distant, so silent, without a word for me. One of his suitcases was sticking out of a cupboard stuffed with books. What was that suitcase doing there, still closed? I attacked it immediately as if it were the enemy. I opened it and dug through it ferociously. The dirty laundry he had grabbed away from me the day before was still there, and lying among it were a hundred or more perfumed letters. The scent of the paper alone was enough to explain my husband's behavior. I opened the first letter: yes, it was his handwriting. And I read, "Darling, darling . . ." But the letter was not for me. Who was this lucky "darling"? I couldn't read another word. My tears kept me from understanding. In my distress, I deciphered only a single line: it said that he couldn't keep his wife from coming to London; she was invited, and it would be cruel and futile to stop her. But if my rival were to ask him tomorrow to spend seven years at sea with her, he wrote, he would leave without even telling me good-bye.

I couldn't bear to read any more. The other letters were from the "darling" in question.

What to do? I had no experience of this kind of situation. Well, I did now. I went to the bedroom, woke him up, and showed him his letters.

"So you went through my things?"

My tears cut short his anger.

"Now that you know, it's better this way."

He lowered his head timidly, like a son in front of his mother.

"What are you going to do?" he asked me.

"Me? Nothing. Something has just been broken inside me; you yourself will never be able to repair it."

I held my hand to my heart, which was beating too fast. I felt idiotic, as if I were in one of those farces where adultery is suddenly discovered. I jeered at myself.

"And you?" I threw back at him. "What are you going to do? I have no reason to reproach you. You don't love me anymore, and that's your right. We had an agreement. I was the one who proposed it: 'When one of us stops loving the other, we'll have to tell each other, to confess.' Love is a fragile thing, sometimes you can get lost in its immensity. . . . And there it is, I'm the one who is lost, but if you are happy with her, I don't wish either of you any ill. Leave as quickly as possible, and for good, with her. Don't ever see me again; go live in another country. Distance will make us forget."

I knew the name of his new country, and I told him so, talking fast without pausing for breath. "If your passion, your love for her is real, you must not leave her. I promise I won't die. I'll try to live and I'll remember that I was the one who allowed you to find your true love. So go, you can go off to sea for seven years or seven thousand years, without saying good-bye."

He was pale and serious.

"I admire you," he said, pulling me slowly toward him. "I'm sorry you found that letter, I should have warned you. I was afraid of making you suffer, very afraid. I love you from the bottom of my heart. I love you as a sister, as a daughter, as my homeland, but I can't escape her. I can't spend a single day without seeing her, without hearing her. She is like a drug to me. She is destroying me, she is bad for me, she is tearing us apart, but I can't leave her."

I lay down again because my legs were wobbling. It hurt, it hurt very badly. We were both crying with desperate sobs, like two children being burned alive in the same fire with no hope for a miracle that might save us.

In the early morning, I was the one who started talking again.

"I will be your friend," I said. "I will go home to my mother's house the way I did when I skinned my knees as a little girl. I'll go and let myself be consoled by my roses, my palm trees, my enormous volcanoes in San Salvador. When you are old, maybe you'll come and see me someday."

He left to stay in a hotel, for we couldn't look at each other without crying, falling into each other's arms, and losing our days to futile sobs. Nevertheless, he looked happy. I took to my bed. My faithful friend Suzanne took care of me, and I made inquiries about the next boat that could take me back to San Salvador.

My husband began writing me tender letters that grew more and more loving, and soon he begged me not to leave. He asked me to wait six months for him, "six short months," he said.

And he swore that afterward he would take me to China, where we would be happy, the two of us, alone together. I believed in China, in our Chinese happiness, and I waited, still suffering, curled deep in my bed.

⋆

ONE DAY HE REAPPEARED with his suitcases. He was tired of living in a hotel. Like a child, like a student who has gone off to spend a few days in a house of ill repute, he set down his two suitcases at the foot of my bed, stood next to them, and cried, "Here I am!"

He let his arms drop along his body. "Here I am. I can't live away from our home anymore. I can no longer live without you. I'm sick. I need you: take me back or I'll die. I can't eat in restaurants anymore—everything makes me sick. I'm drinking too much, and I can no longer write a single line. If I don't work, who's going to pay for our existence?"

Boris came in without knocking, thinking I was alone. He was bringing me the mail. When he saw Tonio, he smiled with joy. He cast a quick glance at me and picked up the suitcases as if he were picking diamonds up off the street. All three of us were beaming. Boris disappeared with the suitcases, put away their contents, and gave orders that the quarters of "Monsieur le Comte" be filled with flowers and made comfortable. He finally had his master back. Even the dog was dancing, and, in his joy, leaving little spots on the rug. My husband didn't want me to punish the poor dog for that; it was in his honor, he said.

But alas, things took their usual course. Once again I waited for my husband to come home at night. One day the dog sat up at the door until seven in the morning; he caught pneumonia from it (he was a very fragile Pekinese) and died within twenty-four hours. After that I didn't even have my dog to keep me company.

The sixth month of this ordeal was drawing to an end. I packed my bags, set the house in order, and, like a soldier who has been conquered but is proud of having done all he could to save his country, I fled.

My husband understood when he saw my preparations. I bought several collections of dresses for my sisters and myself. Therefore, I was leaving. I stepped out onto the terrace. The lights from the Colonial Exposition were gilding the dome of the Invalides.

"Tonio, I'm leaving."

"Yes," he said. "When?"

"I'm sad, but I have to leave you," I continued. "I think there has been a great earthquake in our life, and I must thank heaven for having saved me. I'll go and rebuild somewhere else."

"Yes, Consuelo," he said. "Sometimes that is necessary. I will leave for America, too. I'll make another long-distance flight, and perhaps I will never come back, for I don't feel like coming back. I feel no love, I no longer love . . ."

Without discussion, without a single word more, I took the boat at Le Havre, bound for Puerto Barrios, Guatemala—Central America's only Atlantic port.

THE SEA WAS GRAY, the sea of Le Havre in winter, but I thought it was a magnificent sight. The seagulls were gray, the boat's flags were gray, the enormous heaps of cargo were gray, the people who swarmed around me were gray. My coat was gray, too, a coat made of squirrel fur. The moment came to go up the gangway, which was gray as well.

The horizon the boat headed off into was also gray. My thoughts and my heart alone were sunny, with the sacred light of acceptance. I was being reborn as only Christians can be reborn to another life after leaving this unhappy earth. I might not have deserved this elation, this sense of consolation, but I granted it to myself as a gift, for I had wept so much. I prayed to heaven that I would be worthy of the relief I felt at rolling aside the tombstone of my broken marriage. I promised myself to be happy from then on and never to look back. It was in Paris, and not on the shifting terrain of El Salvador, that I had experienced the greatest earthquake. Now I was going to pick tropical fruit, tame butterflies, and sing along with the rivers. Forever, until the end.

I wanted to be beautiful for my first evening on the boat. I refused to breathe the air of the past. Everything I wore was new, as if I were a newly engaged girl. The chambermaids helped me unpack my suitcases. I stroked the lovely evening gown I would wear for this, the first evening when I had given myself the right to live again as a woman awaiting a sign, which could come from anywhere, that everything would come alive once more.

Ribbons, satin slippers, gleaming jewels, feathers in my hair, a lace mantilla for my curls: I had thought of everything. I dressed carefully, I was marrying my new destiny. I was joyful, happy, happy. . . . The dinner gong rang through the passageways between the cabins. A bit more perfume on my hair! I sprayed a little perfume on the chambermaid who had helped me get dressed, too. I detected a certain teasing look in her eyes.

I walked calmly, with the pleasure and assurance you feel when you know you are well dressed. From my heart to my lace, everything sparkled. I walked through the reception rooms and the bars as if I were dancing, but met only the crew.

A steward walked up to me. "Are you looking for the other passengers?"

"Is it too early? The first bell has only just rung for dinner."

"No," he answered with the same amused look I had seen in my chambermaid's gaze. "You are our only passenger."

A gunshot couldn't have startled me more. I started laughing. I believed and didn't believe his little sally. Touching my arm familiarly, he went on, "Allow me, madame, to introduce you to the ship's doctor, the captain, the second mate . . ."

All of them, standing in a row, greeted me very warmly.

The captain spoke. "You are our only passenger, and the last woman who will ever travel on this ship. We are making our last voyage as an ocean liner. For twenty years, I have been this ship's captain. We had a strike that ended badly. The boat has been punished: it will be converted into a freighter. We were permitted to set out on one last voyage, and by a great coincidence, just when we had received permission to accept passengers, you bought your ticket. You are, therefore, the person in charge of this ship. It belongs to you. We are your crew. If you order us to change course, I will obey you. What orders do you want to give us, to start with?"

"I would like a cold drink, a drink with all of you, to toast our voyage. Dinner can wait."

"Dinner will wait," said the captain.

"*Communiquez,*" the first mate ordered the second.

"*Passez les ordres,*" someone else repeated, and glasses of champagne were distributed to all "my" crew. I didn't know whether to laugh or weep. After a few glasses, the second mate confided in me, "To tell you the truth, we do have another passenger, traveling third class. He's a kind of pirate. He doesn't want to go through Nicaragua, and he is dying. He has a rather strange fixation. He wants to be thrown into the sea before we reach Nicaragua, which is his nightmare. But don't you worry, we'll already have left you off in Puerto Barrios!"

The next day we moved the dining room to the side of the swimming pool, and a greenhouse was built for me. My cabin was next to the captain's. He was an old sea wolf with beautiful lines etched on his face, a laugh that had braved endless storms and stars, and a good-heartedness that was like something out of a fairy tale.

I thought I was dreaming. It was too beautiful to be true. Soon we saw a very colorful island. I asked the captain to set a course for it. He did. It was the island where migrating birds meet. If the captain had asked me to spend my life there, if he had cast the boat's anchor and his heart's right there at that island, I would have found it perfectly natural. But we continued serenely on our way to Guatemala. Even so, I felt that my crew was growing increasingly nervous and anguished as we approached Puerto Barrios.

In the evenings, the captain and I had fallen into our own little habits. We would send away the rest of the crew and, for the thousandth time, tell each other about our childhoods. Like me, he did not want to talk about his adult life. We were grown-ups who were eager to escape reality, especially its ugly side. We spoke in a tone of friendship. He gave me the news of the rest of the world, which reached the ship by radio. I noticed, as we approached Curaçao, that he grew more tender, but his old hands, tanned by the sun, touched me with compassion rather than love when he led me back to the stairs.

In Curaçao, I decided to go for a little walk by myself, to think about my new life. It all struck me as simply marvelous: I saw trees, a new sky, men. Dressed in white and wearing tennis shoes, I set out over the tarred roads of Curaçao, but soon my crew caught up with me. I turned back and shouted, "I want to be alone, to do a little shopping on my own. I'll see you again this evening on board."

The men moved off, but only to a spot about ten yards away. I understood that I was being followed. It was quite a job to shake them off—sometimes there were seven of them, sometimes ten, walking along behind me, pretending to buy fruit, talking to the natives, giving seashells to the children, decking themselves out in strands of shells and flowers. We all felt transformed into children of the palm trees there. The island belonged to Queen Wilhelmina, and that Dutch colony had a flavor of Holland about it, and fresh tulips.

At a bank I changed a little money. The first mate raced to the door, not to open it for me but to rush inside himself, ahead of me. I thought he was crazy. I exchanged a few francs for the local currency, and after a while I went back to the boat. I complained about this not very discreet surveillance to the captain. He laughed and cried at the same time. "You're young and pretty," he explained to me. "The people of the island might have stolen you and made you a child of Curaçao. We can't leave our passenger here on this island."

I believed the gallant old captain. Oh, Captain, if you're still alive, I thank you for your laughter and your tears!

Every day Puerto Barrios drew inexorably closer. When I asked the commander how many miles we had made during the day, he answered sadly, "I would prefer never to reach Puerto Barrios!" The wrinkles didn't leave his brow for a long time after that, and I didn't ask any more questions. The crew, impeccably dressed in snow white and gold, explained the mysteries of the Caribbean Sea to me. For by now we had no more stories to tell one another. Each of us was going toward his final destination. The old sailors would navigate no more. Soon their dreams of life on land would begin. And they were afraid. The children in their rooms, the faithful (or unfaithful) wife always following behind them . . . After so many years of waiting, how would they endure this marvelous repose and familial bliss, this paradise where there would be no more departures or arrivals? Yet this really was the end.

The sailors were transfigured by the overcast sky of the Caribbean Sea. The sky was different in color from the sea. You don't see it immediately, but the body feels brighter, taller, as if transformed by the new light. You slip into this new light as if you were entering a new world. They call it the magic of the Caribbean. People change: those who are violent become gentle, the weak become strong, and you breathe as if you had just been born into a new embrace, a new love. Sometimes the natives begin to sing to this light, as if to give thanks.

When I was falling asleep in Paris, I would dream of seeing my sun again, that light, my volcanos thundering like cannons, the eternal summer. . . . I had long imagined finding myself back in this atmosphere, which was my cradle, my blood. Slowly I stretched out on the bridge and spoke to my old captain about the destiny of the stars, which seem so fragile because our eyes cannot penetrate their mystery. They are like giant bees, and there was no better way to taste their honey than to lie down on the bridge next to this old sea wolf and take in deep breaths of the Caribbean Sea, which reflected the imperturbable stars in the depths of its black waters.

The days were short. We took pictures; we knew that we would soon be leaving these warm waters, that we would soon be separating forever, and we wanted to preserve some trace of this time when our souls met with such intensity, such purity, like the stars mingling in the waters of the sea.

"You will forget me," said the captain, "as all my passengers have forgotten me. That's as it should be. I've loved them all, all the women who stayed close to me for an entire voyage, lying on the same deck chair, full of the drama of their lives, full of their fear of dying. They were all as beautiful and as fragile as my boat's journeys or the life of flowers and butterflies that live only a day, like the glass of champagne you're holding in your hand that will soon be empty but will live on in the bright glow of your eyes. And always the memory, riveted to this skull here"— and he touched his head—"to this skull that, even now, when it's virtually a skeleton's skull, keeps its taste for these fragile journeys, these fleeting lives, the froth of champagne, the glow in your eyes. All of these things are lights—it's light itself that counts, it's light that creates, light alone, bright light."

My body felt heavy. Soon I would awaken in Puerto Barrios, among the palm trees and my family, to reclaim the sun that had watched me being born. I wasn't afraid, but I would very much have liked to fall asleep there on the bridge and gently awake next to God, who can do everything. Even so, I was trembling with fright, for buzzers suddenly went off and the siren sounded from the hold, like someone suddenly barging in on our human dreams, the dreams of ephemeral beings. The siren sounded again, along with a thousand shouts and footsteps. The first mate asked, "*Mon capitaine*, may I come up on your bridge?"

I wanted to beg him not to allow anyone to join us that night, but he, rising like an animal emerging from sleep, crushed his crystal glass in his hand, squeezing it slowly until it had crumbled to powder, and cried, "Yes, come up!"

He had hurt himself. Shards of glass were scattered across the ground. He made his way over to my divan and, for the first time, took my hand passionately in his, inundating my dress with blood. He caressed my forehead with his other hand. It lasted only a second, and then he turned to face his sailor who stood at attention, silently waiting.

"Speak."

"We have a visitor. He is two miles from the boat and demands that we go and pick him up . . ."

"Who is it?"

"The director of the Compagnie Transatlantique. He has an urgent message for the Comtesse de Saint-Exupéry."

"Send for him quickly, reduce speed, lower the anchor in five minutes."

A message for me? Who could it be from but the man I had wanted to bury along with my past, the man who had brought me to life and made me die in Paris? I understood my old captain's tender protectiveness. I felt I was in danger, but what sort of danger?

The whole boat was coming to life, working for this person who was coming to meet us in his boat.

"He couldn't wait until you were in Panama," the captain said to me. "He couldn't wait for you to be free. Little girl, I love you as I love the stars, as I love my memories. When you are far away and you have forgotten this journey, please do me the honor of remembering this night, when I wished I were God so as to stop your tears. But tears, you know, are not always murderous. Tears can purify as well, tears may be the path to grace, a way for women to become angels."

"Oh, yes," I said. "I believe you."

A new bottle of champagne refreshed our thirsty wait.

Meanwhile, the little lights from the boats that were chasing one another enlivened our view of the tranquil Caribbean. As if on a whim, I tried to pick out the thousand tiny slivers of glass embedded in the captain's hand, that hand which had been so kind to me. When I had finished taking them all out, he pulled himself up to his full height and we went back into his cabin, where he turned on a light, put a beautiful commander's cape around my shoulders to hide the bloodstains on my white dress, and called the radioman to ask him to bring in a file. The radioman came in. He was carrying a copper tray burnished so brightly that it looked like gold, on which a dozen telegrams lay.

"All of them are for you. They arrived during the voyage. I didn't give them to you because they would have made you cry. I wanted to spare you the tears."

Trembling, I picked up the first one:

PLANE CRASHED IN GUATEMALA SAINT-EXUPERY NEAR DEATH MUST PROCEED TO AMPUTATE RIGHT ARM YOUR MOTHER WITH PATIENT WAITING FOR YOU YOUR DEVOTED DOCTOR GUATEMALA HOSPITAL.

Then I read the next one:

YOUR HUSBAND GRAVELY WOUNDED 32 FRACTURES II OF WHICH LIFE-THREATENING HAVE PREVENTED AMPUTATION UNTIL YOUR ARRIVAL TAKE PLANE TO PANAMA TO ARRIVE FASTER HOLDING YOU IN OUR HEARTS YOUR MOTHER AND SISTERS.

18

THE OTHER TELEGRAMS were from friends and from the tabloid newspapers, which use tragedy as a way of increasing circulation.

"You've never spoken to me of your husband," said the captain, "your great husband, your famous husband. And there he is, close to death, waiting for you in Guatemala, just where you were going to disembark. You must admit that life is strange."

I no longer knew how to cry—I knew nothing at all. I went on looking at the stars, with death in my heart. The boat had come to a sudden stop. We could hear the straining of the winches, the chains, the ladders that were being made ready to help the Central American director of the Compagnie Transatlantique climb aboard.

I was lying down as the captain paced through his cabin with long steps. Daylight was just beginning to illuminate our drama.

"My name is Luis," cried a man more than six feet tall in a tender, tropical voice. "I've come to take you to your husband as quickly as possible. The president of Guatemala and I, with the help of the Compagnie Transatlantique, are offering you this plane trip, which will allow you to rejoin your wounded husband."

He was a fair-skinned man, still young despite his white hair. He had a laugh that one who was in pain could recognize as that of a kindred spirit. As I was trying to stand up and thank him, I fell into his arms. The captain's cough reminded me that I had to be more of a brave-little-soldier-on-a-battlefield-where-the-enemy's-blows-must-be-born-with-dignity.

"Thank you, monsieur; I am greatly touched by your company's kindness," I told him. "I am glad to have your help. When are we leaving?"

"The boat is waiting for us. We can be in port within an hour."

The captain had pushed all his control buttons, and the entire staff was quietly coming into the cabin.

"One of the directors of the Transatlantique is on board," said the captain sternly. "He will grant us the pleasure of showing him our ship. I place him in your hands, messieurs."

The crew took charge of the visitor. The two nurses, who had no patients except the man in third class, were wearing what amounted to evening gowns. Now, for once, it was their turn to act the part of lovely passengers pampered by the crew—those holiday Don Juans.

I lay down again. The captain paced the cabin as if nothing were wrong. In the distance we heard langorous, intoxicating music, songs, life. I fell asleep, I don't know for how long. I woke up to the eyes of my captain, who gently took my hand.

"Sleep, sleep," he said. "I'll come and wake you at dinnertime. There are no seats available on the plane. Luis will be our guest until Puerto Barrios. This evening, in the great dining hall, we will have our final dinner. We'll even have some passengers from Panama: a group of young women, members of an athletic team. The evening will be a merry one for our guests. You and I—we will command our hearts to wait and sleep. Sorrow is full of mystery. Would you like to be my companion for this dinner?"

I could not refuse such an offer from a man who had shared my pain so deeply and yet would not show me his own.

He kissed my hand. A nurse fetched a bag of ice for my head, the doctor gave me some shots, and a chambermaid laid out an evening gown for me, with flowers embroidered on a fabric as white as hope.

It was hot that evening. The sailors wanted no woman but me at the large table where we customarily sat. They had made a throne for me out of fresh flowers, white flowers they had bought in Panama and had managed to preserve despite the heat. At my place, they had put a simple little inscription: "A fairy." How best to accept this extraordinary gift? How could I help but feel like a flower, even if flowers are sometimes bruised by the night?

Our eyes were radiant, and we were bathed in admiration by those who gave speeches. Oh, how our guest was pampered that evening! Our first mate, the most lovable conversationalist on the Pacific Ocean, asked him questions. Little by little, Luis told us the whole story of his life. He confessed himself to us, to these sailors, who were trying hard to assuage the sadness that the white flowers bedecking this throne had made me feel. Don Luis was crazy about all of us, drunk with the message he was bearing, drunk with his role, drunk with the protection he could give me.

"You see, my captain," he said with all the arrogance of an emperor, "I myself am married, married, married. I have three daughters. One day, I wanted to have my wife and children brought to El Salvador. I waited for the passengers to disembark. My wife was not among them. And yet, the day before, I had received a telegram saying that she was a passenger on that ship. She couldn't possibly have evaporated—when I left her in Paris she weighed more than four hundred pounds! It wouldn't be easy for her to run away. I waited a few more minutes, perplexed, and then I was summoned to the place where the animals were being unloaded. There I said hello to my wife, along with several cows and a horse. Two of my daughters helped her into the passengers' waiting room. She had grown even fatter in the two years since I had last seen her. She spoke in a very sweet voice. At the hotel the door had to be removed so that she could enter the room. And she has stayed there ever since, in that room, and will for a long time to come, no doubt. She can't even turn over or sit down. That, monsieur, is my wife. *Eh oui!*"

This slender, agile, elegant man, married to a monster who couldn't pass through doorways, moved us deeply. Each of the sailors in turn told his story, as sad a story as possible. They were all trying to demonstrate that people sometimes have sorrows that are even harder to bear than the death of a loved one.

★

ONCE IN PUERTO BARRIOS, I thought I was dreaming. I was back in my native country, the country of volcanoes and beloved songs. The president of the Republic had sent a car escorted by two motorcyclists from his official retinue to accompany me on the road so that I would be able to travel more quickly. But I refused to go at such hellish speed. I wanted to stop and drink coconut milk at a little farm where the natives were breaking coconuts open with their teeth and drinking the milk straight from the shell. I took a fresh coconut away in my arms, to drink the milk in the comfortable presidential car. We couldn't leave the windows open because our mouths filled with dust; even with the windows closed we could see nothing but a yellow cloud. I was choking.

We arrived, Don Luis and I, at the military hospital. A little white-haired old woman, very stooped, thin, and sweet, wrapped her arms around me as hard as she could and burst into tears. I hadn't had time to see her face or recognize her: she was my mother.

Our embrace lasted a long time. I was used to so many shocks by now that I thought her sobs were announcing Tonio's death. But no. She led me slowly to a room where a doctor wearing a major's uniform was waiting for me.

"Madame, welcome to the hospital of Guatemala. Your

193

husband has been hospitalized here. He is in room seventy-seven. Come. The danger, the great danger, has been averted, I believe: I mean the danger of death. However, he is very sick. He has many wounds. If you will authorize it, this evening we will amputate his hand, perhaps up to the elbow. It is necessary. I know you are a very courageous woman; I am sure you will share my opinion. A living man with a single arm is preferable to a corpse with two."

I went into the room, which was threadbare but clean. A nurse was watching over the patient. I could hardly recognize Tonio's head, it was so swollen. It was, without exaggeration, the size of five heads. The doctor assured me that they had done all that was necessary and everything had been put back in place. There were devices to realign his jaws in his mouth; his lips were nothing more than mucus membranes dangling above his chin. One eye was almost on his forehead; the other hung down toward the mouth, swollen and purple. He could hardly be seen beneath the cotton and bandages soaked in disinfectants of all colors. Bottles, strung along a complicated system of wires, continuously distilled drops into his wrists, elbows, head, and ears. I had never seen anything like it in my life. And this man was my husband! From time to time he opened a single eye; the other one was completely immobilized by the compresses. Whenever light touched him, something happened in his brain that was impossible to understand: he would start to howl. I sensed that he was battling to save this precious matter that destiny plays at molding, wounding, breaking, transforming. Deep inside his human consciousness—if he still had one—a terrible struggle was going on. Soon I could feel all his wounds within my own being. Sitting next to his bed, on a straight-backed chair, I watched that eye, which sometimes flickered over my clothing or my face. Several weeks went by like this.

I began to feed him, as if he were a baby being given his first spoonful of milk, his first bit of bread dipped in honey. The swelling in his head began to go down. He was very thin. Day by day, he lost more weight. Under the effects of morphine, he often told stories that were so complicated I wondered if I wasn't the one who was sick.

Eventually the doctor authorized me to take him home since there was nothing left but a wound on his hand that would not heal. That hand didn't seem to want to be part of his arm. That was our biggest worry.

The day he left the hospital, our friends thought they would cheer us up by waiting for us at the Palace de Guatemala Hotel with a marimba, a champagne cocktail party, and a hundred waiters. My husband told me, "I'm just going to walk straight through that crowd. Put me to bed in the hotel tonight and put me on a plane for New York tomorrow. I'll have an operation on my face to arrange my teeth and put my eye back in its place, since you can't live with a monster who has one eye on his cheek and the other on his forehead. Don't be upset, everything will be fine."

"But I'll go with you."

"No. We left each other, remember?"

"Yes," I said. "I remember. I'll take you to the plane. Let

me go right now and call to get you a seat on tomorrow's flight."

It was simple, indeed. I wondered if a man really does have a heart and, if so, where it might be located. I had just saved Tonio from death, and he was reminding me that I was no longer his companion. I called on Don Luis to rescue me, and he took care of reserving a seat on the plane and arranging all the practical details.

My body somehow managed to remain upright until three in the morning, when I took my husband, feeble as a skeleton rattling in the wind but guided by the call of a mysterious force, to the airport.

I went home with a fever whose cause the doctors could not determine. It was my turn to go into the hospital, suffering from a strange infection and a mysterious fever. My darling mother brought me back to life, health, and faith. We didn't speak of our womanly miseries; we simply helped each other. Finally one day I left the clinic, and my family took me back to the house where I was born.

The telephone calls from New York to Guatemala came every day. My husband was worried about me and asked my mother to put me as quickly as possible on a boat or a plane bound for Paris, where he was preparing to go. The embassies sent me tender messages, flowers, and gifts from Tonio. But I wanted to see my city again and spend more time there wandering around and finding my childhood friends, my rosebushes growing at the foot of the volcanoes.

"ORANGES, MANGOES, tamales, pupusas . . ." The cries followed me through the little stations the train passed through on the way to Armenia San Salvador.

At my station, the heat had not diminished. I saw children, crowds of children, all standing in rows to greet me, singing the national anthem. The girls were lined up facing the boys; the schoolmistress faced the headmaster. Both were waving batons like orchestra conductors, directing the small childish voices that were singing in honor of their compatriot, their elder sister who had gone through a thousand hardships since leaving Paris to come back to them.

The mayor of my village, Don Alfredo, dressed all in white, was still young, with the placid youth of a small, tranquil town. Many things had changed since I left. The girls had grown up; they were mothers or even widows now, some had divorced. The rich were poor and the poor were rich; the old marketplace no longer existed; the trees had all grown larger, and orange trees now lent their beauty to the streets. Armenia's park had been invaded by bamboo and tamales, and I walked slowly through it, after a month in bed in a Guatemalan clinic, with the line of little boys on my right and the girls on my left. I walked through the sunlight of the tropics, seeing myself as an Alice in Wonderland risen from the depths of a sea dried up by a wicked god—and in that strange way delivered into the tenderness of these children's voices, singing of the joy of life as they walked barefoot over cobblestones burning hot from the sun.

I thought that once I was home I would have a chance to lie down on the cool tiles of our colonial house in the shade of the *madre cacao* or of my favorite mango tree. But my arrival wasn't quite as I had imagined. There was yet another orchestra, three marimbas, the doors of the house were thrown wide open to the whole town, and everyone wanted to shake my hand.

My sisters decided, without consulting me, that my casual attire was out of keeping with such honors. My suitcases and trunks were opened on the spot, and they forced me to put on the most elegant of my ball gowns, at three in the afternoon. One of my sisters put my shoes on, another brushed my hair, the third put it up. My mother gave me a large fan, for in San Salvador everyone is always sweating. I was home.

The only friends whose hands I was happy to shake were the town's three beggars, who hadn't changed at all: el Viejo de la Colbason, el Mudo Nana Raca, and Latilla Refugio. I laughed when I saw that they were all still beggars and asked my mother to take them inside the house. I knew they were my true fellow soldiers in the war of life. El Viejo de la Colbason came to sit next to me, still in pain from the thrashings that are given out to flies, dogs, and beggars.

The house was filled with flowers and palm fronds that formed triumphal arches as if a queen had arrived from abroad. I knew I couldn't play the hostess to all these hearts in search of a friendly queen: I felt myself to be the queen only of great unhappiness. What right did I have to complain? What right did I have to confess to my misery? Little by little I fell silent; little by little I forced my feelings back down into oblivion.

✦

THAT EVENING A PROCESSION of the Isalco Indians who worked on my mother's property filed past me. Each one left me a leaf, a fruit, a bird, an object. It was very beautiful, sad, and moving. I loved all these rituals. But I couldn't play along anymore . . .

The *atamialada*, the feast of tamales, began. El Viejo de la Colbason alone was close to me. From time to time he rubbed his hair against my dress. He was sad that he couldn't shine my shoes, for he gave the best shoeshine in the village. He told me, "We have a fourth beggar here, but she is of a rarer species than ours. She doesn't like to talk the way we do, she doesn't like to eat the way we do. She doesn't live the same way we do. And the others claim she is mad. They call her the village madwoman. She assured me that she would come to see you on her own."

As I was listening to this story, I heard the cries of a woman being mercilessly beaten. I pushed my way through my entourage and ran toward the place the cries were coming from. It was my bedroom. Lying in the bed (which had been carefully made up for me several days before) was a woman who appeared to be about thirty, her hair spilling across the precious embroidery of the lace sheets and pillows. Some servants were trying to tear an embroidered linen nightgown off her. She was being whipped like a dog, and she covered her head but wouldn't move.

It was the village madwoman. Since she wanted to see me alone, she had simply crawled into my bed. Gathering up the last of my strength, I shouted and tried to stop the brutes who were beating her. In vain. My mother told me that the woman was dangerous, that the day before she had put out another woman's eyes and had managed to escape from prison nevertheless. I finally pushed them all outside and stayed there alone with my pure and beautiful madwoman, who, in one movement, stood up and opened her arms to me. I thought that embrace was going to be the last minute of my life. Gently, she caressed my cheeks, my arms, my legs. She dressed me in the white linen nightgown she had taken and opened the door with dignity to leave.

I stayed in my bed, lost to the world.

ONE MORNING a consul arrived to tell me I had to go back to Paris; my husband was demanding my presence.

Once again I walked past my concierge on place Vauban. After all that had happened, I could hardly walk. I was finally home. Tonio was still very thin, very calm, very quiet.

Boris, the butler, laughed his Russian laugh, the same animal laugh that had welcomed me home so many times. The apartment was the same, nothing had changed. Our lives may have been in danger, but our furniture had remained at peace, and the loveliness of this place, as clear and blue as the sky, had been spared. A family dinner reunited me with my husband in silent tenderness. There was a parade of visitors: friends, relatives, my mother-in-law. What did they want from me? I could give them no more of myself. I had come to the end of my string of miseries.

One afternoon, when I came home from my hairdresser's where I had stayed longer than usual, I found the house empty again: everything had been taken away. There was nothing left but some crumpled newspapers floating on the breeze that came in through the open windows. I thought I was dreaming. Where was our furniture? Where were our things? I remember a film by Chaplin called *The Circus*, I think, where you saw only the traces of those who had passed through over the course of the story. I wrung my hands; I tried to understand. I had no idea what to do.

I went down to see the concierge but didn't dare ask her a thing. I went outside to get some air. Maybe there I would begin to understand. Maybe I would find someone to explain it to me. My husband stood in front of me on the sidewalk, like a statue. He took me by the arm and announced, "Yes, I've dismissed all the servants. It was too expensive—I don't have the money to pay the rent."

"But where will we live?"

"I'm taking you to a hotel. I've reserved two rooms."

Once again, life in a hotel. This time it would be the Lutétia.

19

The Hôtel Lutétia was the Left Bank refuge of people from the Right Bank, a place of exchange between one side of the Seine and the other. Our marriage, built on the sands of Africa, foundered on the smooth pavement of Paris. Everything there was flat, gray, and sad. To disguise and embellish this melancholy, we needed tears, champagne, lies, and infidelities.

So we took two rooms at the hotel: one for Monsieur, the other for Madame. It was like something out of the English novels then in vogue.

"Do you really want two rooms?"

"Yes, it will be more comfortable," Tonio told me. "I work at night, and that would keep you awake. I know you."

"All right, as you wish."

At the front desk I asked for two rooms, but not on the same floor.

"You're overreacting."

"No, no. That way you'll bother me less when you come in late."

"Very well, but you will regret it."

"Oh, I've already regretted it. For a minute, just one minute. A single minute. It was when I went home to place Vauban for the last time and all our furniture, all our things were gone. You hadn't said a single word to warn me. Oh yes! That was the moment when I had regrets, I want you to know that. But you too, I think you'll regret it one day, too."

"It's a simple matter of saving money."

"Saving money? But at a hotel we'll pay twice what our rent on place Vauban was, not counting meals. *Enfin*, your accounting methods are mysterious—you must have learned them in the sky. Maybe it is a better bargain, after all. Maybe this way it will be easier for us to separate. There's the savings, I understand. You want to leave me quietly and discreetly. You're so very kind: thank you."

We were shown to our rooms. One was on the sixth floor, the other on the eighth. He gave a melancholy thank-you and muttered, "But who'll give me my shirts, my handkerchiefs?"

"I'll go up to your room when you're there, and you'll have clean shirts and ties."

"You're very kind," he echoed. "You know I broke everything in my body. My gallbladder is damaged and it's impossible to operate—the crash in Guatemala left everything in my body all mixed up. My heart is touching my stomach, and I always feel as though I'm about to vomit."

"Instead you vomit up your life, you vomit everything. What will be left when you're done?"

"Oh, women never want to understand men!"

"Men? *All* men? No. One man, yes: you. I know, you need to be entirely alone. Your days must be entirely free, without meals, without a wife, without a home. You want to come and go like a ghost. Have I understood?"

"Yes."

"Then why did you call me back from Guatemala? Why? To put me up in a hotel room? To wait for what?"

"Me?"

"You've gone too far! I will never be able to follow you! Here we are in a hotel again. In one week your stomach will be upset from the restaurant food, the liquor, the mess . . ."

"I'm already sick. I'm going to Vichy to have my liver looked after."

"Let's go this evening, if you like."

"No, I'll go alone. I need solitude. I'll meet you back here afterward."

"Thank you. And how would you like me to spend my time?"

"Finding us another apartment."

"Fine," I said. "Let's go to sleep."

"In your room, then."

"If you want."

"But if someone calls me on the phone, you'll have to go into the bathroom. You'll let me talk alone?"

"I have never prevented you from speaking on the telephone. The things you ask me to do make me sad. Me, I have nothing to say to anyone, nothing to hide. Let's go to sleep."

His E. continued to dominate him, but not as much as she once had, since he was asking for my help and he was so sad. That night I decided to look for a new apartment.

Something bitter, a rain of ashes and stones, was pounding down on our home. A woman, that's all. There was no laughter left in my heart. I knew this had to end. What were these interludes in hotels for?

By midnight I had forgotten all my woe in his arms. That was how our life was, with all its tos and fros, its love and separations.

✦

THE NEXT MORNING I set out to look for an inexpensive apartment. There had to be one somewhere in Paris, with a kitchen where I could make him vegetables and rice and a little room where he could put away his books. A place where he would always be in my arms, it didn't matter where it was as long as he was in my arms. Half asleep, he asked me again to find a roof to shelter us.

At L'Observatoire I discovered a sixth-floor apartment above the treetops, with no elevator, that was free right away. I waited for Tonio to visit it, groaning with impatience. We went there together. He was ecstatic. He thanked me with tears in his eyes. I was thrilled.

His room had a large balcony from which he could see the park. The rent wasn't at all expensive. We were young, and climbing five flights of stairs was nothing for us. On the balcony I could have birds, flowers. . . . The kitchen was large, with a big coal stove that would heat half the apartment. We'd put a smaller stove in his study, and that would be it. In two weeks, we could be all moved in, just in time for Christmas.

He invited our dear friend Suzanne to visit the apartment with us, and she proved as happy with it as I was. We paid the first three months' rent and were given the keys.

The next day he didn't come back to the hotel but left me a message saying he would be traveling for a few days. I was so happy with my apartment that I didn't worry. Then, around noon, his business manager called and asked me to give him the keys to the apartment at L'Observatoire. My husband had thought it over; he didn't have the means to heat an apartment just then, since the price of coal had gone up.

My God! The hotel was ten times more expensive. I argued, but it was an order. I gave the keys back, weeping.

Three days later, he arrived, pale, haggard, and troubled. One of my friends told me she had run into him in Paris: he had lied again.

I was sad and desperate.

"Consuelo, do you want to find a little apartment again, a pretty one, for you alone? I swear that I really will rent it, and that I will come to see you often."

I understood that he no longer wanted to live with me. It was up to me to decide to live alone.

"Yes, Tonio, I'll ask my agency."

Fortunately, some friends of ours were renting out a two-floor apartment on the Quai des Grands-Augustins, very cheap and with a view of the Seine. Tonio took me to the agency at once and paid a year's rent. I was given the keys. I went to pray at a church, and he went with me. We wandered the quais, looking at books. I was careful not to take an interest in any costly book that he would have wanted to buy me, and I talked about the shadows on the water. On January 1, I said, I would be living on the Quai des Grands-Augustins. He would find the upper floor very pleasant for his work. We would fill it with books and turn it into a lovely little library. He promised he would come back that night. I stayed in his room, but he never came.

Nor did he come the next morning. He phoned me so I wouldn't worry. His car had broken down out in the country, and he would be there for dinner.

That evening, the two of us ate dinner at the Brasserie du Lutétia, without saying much. A great fatigue, a great lassitude had come over us.

"Let's go to sleep, my wife," he said at last. "I want to rest near you."

"Yes, Tonio."

We slept like brother and sister, tenderly intertwined, until noon. He got dressed slowly, begged me to stay in bed, and announced that he had to go to Algeria, where he would be staying at the Hôtel Aletti. He would write me.

He begged my forgiveness for leaving me alone so close to the new year, especially with the moving to do. I didn't even have the strength to protest. My eyes were half closed when he kissed me good-bye.

The agreement with the landlord on the Quai des Grands-Augustins was that as soon as the painters were finished I would move in. I had nothing else to do for Christmas and the painters were finished, so I rented a truck. The movers advised me to move the furniture well before the holidays. On November 26, therefore, the truck loaded with my things arrived at the quai. The concierge greeted us with a scowl and told us that we could not bring the furniture in. I called the secretary of the land-lord, who was on vacation. I had to keep the truck, fully loaded, on the quai, which cost me two hundred francs per day. Finally, on January 2, the landlord came back and informed me that my husband had paid a penalty in order to break the contract and let the apartment go.

I thought I would go mad. But the human body is much stronger than we think. It seems to laugh at the cobwebs of despair that the heart weaves before our eyes in order to blind us to our fate. The body walks and goes on walking. My husband was in Algeria, and I was alone: I bore with my solitude that New Year's Eve. I was learn-ing that I had to live from one day to the next.

With Suzanne to accompany me, I went to rent a stu-dio on rue Froidevaux. I put a table, three chairs, a big coal stove, and my old piano there. And I left the Hôtel Luté-tia, where my husband had never stayed for more than a few hours a week. Some friends informed me that he was back and had rented a small bachelor flat in Auteuil, where the lovely E. spent her afternoons with him. My sculpting was all I had left to console me.

Tonio thought my decision was courageous. My studio pleased him. I heard out his compliments like a dead woman counting the blows of the hammer that is nailing her coffin shut.

So we were separated. The view of the Montparnasse cemetery was chilling, but little by little I grew used to it.

My concierges, father and son, made tombstones. The son worked faster than his father; the old man struck long, slow, muted blows, while the son's little hammer fell to a different rhythm. I listened to the sound of hammers against tombstones from morning to night; those stones would seal off the lives of other people who, like me, had laughed, loved, and suffered.

I explained this strangely syncopated background noise to Tonio. His visits came almost every day but were very brief. I also told him about my anguish.

"You'll get used to it; human beings get used to everything," he assured me.

"Yes, I remember how they make slaves out of people on the Río de Oro. Once you've accepted the humiliation of no longer being yourself, no longer being free, then you're happy, isn't that it? It's the same with me. You've made me get used to living alone, on the edge of a cemetery, on a thousand francs a month. You bring me two hundred fifty francs a week; I feel like a maid on vacation. Why can't you give me the whole amount at once?"

"I'm not rich, Consuelo. I'm earning our living. If I gave you a thousand francs a month, what would you do, little one? You'd spend it all at once."

"I'll work, as poor women do. Maybe I would be happier. . . . Maybe I would earn more than a thousand francs a month."

I was pale and struggling for breath. I spent whole nights weeping, but I didn't want to reproach him in any way. He didn't love me anymore, and that was his right. You cannot berate another person for having ceased to love you. He was helping me survive, nevertheless, in good times and in bad: a thousand francs a month, that covered the rent and the coal. I lived on coffee and brioche, and sometimes only bread and sausage. But the idea of being a slave living on two hundred fifty francs a week was becoming unbearable.

"Thank you, Tonio," I told him one day. "I don't want any more money from you. Is that the only thing you and I still have in common?"

"Yes, I'm afraid so," he said sadly.

"Then, starting from today, we'll have nothing more in common. Take back your two hundred fifty francs and buy a bottle of champagne to celebrate my freedom, if you want: we'll drink it together."

"But tomorrow how will you eat?"

"That doesn't concern you since we no longer have anything in common. But if you're curious, I'll tell you that I am going to find a job."

"Work? You? But you're far too fragile! You only weigh about ninety pounds. You can barely carry a full bottle of wine."

"Give me those two hundred fifty francs. In five minutes I'll bring you a full bottle of champagne, and you will never come back here again to pay me my weekly wage as if I were an employee."

"All right, but don't go out. We can order the champagne over the phone."

"Yes, you're right."

A long moment passed before the champagne arrived.

"To your freedom . . ."

"To yours . . ."

"Tomorrow I'm sure you'll call and ask me to bring you money. It will be difficult because I'm very hard pressed right now. I'll bring you your weekly wage again, as you call it. I earn four thousand to five thousand francs a month, and I have to pay the rent, the telephone, the restaurant bills, and give a thousand francs to my mother and a thousand francs to you."

"You don't owe me anything more after today."

"We'll see."

After this scene, he kissed me tenderly on the mouth the way he used to, then left. He had put some more coal in the stove, he had played the piano, he had made his eternal scrambled eggs in the kitchen. For the first time he had felt at home and had even told me, "If you want me to spend the night, I'll stay. You're still my wife."

"No, no," I cried. "Tomorrow I'm going to work. I'm going to work."

"You're crazy. You really don't want me to?"

"No, I want to work. I want to be free. Enough of this slavery! Enough of being your wife by the month!"

Yet I loved this very large boy who was my husband, and he loved me, I knew he did. But he wanted to be a free husband, and I reproached myself for making him come back to me every time I needed to pay for my room, my food, my telephone. We held each other for a long time, our champagne glasses in our hands, and swore we would love each other forever. He stayed in my bed, but at five in the morning I found myself alone, half asleep. He had left a little note and a pretty sketch that was his portrait: a clown with a flower in his hand, very embarrassed, an awkward clown who didn't know what to do with his flower. I later learned that the flower was me, a very proud flower, as he says in *The Little Prince*.

It was difficult to go from my dream to reality. I had celebrated my independence; now it was up to me to keep my word. I could hardly comb my hair, get dressed, make myself a coffee. I smiled: it really was like a scene from a cheap novel. I was looking for work. What kind of work, anyway?

I went to sit at a table on the terrace of the Sélect to think. It was urgent that I come up with a plan. There were only twenty francs left in my purse, barely enough to buy half a baguette and two tomatoes.

I was at my table in the Sélect, reading my newspaper, when suddenly light flooded into my mind for, as in a dream, Spanish words were ringing in my ears. The café's radio was announcing, *"Cigarillos La Morena, cómpralos, señorita!"* I leaped from my chair. The message was meant for me. I had found the work I needed: radio advertisements in Spanish. I could certainly earn my living that way. I knew a lot of people in Paris. Crémieux gave lectures over Radio-Paris for Spanish-speaking countries; he would help me.

No sooner said than done: the next day I was settled in front of a microphone, speaking Spanish. I wasn't only reading advertisements but also presenting songs and plays.

I was saved.

$\mathcal{T}$ONIO'S FINANCIAL SITUATION eventually improved. His promotion to the rank of officer in the Legion of Honor and the success of *Wind, Sand, and Stars** had made him a well-known, much admired writer. We were no longer living together, but we hadn't separated either. This was our love, the inevitable destiny of our love: we simply had to get used to living that way. He rented me a large house in the country, the estate of La Feuilleraie. He was enjoying his new life, half single, half married. He lived in his bachelor quarters, and I lived in the country. He told me, "You're very happy here in the country. You're better off here than on place Vauban, aren't you?"

He had moved heaven and earth to get coal for me that winter. He was earning a little money writing for *L'Intransigeant,* and he told me that he had written those magazine articles without much wanting to, just in order

---

*The French original, *Terre des hommes,* and the English translation were both published in 1939. The Académie Française awarded the book a prize as a novel, and it won another prize, as nonfiction, from the American Booksellers Association.

to buy me coal: "So we can have central heating installed for you and buy you furniture for the garden, benches and chairs in different colors, lemon yellow and blue."

He came regularly to La Feuilleraie, more often than I wanted him to, actually. He would arrive, and if he found that I had friends over for lunch or dinner, he would go to a little bistro in the village where he wrote me letters ten or fifteen pages long, love letters such as I had never received before.

The garden was marvelous. Lilacs grew everywhere, but I still felt alone. The flowering of spring after heavy rains, the orchards loaded down with fruit, the scent of the lilacs, and the silence of the garden, which was like something out of Lamartine, all cried out for lovers to come and sit on the moss-covered benches.

A faithful old spinster went everywhere with me, sometimes as the cook, sometimes as the maternal comforter of my tears. I also had a pair of old gardeners, Monsieur and Madame Jules, but I missed having someone young around. I asked my dressmaker's daughter to come and live at La Feuilleraie. She was Russian, very pretty, and laboriously earning about fifty francs a week in Paris by spending all day bent over magnificent dresses that other people would wear. I offered her the same salary if she would move into my garden, love the flowers, put away my handkerchiefs, and choose pretty dresses and hats for me. Her name was Véra; she was barely twenty years old. Quickly, she became La Feuilleraie's young girl. She loved climbing the trees, repotting plants in the greenhouse, and growing strange flowers, black orchids or Chinese roses.

Véra began to love me like a sister. She took devoted care of the goats, the ducks, the rabbits, the donkeys, and even a pregnant cow named Natasha, who would soon begin giving us milk. Véra awaited the calf's birth with great concern.

She asked me questions about my childhood, which I answered evasively, for she thought I had always lived at La Feuilleraie. I let her dream. She had an odd way of dressing; sometimes she looked like a Russian ice skater or a peasant woman from the Circassian mountains, sometimes like an Indian.

One day when she had drunk a little more champagne than usual because it was her birthday, she decided to insist: "But why doesn't your husband come to stay? And you, don't you ever visit him in Paris?"

It was a serious question, a problem I couldn't explain even to myself. It was understood between my husband and me that he would live in Paris and I would live here. The answer wasn't very cheerful, and without thinking I told Véra the truth: "Why, Véra, I suppose I hadn't thought of that. I could go and visit him one day."

"Let's go!" she said with great excitement. "I would love to see his apartment. I want to see how he lives, what furniture he has, what neighborhood he lives in. To see his servants."

We were interrupted by the sudden appearance of Tonio himself, who had just driven up with a friend. He was in the habit of making these unexpected visits, for he knew how good-natured my cook was and how much pleasure Véra and I took in welcoming him to lunch, even if we were already having dessert.

That day, our table was covered with forget-me-nots. For her party, Véra had wanted the table to look like a flower bed full of blue flowers. Her name, Véra, was written on it, and mine, too, in letters made from dark mauve violets, along with a heart that had a little metal airplane inside it that she had put there.

"God, how beautiful you are!" Tonio cried out when he saw us. His friend had joined him at the door of the dining room, but he stopped him from joining our intimate lunch party, I don't know why, and abruptly sent him away. "Sorry, old man, my wife has finished with lunch. Thanks for the car. I'll spend the rest of the afternoon here."

He looked like an Arab sheik, and his black eyes shone with a singular gleam that made us tremble. I didn't ask him why he had made his friend go away. Perhaps he wanted this feast of forget-me-nots for himself alone. He sat down at the table as if he owned all the perfumed loveliness around him.

"My children, you are eating flowers," he said. "Flowers taste good!"

"It was Véra who prepared this marvelous table to celebrate her twentieth birthday. We're alone, and you know I have to work this evening. You're welcome to attend her birthday party. Véra was just talking about you: she was wondering what your apartment in Paris is like."

His face closed. He lowered his eyes and, with his right hand, put some violets on his plate, as if to perfume the rice he was eating. Jules arrived at exactly the right moment with his present for Véra. It was a little tortoise; he and his wife had spent several days painting its shell silver. Vera's name was written across the poor creature's back in tiny gold letters. He presented us with the tortoise inside a large seashell. Tonio played sommelier and had us drink more and more. We watched the figure of my giant husband, tall as a tree, moving across the dining room in the dance of a conqueror.

"You are happy here, Consuelo. The light in this room is wonderful. Look out the window at that lawn, those colors—it's like a dream. Here both of you are like princesses in some enchanted tale."

"Why don't you live with us?" Véra asked. "We have quite a number of rooms, you're sure to find one you like. Every day you will have a feast of flowers on the table, I promise."

"Thank you, Véra. Let's go outside and have our coffee in the little pavilion."

"But Madame Jules is expecting us to be here," I said. "She's planning to serve us the coffee and a surprise cake for Véra."

Nevertheless, we walked down paths lined with flowering lilacs, throwing twigs at one another's hair, our cheeks bulging with cherries, for we put whole handfuls in our mouths at once.

Véra and Tonio were both leaning against the trunk of an old cherry tree. They were staring into each other's eyes like young animals who suddenly fall in love and want to prove it to each other immediately. I let them stand there with their gazes full of desire, telling myself serenely that in a harem the sultan gratifies several women in turn. And now it was Véra's turn.

As we ate Madame Jules's cake, we were all as well behaved as children at Sunday school. Tonio was taken aback by the desire of this half-dressed young girl who was openly offering herself to him, touching his hand shyly as if it were the stem of a rare flower. Madame Jules was dismayed. At her age, the old gardener knew what that meant. Tonio was not eating his cake or drinking his coffee. I was concerned for Madame Jules, who, in turn, was worried about me and shed maternal tears as she looked at me.

"But Tonio," I said very loudly, "why aren't you eating your cake? Drink your coffee while it's hot. If Véra is caressing your hand, that's nice, but please don't pain Madame Jules or me. Come on, liven up! I haven't done you any harm. Taste the cake, drink the coffee, it's very good."

The two "children" woke up, and Tonio murmured, "Yes, excuse me, my wife." He pushed Véra's hand away and began eating the gardener's cake.

Véra was melancholy after her twentieth birthday, and I sensed she was in love with Tonio. He began to visit La Feuilleraie less often. Véra was my only friend, my only companion, and to him she was nothing but a child who had wanted to have fun for an hour. He didn't want to destroy the peace and equilibrium that I had managed, with great difficulty, to achieve amid the poetry of La Feuilleraie.

*

THE WEEKS PASSED, and then one day Tonio fell ill. After several days of fever and lethargy, the doctor became concerned: the fever had risen. He warned me that it could become dangerous, even fatal, since Tonio's heart had been severely strained by the airplane crashes. He wouldn't be able to fight off the fever if it persisted.

Véra called him every fifteen minutes to find out how he was. My husband answered her brutally, "I want to speak to my wife."

"Why don't we go and see him?" Vera finally suggested. "He's really very sick."

She had always longed to see his apartment. There is nothing more curious or more tenacious than a young girl head over heels in love. Weakly I answered, "Yes, Véra, you're right. Perhaps I should go and look after him in his apartment."

"We'll bring him back with us to La Feuilleraie," she said. "We'll take care of him here. He's your husband, after all, you have the right and the obligation to take care of him."

She was young. She knew nothing about the terrible scenes, the ruptures, the pacts of silence when husbands are no longer faithful or in love. Carefree young girl that she was, Véra gathered an enormous bouquet of hawthorn blossoms that would barely fit into the trunk of the car.

Bedecked with flowers and carrying a basket of fresh fruit, we left to pay a visit to Tonio at his home.

Véra was outfitted in some sort of folkloric Russian peasant garb. She could barely squeeze into the elevator at Tonio's building in Auteuil. I thought I would die when, for the first time, I rang my husband's doorbell. Véra was sneezing from the perfume of the wild roses she was carrying. A maid opened the door. The huge bouquet went in first, and as the branches of hawthorn pushed the maid back into the room a little gap opened that Véra leapt through.

"He's here," she said, pushing the bouquet against a half-open door behind which voices could be heard.

A door slammed violently, and I saw a bit of green skirt sticking out, the skirt of a woman who had hidden in the bathroom. My husband was red with fever and screaming with rage. "Consuelo, my wife, who asked you to come here? Go away! This is not your place!"

The flap of green skirt was twitching madly. The whole thing was so tragicomical that no clown skit could ever reproduce it. Véra had set her huge bouquet down on the floor. She was pale, crestfallen, confused to see that a woman had hidden in the bathroom. If I hadn't held her back, she would have gone to hide in there too. Tonio was shouting, "Go away! Go away! I want no visitors."

Gently I took his pulse. He let me have my way, telling me, "I want to die, I don't like complications. My wife, I beg you: leave." And he gestured toward the green skirt, which was waving like a flag.

"I'm worried about you," I said calmly. "Nothing else

matters. I was only thinking of your health. Calm down and rest assured, we are going to leave. I came here to take care of you because you are very ill. It's the first time I have come to your home, and you're throwing me out. But you are so feverish, you don't know what you're doing . . ."

"I've never treated you like this before," he said miserably. "Shouting to chase you away . . ."

Both of us were weeping, and Véra was sobbing as she watched.

"You are a monster!" she cried. "If you knew the trouble I went to to make this huge bouquet. All so I could bring it here to you. I'm the one who told your wife to come."

I pushed her out the door. I believe Véra finally understood then that just being pretty isn't enough for a woman to become and remain part of a man's life.

THE DAY AFTER THIS misadventure, my husband called. He complained of sleepless nights but said that the fruit and flowers from La Feuilleraie had brought all of spring to him. His fever was going down, and he begged me to come and have a cup of tea at his bedside, without Véra.

Our conversation at his apartment was very short. I didn't want to stay long. I was afraid of having to go through the previous day's scene once more. His maid looked me over from head to foot. The tea was bad, but I drank it in order to keep up appearances. My husband spilled the teapot onto my clothes. He wanted me to go into the bathroom and dry off my dress, but I refused to go into the room where, the day before, a woman had hidden, wearing a skirt as green as spinach.

That Sunday he paid me a visit with his dog, and since I went to work late at night, regardless of the weather, I asked him if we could leave together.

"If you'll allow me," he said, "I'll stay at La Feuilleraie. But I would like to be alone. I need calm, in order to think about the two of us. Take your governess with you, I don't need any help."

When I came back he was lying in my bed, the way he used to. I was surprised but didn't allow myself to show it. I told him about my radio program and chose, for my own peace of mind, to sleep in Véra's bedroom.

The next day my husband declared that he could not move from the bed, that it was impossible for him to stand up; he needed a man, the gardener perhaps, to help him get to his feet. Véra whispered in my ear that if the servants knew he had spent a night in my bedroom, I would no longer have the right to ask for a divorce.

The idea of divorce had been running through my head. Tonio knew it, and he confessed to me later that he had arranged for a witness on purpose to ensure that no divorce could take place because he had slept in my room, fair and square.

After that deft little piece of staging, Tonio asked my gardener to bring him a yellow bench from the garden and put it in front of the window. I laughed because the room had comfortable armchairs but he absolutely insisted on having a garden bench. So Jules and his wife brought one in. Tonio announced that this room would be his from now on and that it was very important to him that no one else should ever sit on this bench. It would be "the bench of Antoine de Saint-Exupéry."

He spent the day in the henhouse, strolling through the vegetable garden and talking tomatoes with Jules. He left that evening, carrying eggs, fruit, and flowers with him.

In those days I was interviewing a number of famous men on the radio. I began the series with my friend Léon-Paul Fargue. Next, I invited . . . Antoine de Saint-Exupéry. He told Radio-Paris he would do it for a fee of three thousand francs. He added that he spoke Spanish badly but would be willing to say a few things.

My guest was announced. I had my husband led into the sound studio one minute before the red light went on. He recognized me. "What are you doing here?" he exclaimed loudly.

"Silence, please, monsieur. In one minute, the whole world will be listening to you. Here is a script in both languages. I've prepared it carefully. Read slowly. I ask the questions, and you answer."

"But what's going on?"

"Silence. Now, to begin: How did you learn Spanish?"

"In Buenos Aires, with my pilots."

He spoke without stopping, asking himself the questions and then answering them. After a few minutes of this, I took the microphone away from him, speaking Spanish myself now: "You have just heard the famous aviator, your friend Antoine de Saint-Exupéry. He is dressed in light gray, and is very moved to find himself speaking

Spanish. He begs your pardon for his heavy accent, but that is a contract between the French and the Spanish, an unbreakable contract. The Spanish will always roll their *r*'s and the French will never be able to pronounce the Spanish *j*. Monsieur de Saint-Exupéry will now say good-bye in Spanish!"

He was beside himself, and gazed at me helplessly.

"Bonne nuit."

"Now, the next item . . ."

My secretary pushed Tonio out by the shoulders as Agnès Capri began to sing.

Tonio came back later that night to pick me up at the office. *"Madame de Saint-Exupéry, s'il vous plaît?"* he asked a secretary.

"No such lady works here."

"Yes she does; she speaks Spanish."

"Mais non, monsieur, the lady in charge of Spanish programming is named Madame Consuelo Carrillo."

"Thank you. That's the person I want. Where is she?"

"She'll be coming out soon. Today is her birthday, and we're all going with her to her house outside the city. Perhaps you know that her husband is a great aviator but she lives alone in the country, in a big house in Jarcy called La Feuilleraie. And we're all going there this evening."

"But where is she?"

"Here she is. Madame Gómez, Madame Gómez! You have a visitor."

"Thank you."

And turning toward Tonio, the secretary said, "Come along on the bus with us. There'll be about twenty of us.

We're going to have a housewarming party at La Feuilleraie."

He came. But no one knew that the tall gentleman was my husband.

During the party, someone told him a lovely story about me. It was the story of the rose fields on the road from Paris to La Feuilleraie.

"Madame Gómez takes that road home every evening after work," a guest told him. "So of course she's gotten to know all the rose growers. One frosty evening, Madame Gómez saw that her friends the growers were panicked and in tears. The frost was killing the roses. That same night, she sent them dozens of large linen sheets embroidered with crowns. They say the sheets were inherited by her husband, who is an aristocrat, a count, I believe, or in any case the descendant of a great family. You can imagine, white sheets like that, lying on the ground. It was the middle of the night, but she revived the rose growers' hopes. They went back to work. She herself worked alongside them, and with their help, she built an enormous tent, white as snow, to save the roses. The next day, all of us went to help. Each of us, monsieur, took along a piece of wrapping paper, newspaper, it was a real madhouse beneath those 'tents.' We crawled along on all fours, lighting little fires, and, monsieur, it was truly a miracle: the rose crop was saved. Heaven helped them, it can't be denied. The weather grew a little warmer, and the roses managed to survive. Of course the sheets were left in rags, but the love that the rose growers bear Madame de La Feuilleraie, I mean Madame Gómez—that, believe me, is far more beautiful than a thousand sheets, even if they were embroidered with crowns. The growers spent several days at La Feuilleraie to help out in the orchard and the vegetable garden. They cut back the undergrowth. You understand, monsieur, work that is not paid, work that is done out of friendship, out of love for the earth—that is far more precious than any other kind. And everything at La Feuilleraie has bloomed. If you're interested, I can give you the exact figures. Almost a ton of pears have been harvested from the orchard and sold in the marketplace. . . . She loves roses, Madame Gómez, she loves to save them. She herself is a rose."

Part Five

The War, 1940–1941

21

T HE THIRTY-ODD MILES that I went over every day
on my drive through the Bois de Vincennes to Paris
had become a very pleasurable habit. Along the way I saw
enormous fields of beets and vegetables that were trucked
into Paris by night to be distributed in the early morning
at the great marketplace of Les Halles. But the traffic was
becoming heavier and heavier. Something was happening
that all the gallant peasants who were bringing in their har-
vests found tremendously strange. I observed and shared in
their worries. There was talk of mobilization, of war. Soon
France would be going into battle again. We Parisians
clung to peace at all costs; we didn't want to hear the word
"war." No one wanted it to come, but it was already only a
few hundred miles away from us. Our only remedy was to
go on pretending, to ignore the rumors and live in peace
during those last sunny days of the spring of 1940.

Tonio continued to invite himself to lunch at La Feuilleraie. It was the only meal I had at home, among my dogs
and my good friends the gardeners, Jules and his wife.
Jules acted as my sommelier and knew how to pour both
rosé wines and champagne without letting a single drop
fall onto the cloth that covered the legendary table of La
Feuilleraie. My husband was already in uniform; the avia-

tors had been mobilized, though they had no airplanes. Nonetheless, they were preparing for this war, which promised to be more of a farcical butchery than a war, since they had no weapons with which to combat a nation that was armed to the teeth.

The months went quickly by. We avoided mentioning the war but spoke instead of the hawthorns that were in bloom, the preserves that needed to be put up, the hunting lodge that would have to be repainted. One day I told Tonio I was going to use all my savings to buy grain to feed my hens and the other animals.

"I'm also going to convert the tennis court into a henhouse, to increase production. And use the pond for raising ducks."

I spent my afternoon in the car, transporting enormous sacks of grain that I bought here and there, for the peasants were already doing as I was and hiding what they had.

Then France went to war and was defeated in a flash of lightning. My mother, who was in San Salvador, sent me a telegram ordering me to leave Europe as quickly as possible and come home like an obedient little girl.

I told my husband about that telegram. For the first time he begged me, like a child in tears, to stay in France whatever happened. I must not abandon him; if I left he would feel completely unprotected, he would be shot down on his next mission. He would lose his hold on life.

I promised to do as he wished. Since it was almost impossible by then to reach Radio-Paris by the roads, I had decided to live in the city in order to go on working. But

Tonio persuaded me to give up my work at the radio station and stay at La Feuilleraie, to feed my rabbits and make jam. I accepted, for Tonio's airport wasn't far from the estate and he often came to stay there, one or two days a week. Despite the instability of our lives, we had several days of happiness among the ocean of leaves and roses that was La Feuilleraie.

The Germans bombarded the little train station at Jarcy, about half a mile from the house. Several coaches of a train were blown up, and my cook went mad from fear. The valet had to join the army, and Monsieur and Madame Jules were the only ones left to keep me company.

One Monday, I'm quite sure it was the tenth of June, my husband arrived at the house, frantic.

"We have to leave in five minutes," he told me.

"Where?"

"Anywhere. It isn't serious; bring along a little suitcase, just what you need for one night. You'll soon be back home, I hope. But I don't want you to stay here alone. The Germans are closing in on Paris. You can hear them already . . ."

"Yes, I hear them, especially at night. The other day we saw some planes fighting just above the edge of the property."

"Hurry; you'll take the little Peugeot. Bring as much gasoline as you can, so that you can go as far as possible. I think the best place for you is Pau."

"Pau? But I don't know anyone there."

"Doesn't matter, you'll soon meet good people. All the

gold that belongs to France is being evacuated to Pau in armored trucks. Follow one and stay close because the Germans will never bombard France's gold. They've been informed and know it is going to be stored in a safe place. So they will know where to find it after the negotiations. It's in their interest for that gold to be well guarded."

And so I left in the car. I was trembling with fear and cold.

"I beg you, no tears," he repeated. "You'll have plenty of time to cry later. If you want to know how I am, you'll have to be in the free zone. If you stay in Paris, you'll never hear a thing, even if I'm dead."

I still wonder by what burst of energy, what mysterious intuition, I managed to follow his advice and, like a sleepwalker, struck out on the road to Pau.

I left him with my eyes closed so I could hold on to the memory of his face, the smell of him, his skin. We went in opposite directions. Gréco, my favorite dog, followed me for several kilometers, running behind the car, but thirst and exhaustion discouraged him, and I soon lost sight of him, too.

I ARRIVED IN PARIS but couldn't go any further without sitting down one last time on the terrace of a café where I had so often sat before. At the Deux Magots, the tables were as crowded as ever, and everyone was talking about leaving Paris. Evacuate Paris: that was the order.

A voiceless rage rose up inside me. Why run away?

Why leave your house to your enemies? Why not stand up to them? Even with a gaze? I found those orders very unwise. My own case was different. If I wanted to have news of my love, I had to go to Pau. I could not live without any information on what was happening to him in the turmoil into which he and his squadron had been thrown.

In one minute I had lost my house, my husband, and this adopted country that I loved and respected. My mouth tasted of ashes, and nothing, not even liquor, could quiet the feeling of hatred and defeat inside me. For the first time I was running away. It was a strange feeling. You run from the enemy, you go anywhere you can, and you feel even more threatened. It was my turn to be engulfed in the panic experienced by the forty million French people who had received the order to evacuate their homes, their beloved villages, to mill around in circles like animals, using up the last of their energy without suspecting that their strength and their resistance was leaving them.

I was going to Pau, then, so I could receive letters from the man I loved. I would willingly have stopped anywhere. I would willingly have laughed in the face of a German who would then shoot me against a tree. The only thing that frightened me was the poor Frenchmen, once conquerors and today fleeing through the streets like a flock of sheep without a shepherd, at random, with no star to guide them.

It was impossible to think in the uproar of the bombardments the Germans were raining down on the endless progression of human beings who spilled out over the countryside and roadways of France. Each one believed he was going somewhere, but if he had taken one minute to think it over he would have stopped wherever he was, because it was a delusion to believe that the millions of people who were all on the move could find the food and lodging they needed somewhere else. But they continued pushing against one another, like beasts being led to the slaughter. You could hear the moaning of those who fell beneath the bombs that were dropped on us almost at point-blank range. Only the armored trucks that were transporting the gold were spared. Tonio had been right.

I managed to slip in between two of those trucks. In the night, we received the order to crawl under our cars and switch off our side lamps, which had already been painted blue or gray in order to be invisible from a meter away. By then we were used to seeing in the dark.

I fled like that for five days. At my first chance to go to a post office, I asked if I could send a telegram to my husband. After being questioned at length and showing my papers, repeating my husband's name, with his rank of captain in the French Army, writing it down on several forms, and carefully specifying the name of his squadron, I was finally authorized to write out a telegram to him without having any guarantee that he would receive it. But I seized this slight chance. I needed to write his name down on a form, not in ink but in tears. Then I stopped in a village to write a letter.

I finally reached Pau. My landing place had been arranged; I was expected. The next day, I went to the post office. It was like a religious duty I was fulfilling: every day I would go to the post office, where I would wait for news of Tonio. Since heaven had allowed me to cross the distance from La Feuilleraie to Pau, heaven would also send me a message. Hundreds of people were waiting at the post office just as I was, hoping to find a letter there. In this jumble of uprooted beings, far from all that was dear to them, people started making one another's acquaintance. None of us was proud to tell the story of our flight, our defeat, or the tearful hope that made us stand at the post office waiting for a letter that would connect us once more to those we loved.

I vaguely recalled, as if it were the distant cry of a drowning man, the few words Tonio had spoken to me before we separated: "Monsieur Pose, the director of the Banque de France, is a friend. Remember that name: Pose, like Pau. You'll go to the window of the bank to ask him to help you if you lose your money. He knows us. I'm sure he'll help you." I ran to Monsieur Pose's bank and shouted at the windows, "Monsieur Pose, Monsieur Pose, Monsieur Pose!" An employee asked me what I wanted.

"I only want to see Monsieur Pose. I am Madame la Comtesse de Saint-Exupéry."

"He is in a meeting, madame. He told me to help you. He has had a message from your husband. What do you want? What would you like?"

"A room—I'm not finding anything. I cannot stay with the people who have taken me in, and I've tried all the hotels."

He asked an employee to go with me. The government had requisitioned some more-or-less habitable rooms in private houses, cold attic rooms with no running water.

But I was very happy to find a bed in the home of a local woman, who had me sleep in the same room as a soldier and an old woman.

My stay in that attic was difficult, but waiting for news of Tonio, who had gone to fight in North Africa, was worse. I didn't know what saint to commend myself to in order to get news of him, and my emotions subsided from anxiety to resignation, and finally to the patience that would allow me to endure this ordeal.

On a day like all the others I was at the post office, waiting my turn among hundreds of idle people who had been arriving since seven in the morning to take their places in line at the windows. The employee, who knew me, sometimes gave me a wave of the hand to let me know that there was nothing. That day, I heard his voice saying, "A letter for Madame de Saint-Exupéry." I felt as if a shooting star had stopped for me in midflight. The sun was shining for me alone, among all these wan, lonely faces waiting for their letters day in and day out.

An old woman took me by the arm, and, going to the window before my turn, I accepted the envelope. All eyes were on me, on my clothes, my feet, my face. Their envy was so strong that I fell down in a dead faint on the marble floor of the post office. All the people standing in line ran to help me up, but what each of them really wanted was to catch a glimpse of the handwriting on the letter, which I was clutching against my chest as if someone had been trying to rip it from my hands.

The old lady who had led me to the window helped me down the stairs and went with me to a nearby café. She adjusted her glasses and advised me to stay calm and take some time to think before opening it.

"I'll go with you to the church to thank Heaven. Now read your letter, my child," she added, deeply moved.

I recognized Tonio's handwriting, but it was impossible for me to see clearly. I no longer knew how to read: I'd gone blind. Lights of all colors danced in front of my eyes, and I was shaken by a fit of weeping. The old lady took the letter from me and told me that he had arrived safely in Africa, that he had sent this letter by the one and only mail delivery to France, on the last France-bound military flight out of Africa. "I promised I would let you know how I was," he said. He promised to see me again and never again to leave me.

Until late in the evening we sat in the church; it was the only place where it was still possible to relax, for the city had ten times its normal quota of inhabitants. When the old woman left, I wondered why I hadn't asked her for her name and address. By then it was too late: she had disappeared into the crowd.

I laughed all alone, chanting Tonio's name. I caressed the letter as I would have caressed my own child. I decided to choose a good restaurant and have a real meal at last. I was full of courage. Since leaving my first hosts' home, I had not had a chance to sit down at a table, for the restaurants, though they had three seatings every meal, would not give a table to a person eating alone. But that evening I was determined to sit down in front of a white tablecloth and savor a meal that would make me wait for my husband in all serenity.

He would see me again. He would see me again, and he had said he would never leave me. God was showering me with gifts. Tonio's love had come back to me. I felt blessed, singled out from the crowd, I felt like giving thanks to God out loud in the street. My joy was hard to control, and I walked in a zigzag along the sidewalk of Pau's main avenue. The faint electric blue light of the blackout led me to a restaurant. A long stream of famished heads were jostling against one another as they surged through the door of the restaurant. When my turn came, I headed for the bar. The smoke, the light, the smell of food and people almost made me sick to my stomach, but I had been hungry for days, eating only dry bread and cheese that I bought from peasants, without even a glass of cool water.

A middle-aged man, dressed in gray with an absurdly gaudy tie, asked me, a certain malice in his voice, if I was alone. "You're sitting at the bar," I answered. "Would you like to order me a port? Or make that a double port. I'll pay."

He smiled, ordered a double port, and told me, "It's on me, mademoiselle. I'm alone. With two people, it's easier to get a table. I'm from Pau and I know the maître d'. He'll give us a table at the second sitting. Here, take my bar stool."

He grabbed me around the waist, more affectionately than even a friend would, and lifted me up onto the stool. I began savoring my port, dreaming of the African sky that would protect my husband. I forgot the gentleman in gray who had touched my bare arm so familiarly. He insisted I have another port. I accepted, and we went on drinking. I heard him telling me that he was making a fortune selling old ties that he would never have been able to sell in his boutique in peacetime, and that business was very good.

I was too happy to be shocked by his familiarity. I was finally going to have dinner in a restaurant, for the first time since I had left Paris. I had to start living again! I looked around at all the faces. Perhaps a friend would turn up among the other clients. Faces and more faces went by, but I didn't recognize any of them. My shoulders drooped. I bent over the bar, ordering another port every fifteen minutes. I had my letter against my heart like a talisman, so I was afraid of nothing.

Heavy, muscular arms seized me, and I heard a shout, "Consuelo, Consuelo, is that you? Come with us."

"Consuelo, how long have you been here?" asked another voice.

Soon I was sitting in front of the white tablecloth I had dreamed of, surrounded by three old friends of Tonio's, three soldier friends who had risked their lives in this war, a captain and two majors, all three wounded, two in the leg and the third in the arm. They were bandaged and walked with canes, which meant that we had better service and a better meal than the rest of the clientele. I realized that I had abandoned my gray fellow without a word. None of the three men knew what had become of their wives after the evacuation of Paris. No communication was permitted, and they had had to stay in the hospital to attend to their wounds. They had initially been in Biarritz, but when the Germans invaded that city they had escaped to Pau in an old truck driven by a nurse they called the "virgin of Biarritz."

I thanked heaven for having sent me these true friends. We wept as we talked about the French defeat, and at the end of the meal all three of them declared at once, "You're coming with us. We have some rooms in a little hotel. There are five of us, and with you that will make six. The women have beds, the men sleep on the floor."

I followed them like an animal that has finally found a cave to take refuge in. We went in through the courtyard, for the rooms were all tiny attic rooms without curtains or running water: maids' rooms.

When I had recovered from my emotions, I had an offer for them: "I'll take you to my country house outside Pau."

"What? You have a country house near Pau? A real house? In the country? That's too good to be true. Are you joking?"

"No, not at all. Today, for the first time, I received a letter from my husband. I ran through the streets to the garage where I had left my car so that I could hide my treasure there, my letter. Well, just imagine, I had ten liters of gas left. Since I have a small car, I could go as far as a hundred kilometers on ten liters. I set out for the hilltop fields where a Greek family I know lives. 'Why don't you come and live out in the country?' their maid suggested. I don't have a house in the country. Her parents, she thought, would rent me the Castel Napoli, a house on their farm, a very old house surrounded by large wells of potable water and fig trees. I went to see her father, and for a thousand francs a month, I rented the house so that Tonio could have a place to rest when he came back. Tomorrow I'll take all of you there."

"Not tomorrow!" my friends shouted. "Right now! We're sick of sleeping on the floor!"

Like an infantry unit, they buckled up their satchels and piled into their car. As wounded soldiers, they were entitled to a certain amount of gasoline. We invaded the Castel Napoli. Each one took a bedroom by assault, and we all lived on the large farm as a family. From time to time we heard news from soldiers who were leaving the army in Africa to go to England, where they would continue to fight the war.

My wait at the post office was shorter now because soldiers were given priority. But I had no further word from Tonio.

Then, in a café, we learned from a pilot that Tonio was back in France. It was as if I'd been struck dumb. How could he not have let me know? It was impossible! I had received a letter, my letter, his last love letter. A letter of fidelity. He had sworn to me that if he came back alive, he would never leave me again.

I had just spent three months in perfect serenity with my soldier friends. One of them, understanding my chagrin, had tears in his eyes. The handsome pilot who was talking to us did not understand the damage he was doing, for my chest was heaving and a torrent of tears was flooding my cheeks. The major questioned him about my husband's demobilization, and he gave us all the information he had, adding that he was quite sure he had heard Saint-Ex say he would rejoin his family at Agay, in the Var.

I was in despair. I could hardly stand up, overwhelmed with fever and anguish. My legs were collapsing under me like the legs of an animal lying down in a field to die. Only death could free me from this fever of waiting.

★

A FEW DAYS LATER I received a telegram from my husband, telling me to meet him at the Hôtel Central in Pau. I went to that meeting like a sleepwalker. From the moment I had received the message, my friends had kept a close watch on my every move. My rendezvous was theirs as well. They sat in a circle in the farmhouse kitchen, begging me to come back quickly with Tonio.

There was no mirror at the Napoli farm, so I couldn't look at myself. They served as my mirror and gave me advice on my looks, which had taken a turn for the worse since I'd fled from Paris. The women loaned me a handkerchief, a comb, a brooch, and even a pearl necklace.

When I arrived at the Hôtel Central, I was told that my husband had asked that I go directly up to room 70. A bellboy was waiting for me and showed me to the door of the room. I knocked softly. A hoarse voice shouted, "You can come in." The bellboy jumped and ran away on tiptoe, repeating, "Go in, go in!"

I couldn't manage to turn the handle correctly. Tonio's voice repeated, "I'm in bed, turn the handle to the right, come in."

He was, indeed, in bed.

"I've turned the light off," he said. "I'm about to go to sleep. Turn it on if you want, the switch is to your left, near the door."

"No," I answered. "I don't need light."

I hadn't seen him since La Feuilleraie. He was lying down, his face very pale and burrowed into the pillow, his eyes half shut.

I wanted to kiss him. I wanted to take him in my arms, I wanted to tell him all about my wait, my love. He closed his eyes and murmured, "I would really like to sleep."

Slowly I began to undress. He sat up abruptly and stopped me, in the same hoarse voice. "No, don't bother. It's one in the morning, and I'm getting up at three. I have a train to catch. I'm going back to Agay. So, darling . . ."

"Then I barely have time to go and get my things from the farm," I suggested naively.

"No, I'm leaving for Vichy right away. When I come back, I'll spend more time with you. You're best off going back to your friends now."

I explained weakly that there were no taxis at that hour, that on foot it was a half hour's walk across the fields and the road was completely dark.

"Listen to me," he said in a very serious voice. "I strongly advise you to go back."

My heart sank, all its flames suddenly vanishing into ashes. There was nothing left. I closed my eyes. I didn't know whether to cry out or to weep. In my bag I had his last love letter, the one that said he would never leave me again. I took it out, reread it, and left it on his pillow. He looked at it and without a word or a sign let me leave the room and set off through the dark night toward the Castel Napoli.

My friends were still sitting in a circle in front of the fire. I came in like a beaten woman, without tears or hope on my face. Something inside me that was ruined, shattered, manifested itself in a continual movement of my head from left to right, like someone who has a tic that makes him signal no, no, no, no.

I had seen Tonio again. Had I really seen him? It wasn't possible. No, my head shook from left to right and back again. I went over to the fire, not even looking at the faces of my friends, who were anxious about the trembling that was slowly moving down across my entire body. Soon I was able to say, in a very low voice, "No, no."

"What? No, what? Tell us, Consuelo, what's happening to you? And your husband, have you seen him?"

"No, yes, no, no."

"Are you mad?" the major exclaimed. "You're scaring us, explain yourself."

"I have nothing to explain. I don't know, I saw him for a few minutes. He told me he wanted to sleep, that I should come back here and go to bed, that he would come back someday to see me. I didn't even give him my hand, and he didn't give me his."

As I spoke those last words, I was finally able to weep in the major's arms.

"There, there," he said. "Pretend you never saw him at all. Here, drink this glass of whiskey."

It was the bottle I had begged from the Marquis de

Guatalmine for Tonio. The major had found it, even though I had hidden it away after writing "For Tonio" on the label. He had discovered it and was offering drinks to everyone. But that was fine with me now. My nerves got the better of me, and I began laughing very hard. The other women burst into hysterical fits of giggles at their inability to console me. We threw more wood on the fire, and far into the night, the major, who had been decorated by the Legion of Honor, was still singing, *"Il reviendra à Pâques ou à la Trinité!"* ("He'll come back at Easter or at Trinity!")

I didn't stir from my armchair, and the sunrise over the Pyrenees found me still seated in front of the fire, trying to comprehend the deep mysteries of the human heart. The major watched over me. From time to time he put another log on the fire or stirred the embers, and sometimes he caressed my hair without saying a word. In the morning, he brought me a cup of coffee to drink. My throat was dry. I loved the smell of café au lait. I looked up at his manly face and found it handsome and good. He held out the steaming white faience cup. I stood up slowly, and he spoke these words: "If you love me, kiss me and we'll get married. I will never leave you."

AT NOON I WOKE UP next to a river. The major was peering into my face and tickling my forehead with a twig.

"You sleep like a child; look what I've caught while you napped."

Crayfish were jumping in a bowl at my feet.

"Come on, let's cook them. Pick up some stones; we'll light a fire, and this will make us a good lunch."

He made for the house, carrying me on his back, suddenly moved by my fragility and my folly and deeply distressed by the mad love that was breaking my heart. He wanted to save me. I asked him how I had come to be in the field, for I had no memory of it. He told me he had carried me there, fast asleep in his arms, that he had washed my face and given me cool water to drink and then sang songs to me until I fell into a peaceful sleep. While he waited for me to wake up, he had taken off his shoes and fished for crayfish.

Feeling more like myself again, I combed through the grass, trying to make a little bouquet of wildflowers. I found some four-leaf clovers. We each took one, and I'll always remember the advice he gave me then: "Never look back; remember that in the most wonderful legends, the person who looks back is always changed into a statue made of stone or salt." Whistling a military march, he led me deeper into the green countryside, toward the forest.

THEN ONE DAY I received a letter from my husband, inviting me to lunch in Pau. I showed it to the major.

"Do you really need to go?" he asked me.

I let out a long sigh.

He sighed in turn. "I don't think you've seen the last of

246

your suffering. Go ahead, I'll drive you to the village and wait there to bring you back."

There we were, my husband and I, sitting across from each other as if nothing had happened, exchanging the familiar phrases of an old married couple: "How is your family? Were there a lot of people in the train? It was hot. It looks like the sky is clouding over, it's going to rain. Are you hungry? You should eat a little more rice. It's hard to get rice right now . . ."

He noticed the four-leaf clover I was wearing in a locket around my neck. He was more interested in this piece of jewelry than in all the rest of me put together. He opened it very easily with his magician's fingers and was astonished. "Is it a romantic souvenir?" he asked with a somewhat melancholy laugh.

"A little more than that," I answered seriously.

"May I know?"

"Yes, I was going to tell you. I am engaged."

"To a clover?" he said ironically.

"To the gentleman who gave me the clover."

"Since when?" he went on, less ironically.

"Since the other night, when you advised me to go home and go to sleep."

"But I told you, Consuelo . . . my wife . . . that I would come back to see you. Here I am."

"It's too late. Too late. I'm engaged to one of your friends. It's probably best for both of us, since you'd rather be far away from me than with me."

"Or so you say."

"I'm not saying anything, I'm not arguing. I want a companion. I don't want to be alone anymore. Excuse me, it's late. Someone is waiting for me."

"I came because you wrote, in a letter I received in Algeria, that you had made a vow to go to Lourdes if I came back from the war. Since I'm back, alive and here with you, now is the time to fulfill your vow. I know that you were serious about it, and we have plenty of time. We're only about an hour from Lourdes, you can easily be back home tonight."

Yes, I remembered. I had made that vow on a day of despair as I was fleeing among the lost souls on the roads of France. I had fallen to my knees beneath a sky charged with misery and saturated with the smell of the enemy, crying, "Lord, Lord, bring my husband back to this land safe and sound. I promise that when he returns I will lead him by the hand to Lourdes to thank You humbly."

So I went with Tonio to Lourdes, taking him by the hand to fulfill my Christian vow.

He took it very seriously. We baptized each other with the pure water of the fountain of Lourdes. Then my husband started to laugh and declared, "It's done! You no longer owe anything to Heaven, but I'll ask you to have dinner with me one last time. I think we have quite a few things to tell each other."

"No, Tonio. I have nothing more to say to you."

He laughed again and led me by the hand to the Hôtel Ambassador, assuring me that the port there was very good. The hotel was owned by a captain.

As if they'd been waiting for us, the staff ushered us

into a private dining room. I was a little shocked by this since I was engaged to another man, but Tonio explained that if you wanted to eat and drink well it was a good idea to hide away in a private room, since food was becoming scarce in France.

He was in an expansive mood and began to talk about the miracles of Lourdes. I was treated to a whole dissertation on the word "miracle" and the effects of miracles. The port was good, and I felt reconciled with life. I was happy to see him calm, tender, and good again, as I had once known him. In fact, neither of us was at fault. That evening, we were just as we had been when we first met. I was delighted, and I thanked him with all my heart for this miraculous little trip, which had proved to me that I hadn't been wrong about the nobility of his heart and the honesty of his character.

The port was followed by a sumptuous dinner. Everything smelled wonderful. The owner came to join us. When the electric lights went on, I realized that a lot of time had gone by, that I was in a different city than Pau, and that my major was still waiting for me. My husband read my sudden anguish in the wrinkles on my forehead.

"Do you need to call him? Don't get up, I'll go. Give me his number. I'll explain to him why we came here."

And he disappeared in the direction of the telephone. I waited for almost an hour. The owner poured me glasses of mirabelle, which was very flavorful.

Tonio finally reappeared and announced in a grieved tone, "The major wants you to know that he's no longer waiting for you. He's rather upset. Listen, Consuelo," he added with a smile, "would you like to become my fiancée?"

The liqueur on my lips had taken on a bitter taste since I'd heard the hard-hearted response of the major, who, for a little trip to Lourdes, was sending me to the Devil.

"Don't be angry; men are all alike," Tonio said, still smiling. "Be a good girl and promise to marry me, with the same clover."

Before I could say a single word he had taken the locket from my neck. And I soon found myself in a magnificent suite at the Hôtel Ambassador, not just engaged but re-married to my husband.

THE NEXT MORNING Tonio was the one who brought me steaming hot café au lait, as he murmured in my ear, "My Consuelo, I beg your forgiveness for all the pain I have given you and will give you again and again. Yesterday, I never phoned the major."

The coffee fell from my hands.

We spent another night in the hotel. But my husband truly was a bird of passage. The next morning, he announced, "My darling wife, I must leave you and perhaps for a very long time. I've been given a mission outside France, and you must stay here alone to wait."

22

J TOOK REFUGE IN THE VILLAGE of Dieulefit, a place admirably well suited to a life of seclusion. The trees bathed me in peace and hope. The crops were starting to ripen, and the scent of the harvest was in the air. I wept as I dreamed of the orchard I had left behind in Jarcy, which must have been filled with pears and red apples just then. Who would eat my fruit? I was overcome with a frantic love of nature and wondered when I would ever return to the sweet shade of my apple trees.

My loneliness grew every day. In vain I told myself that God has given us the whole earth and that it is up to us to be wise. I struggled to believe, to believe to the very last, but I felt a need to resist, which insinuated itself into me almost against my will.

In the evenings I went on long walks, rich with all the wealth of the earth. I imagined Tonio close to me in a thousand ways, but I never found anything but emptiness when I tried to seize his image. We were separated by oceans, and I could only cross them in my dreams.

Then, like a sign, an offer came from Bernard Zehrfuss, an architect friend I had met during the debacle in Marseille, to revive an old stone village, fill it with artists, and thus resist defeat and the terrible blows being dealt to civilization. That was how I went to Oppède.

Oppède: a small hamlet in the Vaucluse with houses dating back to the Middle Ages, all abandoned or in ruins, and a château built by the Comte de Toulouse, Raymond VI. That was where we settled to found our little community of artists and perpetuate our art. I decided to call myself Dolorès.

The old utopian ideal of fraternal, monastic, or socialist communities was taking root in me. My friends in exodus had convinced me: "It's marvelous," they said, "they're planting gardens, building houses, hunting wild boar, they've reopened the wells. They're living, in short! Think of it: they are completely free."

And so I arrived in that beautiful, mad village in the middle of a howling mistral.

Bernard Zehrfuss, the young architect who had won the Prix de Rome, welcomed me. "We must take each other by the hand, Dolorès," he said. "We must form a chain. We're going to become stronger. Oppède, you'll see—it's nothing, and it's everything. It is our heart and our strength. Our civilization is being dragged through the mud right now, but it has left us its teachings. It has given us a taste for form, for design. When the world collapses, when there is nothing left but ruins, all that matters is workers or artists, whichever term you prefer, I mean the people who know how to construct."

The glow of the setting sun played over the buttresses and the walls with their high, arched windows. This pile of giant stones seemed utterly improbable, rising over the pure bluish line of the Lubéron mountains. That was Oppède.

I clunked around in wooden shoes that I wanted to take to New York, where you were, Tonio, to show you.

In Oppède, I learned about life. I thought I already knew everything, that I had learned everything on my father's coffee plantations, but this apprenticeship still remained. I asked myself a thousand questions, all centering on you, and as I watched the eagles circling the château, diving in through the gates and escaping through the windows, I wondered where you were at that moment. But I knew you were safe, there in America. Every day I waited to hear from you. I especially loved your telegrams, which were always searing, anguished, loving.

I thanked you, my angel. You do not know what those telegrams meant to me. You called me Consuelo, *ma bien-aimée.* You told me that spending Christmas far from me had plunged you into despair, that you had aged a hundred years just thinking of me, and you claimed to love me more than ever. "Be certain of my love," you said.

I thought again of the last time we had been together. When I told you I was going to live in Oppède, you had invited Bernard Zehrfuss to come see us. "I'm leaving you my wife, I'm entrusting you with her. Take care of her, for you will have to answer to me if something happens to her." Then Bernard said, "Listen, if you really care for your wife, give up your trip to America and stay with us. We will form a resistance here, among these stones that cannot speak." But we could not hold you back; I stayed in Oppède alone. I was proud to be here: our community would awaken these stones.

I spent my time writing you letters, letters that did or did not reach you. I received only telegrams. All of those messages made me live with you again, made me understand all that united us. And all that separated us, too. Especially the lovely E., who nonetheless had once been my friend. I was the one who asked you one day to read her manuscript because I was moved by it. She was charming to me then, as all women are to the wives of the men they intend to seduce. I even gave her my aviator's helmet to wear in our little airplane, so you could teach her to be a pilot. I wasn't jealous of her, I never thought you would betray me with her, and I still don't believe you have betrayed me. I thought it was a great friendship; I wanted to ignore the malicious tongues.

One day you told me, "Listen, my wife, I often go out alone. I go to dinners with people who are a bit outlandish, because in *N.R.F.* circles—where you are well liked, by the way—there are some rather odd people. You remember once when one of the guests took you into the library to show you the deluxe first editions, and also *Le Con d'Irène* [Irene's Cunt], which shocked you a great deal. That's why I don't take you with me anymore."

Yes, that was true. . . . I also remember that some of the gentlemen were trying to put their hands down the front of my dress, which was easy to do since I was wearing an evening gown. I let out a little shriek, and you heard me and came to my rescue, although a woman friend of yours was sitting on the floor at your feet with her guitar, singing very beautiful melodies. She'd even let her hair down and was leaning her head between your legs, with funny little jerking movements: it all made a delightfully erotic tableau. I was too young; I wasn't used to the lax ways of Parisian artistic circles—the "high life"— and you told me, "Go back home, *ma petite fille*. I know you're shocked by certain types of behavior, but they're entirely natural. It's just that I need my freedom. Consuelo, stay home. You love to paint, even at night—I'll install a light for you that will be exactly like daylight."

Perhaps I was behind the times, but I remember my bitterness and anxiety when you would come in late at night, or at dawn. Ah, Tonio, such anguish! I didn't know which you preferred: to be lost among the stars in the sky or among the pretty blond heads of Paris.

To all the flatterers who surrounded you I was always little Consuelo, the Spanish woman who made scenes. Even though it wasn't true, you would say, "Excuse me, I have to go home because otherwise my wife will make a huge scene." In fact, you went home to write, for you had so little free time in Paris. Whenever you were at our house, it was always with other people—men, women. At four in the morning you'd announce, "I'm going out for a walk with Léon-Paul Fargue," and you'd go all the way to Versailles on foot. You would stroll for hours, until just before dawn, and then you'd call: "Come pick us up in the car, we don't have money for a taxi."

You see the kind of life I had? But I'm not complaining, my darling, because you never wasted your time; as soon as you had an hour you would work, anywhere, even in the bathroom, if you had to work out an equation for some aviation problem. My God, being the wife of a pilot is a whole career, but being the wife of a writer is a religious vocation!

We would go through difficult periods. There would sometimes be a tempest in my heart, and to soothe me you would stroke my forehead with your hands, your archangel's hands, and speak to me in those magical words of yours about love, about things that are sacred, about tenderness, fidelity, and it would all begin again.

"Don't be jealous," you would say at those moments. "My true career, as you know, is to be a writer, and when your enemy is kind enough to send me some little gift, a pair of ivory dice or a suitcase embossed with my name, my heart softens toward her and to thank her I write her three or four pages, do some little drawings, and that's all. But don't be afraid; I know what you have gone through for years, and I thank you for it, my wife. I am joined to you by sacrament, so don't ever listen to what people say."

But at that point, in Oppède, I had to keep busy. There were ten of us by then. We made our own bread, we spun wool, we knit sweaters out of wool recycled from old mattresses. We didn't have much left to eat, we were so strictly rationed. But a miraculous idea came into my mind. It was like a revelation. I remembered a conversation with Tonio at Pau when he told me that the Germans were buying the peasants' crops "in the field," which meant that they bought grapes, for example, before they were ripe and took delivery of them only once they had ripened. Since they were printing up as many ten-thousand-franc notes as they wanted, it cost them nothing to pay out whole sacks of banknotes. The peasants were satisfied, and that way the Germans were sure of starving the French. After having sold our jewels and watches to the peasants—eggs cost three hundred francs apiece—we had to resort to eating the fragments of asparagus they left in the ground and melons that grew almost wild. We couldn't survive like this for long. We held a council: Florent Margaritis and his wife, Eliane; Bernard Piboulon and his charming wife, who was also studying architecture; and Albert Bojovitch, whose brother was the editor of *Vogue* in New York but who had no desire at all to leave for America; he wanted to stay and resist. They decided, "Let's go back to Paris, because things have become impossible here."

"Wait another twenty-four hours," I asked them.

"I'm leaving for Avignon," I declared the next day. "That's where the Germans store the crops that they buy, in trains. We'll steal them. The cars are full of salt pork, mutton, and butter."

I climbed over rocks and low stone walls until I finally reached the trains. I managed to board one, though the steps were very high. I found a pig, which I dragged over the rails. A sentry saw me but didn't shoot. Why not? I went home with the pig and the friend who had been keeping lookout for me. It took us four or five hours to get back to Oppède. The cook, who was Moroccan and, unfortunately for him, did not eat pork, nevertheless resolved to prepare the animal: "I'll cook it for you, I know how it's done. You'll eat well this evening."

Our feast was marvelous. There was even wine, old red wine, stolen from the cellars of abandoned houses. I made the trip to the trains several more times; after that, the young men went. No one was ever killed.

One day a car appeared, and we were very much afraid that the authorities were coming for us. We had binoculars and could see from the ramparts that a woman was driving it. She was named Thérèse Bonnet, and she was coming . . . to get me.

"I know you're settled in here," she told me. "But why aren't you with that fine strapping husband of yours in New York, where he's doing card tricks and going out with every millionaire American blonde in the city? What are you doing dying of hunger here?"

I gestured toward my friends. "Here we are," I said. "We're a group, all for one and one for all. I'm waiting for my husband to send me money or a ticket, to give me some way of joining him."

Soon after that, I went to see my mother-in-law in Marseille. She spoke to me in a grave voice. "Tonio is ill," she said, "and your duty as his wife is to be at his side."

I had indeed received a telegram. My husband was in a bad way and could not be operated on because his organs were all mixed up after the accident in Guatemala: if he was alive at all, it was only by the will of heaven, and his own will. "I don't have any papers," I answered his mother.

"You're from El Salvador, your consulate will give them to you without a problem."

"No, I'll wait; I'll wait for Tonio to ask me."

At last I received the telegram: "Go to the home of Monsieur X to pick up money for the trip; all your papers are arranged. Our friend Pozzo di Borgo has received instructions to give you."

Suddenly the sky looked brighter to me. I announced the good news to my friends: Tonio was finally asking for me. I had been at Oppède for eleven months. They all raised their eyes to the sky and exclaimed, "You know, if you leave, we'll all leave; we won't stay here any longer."

I WAS HAPPY to be going back to you, but my heart was torn; with my friends at Oppède I had experienced a state of honest intimacy, a different way of thinking, and the idea of leaving Bernard made me particularly sad. He was a great and noble gentleman, a young man not even thirty years old who sang from morning to night, who saw to it that we were all cheerful and that our community worked well and at a good rhythm. The workshops were immaculate, and beautiful things were made in them.

The day I left Oppède I felt more imperiled than ever. A poorly transmitted telegram from New York was enough to make me imagine that everything there was more dangerous and menacing than my beautiful stones, which were stable and eternal. Once more I was on the road, unable to explain to myself why I was on this new mission or to clarify the mystery of my errant life. I desperately needed to find some outlet for the anguish in my heart.

Once I was on board the airplane, I thought about my reunion with Tonio. It had been more than a year since we had last seen each other. Despite the comfort of the German plane that was taking me to Portugal, I imagined that an accident might still deprive me of him. I so longed to see him again! I'd been told that if I was lucky, once I was in Portugal I'd be able to continue my journey to New York by boat. If I'd been given a choice, I would have preferred to wait for us to be reunited among the stones of Oppède.

I felt weak from lack of food and also from a fear of seeing him again. My inelegant appearance brought a childish smile to my lips—I didn't feel like an adult. I would have wished to be glamorously arrayed, as if for a ceremony. But my heart was drab. I said to myself, "If only I would turn into a woman made of glass when he looks at me . . ." My mind was overpowered by bizarre images, and I gazed longingly up at the sky. I caught a glimpse of myself in the plane's opaque windows and saw my poor hair, which was cut very short; I had had to cut it myself in Oppède. I dreamed of the latest hairstyles in New York and was irritated at being out of fashion. My hair wasn't going to grow back overnight! I was thin, very thin: less than a hundred pounds with my clothes on. I felt ill at ease in the goatherd's clothes I was wearing. There was a woman on the plane who never took her eyes off me: Was she a spy?

Barely an hour after takeoff, the loudspeaker announced that the flight was being interrupted: we would be stopping in Barcelona. The following day some of the passengers might be able to continue on to Portugal.

The airport restaurant in Barcelona was no great affair, but the meat and soup smelled good, bread was set out on the counters for the taking, and all the passengers who landed rushed there immediately to take the edge off their hunger. I had just ordered a bowl of soup and a plate of rice when the barman asked me what currency I was planning to pay with. I was in the depths of despair, for I had no pesetas. The waiter understood my problem and took the steaming soup, which had just arrived, from under my nose.

The "spy" saw how confused and helpless I was and gave me a hundred pesetas. I used the money to leave the airport and look for a hotel in the city. The concierge's first question was "What currency are you traveling with?"

I took a box of syringes from my suitcase; at the bottom, underneath some cotton, I had hidden three five-thousand-franc bills. It had been a year and a half since I had had a full meal, a hot bath, or a bed with sheets. That hotel was paradise for me. I would have liked to spend several days there; the staff was very pleasant, and I saw nothing of the legendary misery of Barcelona. There was dancing in the dining room, and lovely women in evening gowns flowed by with that smile of ease that everyone you pass in the corridor of a hotel is wearing. I ordered a bottle of wine, a roast chicken, and an assortment of desserts. I couldn't help thinking of our garlic soup in Oppède. I was melancholy at the thought of having left Bernard and my friends, who weren't sharing my chicken, and a whole series of memories flooded over me as I drank my bottle of wine alone. I saw each of their gestures again, weeping as I listened to old waltzes, and told myself that it was as if I'd left my childhood home. However, I had to move onward, forever and forever, until I became an old woman somewhere on the planet.

The luxury of my bedroom felt alien to me. I wished I wasn't alone. I couldn't sleep, and I was increasingly feverish. I was about to call for help when the door opened and my companion from the airplane, my "spy," said my first name and whispered, "I arranged to be on the same floor as you. Let's run the water in the tub and speak very softly."

We sat on the floor next to the tub, like two thieves, and began exchanging words, almost into each other's ears.

"Oh, how lovely of you to have come to visit me."

"I'm feeling down, too. I'm not allowed to speak to anyone."

"I could make you lose your job, then?"

"No," she said, with a bitter smile, "my head, more likely. I've had it with espionage. It's not even dangerous. It's boring."

I was rather alarmed to learn that my new acquaintance's job consisted of informing on people. Meanwhile, she found it merely boring. She took a bottle of liqueur from a small attaché case and poured each of us a glass.

"Yes, it disgusts you to drink with a spy, doesn't it? I can see that. But it pays. If you want my advice, stay in Spain. You speak Spanish, French, and English well. You can have a good salary, make yourself a small fortune, and retire after the war. In any case, I know it's not going to last much longer. And that way we could work together . . ."

I had taken a single swallow of the drink she gave me, which had a funny smell. It was odd—I was having a hard time making out what she was saying. Then I realized that there was a powerful narcotic in her liqueur, and that she wanted to go through my suitcases. I had demonstrated my skill at concealing money in my luggage, and she undoubtedly imagined that I was also concealing plans. Panic gripped me as I remembered scenes from spy movies I had watched. What effect would the narcotic have on me? I struggled to make a decision as quickly as possibly. She was habituated to the narcotic, and it no longer affected her. She wanted at all costs to make a thorough inspection of the contents of my luggage. Since I was carrying nothing that was at all compromising, it was best to let her do so. I told her I was going to the hotel pharmacy to buy some cosmetics and asked her to be patient and wait for me if it took a few minutes. I added that I had promised a dark-haired man who had eaten dinner next to me that I would chat with him in the lobby for a bit, but that I wouldn't be long. She started to laugh, and I thought I heard her say, "You can take care of all of that quickly, because I know how to work fast, too."

Before I went out, she handed me a glass of cold water and told me, "Drink this down in one go."

When I returned, there was no one in the room. I

found only a note, in Spanish. "I like you because you're not an idiot. Thanks. Don't worry about your trip to Portugal. You'll leave tomorrow. Signed, Liliane."

★

THE PLANE LANDED in Lisbon on a windy day. My body was numb. Drunk with fatigue and emotion, I couldn't control my limbs, and I sprained my ankle getting off the plane. I limped through my entire stay in Portugal.

The evening before my departure, I finally succeeded in phoning Tonio, but we couldn't talk because no one was allowed to speak over the phone in any language other than English, which Tonio didn't speak. I heard only "Consuelo," and I answered "Tonio." The operators left the line open a few minutes longer, but we were as mute as young lovers who are transfixed with each other.

Just as we were boarding the ship, a rumor made the rounds: there was a fire on board and the ship wouldn't be able to leave port until the following morning. Several travelers went home with their wives, children, and luggage, but I had seen no smoke so I stayed close to the boat, waiting for the end of the story. I had my reward: we left the port that evening.

We had no electric light during the entire trip. We were forbidden to use a match or possess a camera. Every morning, floating on the gray winter sea, we saw bits of wood and debris, all that remained of the boats that had been destroyed a few nights earlier or that very night as we slept on the bridge. We were usually roused two or three times a night by a bell, an exercise intended to keep us on the alert, so we would get used to the gymnastics of running for our lives and be able to take our places in the lifeboats in orderly fashion should the torpedoes the German radio broadcasts threatened us with come down and surprise us on the open sea. Preposterous rumors circulated among the passengers: the boat would not be sunk because it was carrying spies to America. A few of the bolder and more imaginative gossips claimed that the entire boat was a pack of spies. Or they said that the ship's prisons were choked with travelers and that it wasn't seasickness that was diminishing the number of sleepers on the bridge. . . . I knew that the captain was in fact uncompromisingly severe with people who broke the rules by turning on a flashlight or even striking a match. Even so, a strange feeling of security prevailed; we were not afraid.

As we arrived in Bermuda, a pregnant woman gave birth in the darkness of the bridge, not far from me. The doctor did his duty: it was a difficult case, a pair of twin girls whose mother had the courage to name Bermuda. Our twins were the great event of the day. When we arrived in port, we were forbidden to go on land; we were held there on the boat for several days because it was the last American ship to leave Lisbon since the war broke out. The orders were strict; all books and letters the passengers were carrying with them had to be examined. We all had to hand over our papers. Jean Perrin, a great French scholar, was on board; he saw all of his calculations and equations confiscated and watched in despair as they were crumpled up by ignorant, unscrupulous hands. His poems were cause for great concern, as were his geographic maps and the little doodles he would make in the margin of a book when something he'd just read suggested an idea.

We were all afraid of being ordered to leave the ship in Bermuda. We had already suffered so much in France that we felt like guilty sinners. Three anguished days passed, but the inspection of the scholars' and writers' papers turned out to be completely fruitless. We set off once more our journey.

Every hour brought me closer to Tonio.

23

THE DAYS WERE GROWING COLDER and grayer. Winter was on its way when New York finally came into view. We were very far north. The water seemed denser, as if made of steel. The boat glided gently toward the city lights, reflected in the clouds. Our minds were blank. We passengers had nothing more to say to one another. We were in a hurry to arrive: the final minutes of a journey are always the hardest.

While we were still in the choppy waters of the bay, I was called over to the table where the officers were checking our passports. It's always unpleasant to be asked if you are indeed yourself and to have your signature verified. The boat had stopped moving. No one spoke. I admired the orderly way in which our arrival took place, the American sense of organization that presided over everything. We poor sheep, lost in the storm on the other side of the Atlantic, had by the greatest of good fortunes been sent to a safe land.

I'd grown friendly with one of the other passengers, S., a man in his forties, tanned as a Portuguese, levelheaded, full of good health and good spirits. He too was traveling to be reunited with his wife, whom he adored. Not a day had gone by that he didn't show me a photo of her and of their little cat. Smiling, he told me with some embarrassment, "Yes, I have great affection for that little beast. We call her Maria—I don't know why. A cook gave her the name. I must confess that I'm a little ashamed of my feelings for a cat at a time when thousands of children are dying of hunger in Europe. I was employed by an organization that worked to save people, especially Jews. We were ordered to save the intelligent men. How was I to know who was intelligent and who wasn't? How could I possibly intuit such a thing when a man stood there pale with terror, stammering incoherently and begging, 'Save me, save me, give me papers, otherwise I'll be sent to a camp'? I sometimes asked people their profession, and they had forgotten even that. All they could do was live and hope to save their remaining hours on this earth."

As he spoke, he was looking for his wife through a pair of binoculars. Suddenly, he caught sight of her.

"Ah! I see her, and it looks as if she's holding Maria in her arms. Let's hope Maria doesn't scratch her!" He let out a hearty laugh.

"I'm afraid my husband won't be at the dock and I won't be allowed off the boat," I confided.

"I'll take care of you," he said. "If they lock you up in Sing Sing I'll soon come to your rescue. I will prove who you are. I will find your husband. Don't spoil your arrival in New York—have faith. America is a good country."

In the end my fear won him over, and by some means he sent his wife a telegram from the boat, asking her to warn my husband to be at the dock when we landed. I believe we received an answer, but the wait on board the boat alongside the lone seagulls floating on the oily water was still an anguished one.

Toward four in the afternoon, we were finally allowed to set foot on land, but only within a space closed off by barricades. We were locked in like hens in a henhouse, and only those who were claimed from the outside by a husband, a father, a friend were allowed to go free.

My turn came. The fellow asking for me was a stranger. From afar I saw a short, fat man wearing enormous glasses whose loud laughter reached me sooner than the features of his face. I saw that he did indeed have the papers that gave him the right to pick me up.

Closer up I recognized him; he was a friend of Tonio's I hadn't seen for at least twelve years. Yes, it was Fleury in the flesh, carrying with him all the sands of Africa. In my mind I saw him again as he had been back in the days when the airmail service was inaugurated. Now he looked like a caricature of himself; the twelve years that had separated us hadn't made him any younger. He had been living in Brazil and drinking too much. His laugh grew louder and louder. "Consuelo, don't you recognize me?"

I couldn't answer. So he was the one who had come to welcome me in Tonio's place. Why? Toward what new mystery was life propelling me? He squeezed my hand, and we began to walk through the hustle and bustle that always accompanies a ship's landing. He went on talking in my ear, with occasional little spasms of coughing and laughter. "Your husband forbids you to speak to journalists. Do you understand? He forbids you to speak, to give any interviews whatsoever. Listen to me carefully: the journalists will come with their cameras, and I will tell them that you understand neither English nor French. You are deaf and dumb. Otherwise Tonio will send you away again, I don't know where. We are at war. Forgive me, your silence is making me nervous, but this is serious. Tonio would never forgive you if you spoke."

An American, accompanied by some policemen, came forward with that glacial smile journalists always have. "Bonjour, Madame de Saint-Exupéry?"

"I'm not Madame de Saint-Exupéry," I said. "I'm her maid."

The cameras, which were about to spring into action, were stopped by the journalist's guttural cry, "Wait, there's a mistake, this is the servant of Madame de Saint-Exupéry. Madame de Saint-Exupéry is still on board!"

I moved calmly past them, and they went on waiting for my "mistress."

Relieved to be walking on solid ground, I slowly collected my thoughts. Now I understood Fleury's little comedy. He had come to collect me at the foot of the gangway to make sure that no photograph was taken of my arrival. It would have been difficult to claim that we were not Monsieur and Madame de Saint-Exupéry if we were in each other's arms. So Tonio did not want to be seen with me. Why? No doubt he was trying to spare one of his girlfriends the sight of a legitimate wife in her husband's arms . . .

Bitterness was making me ugly. I began to hate life. And to think that in a few minutes I would see the face of my husband, who was fleeing from our reunion! Yet I couldn't reproach him. The shock was too strong. After all I had been through during the war, after two years of absence, to find myself in front of my husband in flesh and blood . . . I took a deep gulp of the bitter, salty air of the dock. I wanted nothing to remain inside me but goodness, peace, and love. I loved him. Yes, I loved him still.

No amount of quibbling about interviews and photographers could change my feelings. But my heart grew weaker with every step. My ears started to ring, and my legs were no longer holding me up; they seemed to be made of cotton.

Soon I could make out nothing more than shadows and cries. I shut my eyes for a few seconds and clung tightly to Fleury's arm. He helped me lean against a wall and comforted me. "Don't faint now," he said. "You've handled this very well so far. A little more courage, and you'll see your husband. He's just over there, behind that large column. Open your eyes, I beg you."

I breathed deeply and let my arms go slack. The idea of seeing my husband again gave me back my strength. Had I been ordered back onto the boat to spend two months on a stormy sea, I would still have opened my eyes and walked, until my life's last breath, back to the man I loved.

I stared at the column, which seemed to grow taller and taller. A hundred yards still separated me from Tonio. I saw his outline, like a tall tree, standing between some pillars. I began to make out the curves of his silhouette, his shoulders, which were a little stooped, as if he were holding up the column. He watched me approach, motionless.

This man was my husband. I could see him ten feet away from me, pale, wrapped in gray gabardine, locked up inside himself. He was wearing neither a hat nor gloves; he didn't move. Finally I managed to touch him. He didn't look like a living being. It had been a thousand years since we had seen each other, kissed each other, questioned each other with our eyes. I was right next to him now, and his arms were made of iron and my voice had fled beyond the mystery of life. It was he who abruptly opened his arms and held me tight enough to strangle me, shouting, "Let's go! Let's go right now."

But like everyone else we had to wait for a taxi. We waited for almost an hour. I began to enjoy the courtesy that prevails among those standing on lines in New York. People are simple, patient, polite. No one grumbles or breaks in ahead of anyone else. This comforted me and calmed my nerves.

The first question Tonio asked me was "Who was that with you? Why did you give an interview?"

I was weary. "Listen," I answered, "I didn't speak to anyone."

"But I saw you, I saw you speaking to someone."

"Yes: I told a journalist that I was Madame de Saint-Exupéry's servant. That's all. Don't interrogate me any further," I pleaded. "I endured enough questioning over my papers when we landed. I got up at five this morning and was so nervous I haven't eaten all day."

In the taxi, we didn't exchange a word, paralyzed by this reunion. The magical conversation I had been waiting for did not take place. Two beings who had just resumed their life together continued on, identical to themselves, not understanding each other, not connecting, walled into their silence as the taxi hurtled into the heart of the noisy city.

I didn't know where my husband was taking me. My destiny was entirely in his hands. My heart could neither laugh nor weep.

"I'm taking you," Tonio announced at last, "to the Café Arnold."

"Why to a café?"

"Because people are waiting for us there. Some friends are giving a cocktail party for you. My editor, his wife, and some other people."

"But I have to freshen up a little, do my hair at least," I said shyly.

"New York is very spread out, distances here are large, and anyway, there's a bathroom in the café where you can wash your hands."

I had no choice but to obey. A few minutes later the car stopped in front of the Café Arnold at 240 Central Park South. I was bundled out, bellboys opened a series of heavy doors, and I found myself facing a dozen people who were laughing joyfully, curious to meet the wife of the great writer.

★

THE CAFÉ ARNOLD is a French café. Its waiters are attentive and will serve you French apéritifs, absinthe, Chambéry-fraise, Martini, and of course the whole gamut of American cocktails, those erudite mixtures that the black barmen concoct for their thirsty customers like sorcerers brewing poisoned philters.

My shabbiness stood out against the polished good looks of the women in low-cut dresses who were questioning me about my trip and about France, all of them perfectly at ease in the company of their friends and husbands. Little by little, warmth, confidence, and pleasure in these beings who were surrounding me with their noisy friendship began to steal over me. The meal was copious. I saw mounds of butter on the table, breads and meats I hadn't tasted for a long time. My husband was there beside me, as in the old days, and I was enjoying myself, surveying the hair, jewelry, and dresses of the women. It was difficult for me to imagine Oppède, to think back to my stone village. Was I alive? Was I dreaming? Or had my string of misfortunes simply come to its end? My husband was entertaining the guests with his eternal card tricks.

"It's late," a lady said finally. "I have to wake up early. I must go."

My husband jumped as if wound up with a spring. "You, too, Consuelo," he said. "You must be tired. Let's go."

A simple signature on the check sufficed to bring this sumptuous evening to an end. We took another taxi, and I heard my husband tell the driver, "Barbizon Plaza."

Followed by the hotel manager, I walked through a three-room suite that struck me as the height of luxury. I was surprised to be in a heated apartment with a bathroom, but even more surprised by my sense that no one was living there. Then Tonio said, "Good night. I'm living in another apartment that's too small for the two of us. I'll call tomorrow to find out how you're doing. I hope you have a good rest."

He shook my hand and wished me good night. It all happened very quickly. I stared at him like an animal, without understanding. He repeated again, "Sleep well. See you tomorrow." And I found myself standing there alone in the middle of the room, among unfamiliar furniture, in an unknown city.

★

Part Six

★

New York, 1942

★

24

ট WAS HARD TO FIND ANSWERS to all the questions that besieged me. This was truly a nightmare. I
had left my friends in Oppède, and now I was alone, on
the edge of a bed, in the chill of a hotel room. I couldn't
believe it. I sat on the floor the way I used to as a child
when I had just broken a pretty doll or couldn't understand some new game. I don't know how long I stayed like
that. I wished I could fly like a fairy out the window of my
twentieth-story room into all the beautiful lights of the
skyscrapers and go straight to God, where the angels
would have been much better company than my husband.
I didn't even know his telephone number. Where could I
find the comfort of a friendly word? My body was in a
state of collapse, and my mind went feverishly back over
the life I had led since I had married Tonio.

I paced through the icy suite, gazing at its porcelains,
its engravings, those anonymous objects that are the same
in every hotel room in the world. I looked out at the
buildings of New York, all lit up. Which window was my
husband's? I was weeping softly when the door of the
suite opened and a waiter peered in; he was bringing me a
telegram and begged my pardon for having used his master key when I didn't respond to his knocking. It was from

Bernard Zehrfuss: "The knights of Oppède are with you in thought on your arrival in New York. We miss you terribly. Letter follows, your devoted Albert, Bernard, etc."

Oh, how badly I had needed this message! Somewhere in the world were the hearts of friends who were thinking of me. I began a long letter to Bernard in which I was finally able to say everything that was overflowing inside me. The night went by in a kind of daze. Why was Heaven treating me so strangely? The day found me like that, still dressed, stretched out on the sofa.

Guests at the Barbizon Plaza were served a French breakfast, slipped through a slot in the door. There were several cupfuls of café au lait, along with bread, butter, and jam. I drank the steaming hot milk like a robot, still trying to define my situation. Where was Tonio? And who was he?

I gathered up the crumbs I had dropped on the floor. It was a pleasant task to reassemble the little bits of bread that were scattered across the blue carpet: this simple gesture brought back a kind of consciousness of life.

I had an answer to send to the telegram from my faithful knights. They were my wealth. My steadfast love. I wasn't alone in this suite of icy rooms. I could think of them and love them, since they allowed me to show them my love. The telephone rang, and its ringing snapped me back to reality.

"Hello, hello, Madame de Saint-Exupéry? Your friend from the boat here—the Portuguese. I've just learned from your husband that you are alone at the Barbizon. Is there anything I can do for you?"

"Come and see me," I said. "If you have time."

Fifteen minutes later, S. was sitting in my living room. We spoke of this and that. He asked me if he could bring his wife over for dinner. We remained silent on the question of my husband, though I was tempted to confide in this man who was so kind. When he left, he kissed my hand, and I had to snatch it away because tears were welling up my eyes. He slipped away discreetly, as if he knew he could do nothing for me. All I knew about him was the telephone number of his office. That way we would be able to talk sometimes. For me, even that meant a great deal.

The telephone rang again. This time it was my husband. He informed me that we didn't live very far from each other, which meant that if I wanted to stretch my legs a little I could come see his apartment. I was touched and accepted his invitation. He barely gave me time to catch a glimpse of his place, told me he was busy for lunch, and recommended that I eat at the Café Arnold, down below his apartment, where we had gone the night before. After that, I adopted the Arnold as my own.

My husband was feeling the same anguish and exhaustion that I was. I felt sorry for him, and he realized it was cruel to make me live apart from him. I didn't want to be the one to bring it up. I did tell him, however, that I wanted to go back to Oppède. I had nothing to do in New York; I was terribly bored already, the streets were alien to me, and I had no friends. He assured me that the next day, a Sunday, he would drive me to the country home of one of our friends, Michèle, who would undoubtedly be happy to serve as my guide to the city.

And indeed we went to her house the next day. There I found trees in bloom, young people drinking, and the atmosphere of a real home. The day passed quickly, and I went home that evening to my solitary apartment.

My mother asked, in a letter from Central America, why my New York address was different from my husband's. I showed the letter to Tonio, and as quickly as possible, he managed to procure an apartment for me with an address almost identical to the one at 240 Central Park South, where he was living.

And so I began to settle into New York. From time to time my husband would come eat a meal with me at some strange hour, for he ate around two or three o'clock in the morning. I had wisely resolved to work. Work is the only thing that will allow you to keep your balance and find your way out of the confusion of events. I decided to go back to sculpting and enrolled at a school just two buildings away from mine: the Art Students League.

By the end of my first week, I had befriended several young people who were devoting themselves very seriously to art. Some of them went with me to the movies; we ate meals together and even had fun reading the old French newspapers we managed to dig up. These friends were a great comfort to me. I still felt unable to sculpt pure forms, but the professor pampered me a great deal; I was a refugee, that much was clear from my skinniness and the gratitude I displayed at the least sign of affection from him.

My husband would come to visit me at the school. One day I was glad to see him peering down at my most recent statue. It was a little askew, like a tightrope walker. He told me not to despair. With great assurance, he predicted that if I touched it with my fingers every day, if I learned how to caress the clay just right, the statue would soon become beautiful and straight. I looked into his eyes with astonishment. His advice gave me an idea: if I were to go see him every day, to caress him with my loving gazes, if I went every day to show him my fidelity, my faith in the sacrament of marriage that had united us forever, perhaps in the end he would listen to me and be my husband again, as he once had been.

Meanwhile I continued to sink into a kind of depression. I often went into churches on little pilgrimages. Sometimes I laughed about it, sometimes I thought I was going mad. I went to confession and told the priests my secrets.

I had a lovely apartment and on the surface lacked for nothing. Sometimes I reread Bernard's letters from Oppède and remembered the privations, the fear, and the cold we had gone through in that stone village, swept night and day by the mistral that constantly carried the sound of the enemy to our ears. Then I thanked heaven that I was there, safe and sound in a sunny white room. But the comings and goings of my husband-neighbor, certain sounds, certain female voices, certain laughs, certain silences that I perceived through the thin wall made me shake with jealousy, asphyxiating in my solitary existence as a neglected wife. I felt a bit like a queen who is not stripped of her title although she's sent into exile. At moments like that all the white tablecloths, all the luxury, all the lights of the skyscrapers were unbearable to me. I wanted only one thing: a shoulder to sleep on.

During that period, I reread *Letters of a Portuguese Nun** and certain other works that made me burn with love for Tonio all the more. I realized that it was unhealthy to live so near him that I could see the lights of his apartment from my windows.

I asked him, very calmly, to find me another place to live, farther away from him. I explained that I couldn't be indifferent to what went on at his place, that seeing pretty women coming and going from his apartment was torture.

He took me silently by the hand, kissed my hair, and told me, "You are my wife, *ma femme chérie*, for I cherish you at every hour of the day. You must come to understand me as a mother understands her son. That is how I need to be loved. I've done great things in aviation, but as you know I've broken my arms, my shoulders, and my ribs, and sometimes I feel as if my head were splitting open. The first time I crashed, when I was learning to fly, I must have damaged something inside it. Ever since then

**Lettres d'une religieuse portuguaise,* first published in France in 1669, was a collection of love letters purportedly written by a Portuguese nun and translated into French. For centuries, writers from La Bruyère to Stendahl to Rainer Maria Rilke hailed it as a great work of literature spontaneously created by the passionate outpouring of a woman's heart. Not until the twentieth century was it determined that the book had in fact been written by a Frenchman, a minor literary figure and sometime French ambassador to Constantinople named Guilleragues, whom some editions had billed as its translator.

I've suffered from terrible migraines that make me fall silent or fly into a rage.

"It does me good to have you there with me, not speaking or moving, asking for nothing. It may be that there's nothing more I can give you, but perhaps you're the one who can give me something—make me grow, plant your seeds in me, enrich me, make up for what I'm losing so that I can create, so that I can go on with my great poem, the book I want to put my whole heart into. You're the first to have believed in me, you are the woman for whom I wrote *Night Flight*.

"Do you remember the letter I wrote you during my stopovers in tiny South American villages? You understood that letter. You told me, 'More than a declaration, more than a love letter, this is a cry for help to the only being who can help you—help you during your hours of solitude in the sky, help you when you're endangered by the stars, which in your exhausted state you confuse with the lights of mankind on the earth, help you when you are once again among men and have to learn again how to live, help you not to forget that you, too, are a man of flesh and blood, an ephemeral man.'

"You were the person I was looking for. You were the port where I could take shelter from the storm, and you were also a very beautiful young girl, already anguished by my night flights, anguished by the threat of the end. So if you love me even a little, protect in me the essence of the man that I am, because you believe in its value. One evening you said to me, 'You have a message to deliver to mankind. Nothing must stop you, not even me . . .' That day I decided to marry you forever, for all of life and for all the lives we will be given to live beyond the stars. And you began creating a world where I would walk straight toward that message, which you believed in.

"Often in the bitterest moments of our separation I walked again, full of confidence, alone in the big attic room in Tagle, back in Buenos Aires, where you used to lock me up in front of a table to write, to write a page of *Night Flight*, like a child being punished. Even in my moments of anger with you, my lips can still taste the port that you would serve from a small cask whose golden spigot looked so pretty in that loft where you condemned me to forced labor. Consuelo, I haven't forgotten any of your tenderness, your devotion, your sacrifices. I know how deeply you've been wounded by the anguish, the torments, the difficulties of the wandering life I have made you lead. I know how hard your women friends have been on you when it came to criticizing our relationship. They judged it only with their feminine minds. But you, you understood me, and later you loved me, but you were painfully bruised by the struggles of our daily life. Your impatience grew out of your weariness, and mine as well. Worry took the place of love, and I left you in order to protect us from each other. Our friends have been wrong to hold you responsible for my happiness or unhappiness. You must know that I have never stopped loving you. But I see your forehead wrinkling up, I hear you raising your voice, which is about to separate us again."

"No, Tonio, I am not bitter," I said. "I learned a long time ago to digest the venom of jealousy. There will be no more arguments between us, no more crying. I want to see things clearly. I came from far away to be near you, and the days go by without our even having a meal together. I do not know how I can be of any use to you, living in a different apartment, forever outside your door. Even a dog is allowed to gaze on its master."

"Be quiet," he cried, "you're hurting me! I'll find you an apartment in my building today. That way we'll see each other every day, and we'll go on talking about us."

And so I moved again, this time into an apartment that was like a greenhouse. My husband sent me flowers, plants, a silent typewriter, and a Dictaphone. "That way, when you're alone you can tell your beautiful stories to this machine," he said, "and if I feel like listening to you, I'll put one of your recordings in and hear your voice. For you are a great poet, Consuelo. If you wanted, you could be a better writer than your husband." My housewarming party was very lively. My husband brought some friends, and we had a pleasant evening.

After the move, he changed. He came to visit me every evening before going to bed, to prove that he was going back to his cage every night. Sometimes he would phone me to read a few pages he had just written, and he would talk to me about the future as if we were going to be together until the end.

25

MEALTIMES IN OUR HOUSEHOLD were a bit of a muddle. Tonio would say he was coming to lunch or dinner, but he would never show up. My mood was certainly not pleasant. Often I fled in anger from the table I had prepared and went down to the Café Arnold to eat by myself. And there I would find him, surrounded by men and women, striving to amuse his guests—he, the most melancholy Frenchman in all of New York. He didn't like to see me sitting alone at a table in silent reproach. He would ignore me, and if by chance someone who knew me was there and gave me so much as a quick handshake, I could see something approaching hatred for me in Tonio's stare.

No matter what transpired during the day, it had no effect on our nightly conversations: he would come to me or call, speaking in his tender voice, wishing me good night and talking about the day to come with love. But happiness was always postponed.

On the first day of spring I risked going to his apartment. Though I had moved into the same building, I had yet to be invited there. He was always the one who came up the three flights of stairs that separated us. That day, the fresh sunlight shining on my green leaves and flowers had encouraged me to put aside all shyness and run to him. The door was never locked. I went in and found a dozen people there, just finishing their lunch. Immediately I put them at ease by informing them I had come to serve the coffee. The light touch with which I returned to my role as lady of the house amused Tonio. But the relaxation I had noticed in his expression didn't last long.

Among his guests was a musician friend who was giving a concert at Town Hall the next day. He insisted to my husband that I attend. I pretended to forget the invitation, but Tonio wanted, for the first time, to be seen with me in public.

We had seats in the orchestra section, very much in view of everyone. The entire French community of New York was there, since our musician friend was their compatriot. I was happy to be listening to good music, but I could sense that my husband was terribly nervous because of the smiles and sly remarks of the people around us, who were seeing him out with his wife for the first time. At the intermission, he fled without a word. I found myself alone and all the more exposed—even the musician, busy conducting his orchestra, noticed it. I hadn't brought my purse with me, thinking Tonio would take me home.

After the performance I felt lost, both in my heart and in the streets of New York. I walked along the sidewalks in my evening gown for half an hour, my eyes full of tears, passersby staring at me, until I happened to meet my musician friend, who was stepping out of his car to go into a large restaurant. He took my arm, and I followed him. From that day on, I had another friend in this city where

I felt so foreign, and again I began to think long and hard about life and the hearts of men. My friend made me understand, little by little, very gently, that if one member of a couple is at fault, it's the other one who has to make things right, whatever the cost. He took me to the country and showed me the beauty of the American forests. When I returned to the city, I felt more sure of myself.

My husband was a little disturbed by this three-day absence, which I had informed him of laconically in a simple note. Our conversation was friendly but rather ironic. Normally, he was the one who went away on the weekends, I didn't know where, but this time it was me. In appearance, nothing had changed between us. I gave it a lot of thought, and one evening I asked him if he would grant me an hour so we could talk seriously. He wanted to put the conversation off until the next day. I accepted, on the pretext that the delay would give me a chance to see a great singer who was appearing in a club. Immediately he changed his mind: he would come see me that evening.

For the first time he showed up exactly when he'd said he would. I offered him a large glass of milk, as usual, but he asked for a whiskey. We drank several whiskies and then I told him I had finally understood what I had to do: divorce him.

A few days later, we met with a lawyer to resolve our situation. The lawyer insisted that I move to another building immediately. My husband told me to answer in English—I was the one doing the interpreting—that this could not be done. He would agree to give in on the question of money, but he didn't want me living anywhere else.

The argument grew heated; the lawyer told him in bad French that he was treating me like a mistress, not a wife, and that he, my lawyer, was prepared to defend me.

My husband stood up and planted a kiss on my lips. It was the first kiss he had given me in the six months I had been living in New York. It made me angry, because he wasn't doing it seriously.

"I don't give a damn about laws," he concluded. "I love you." Furious, he slammed the door.

And so it all began again. I remembered Almería . . . the orange trees in flower along the coast . . . the love of our young lives . . .

26

IT WAS SUMMER, and the heat was tropical. "We have to leave New York, you see, and live out in the country," I suggested to Tonio hesitantly. "You won't be able to stand it here."

"I dream of being in the country and feeling cooler. Not going anywhere, just working, writing, night and day."

"Give me some money," I said. "I'll ask an agency for information."

"No," he said, "I'll take you to the train station. You'll

get on a train heading north, a lovely electric railcar, the fastest one."

At Grand Central Terminal in New York, I climbed aboard a train without knowing where it was going. I looked at the names of the stops and read "Northport." There, I said to myself: it's north, there must be a refreshing breeze.

I bought a ticket to the last stop on the line. I remember, Tonio, that you paid quite a few dollars, so I could go to the ends of the earth, but the ride turned out to last only forty-five minutes.

When I stepped off the train, I looked around for a taxi to take me into the city. No taxi. But I had a little trick, à la Consuelo. I was the only woman in New York who could find a taxi when everyone else was looking for one. Among the cars stopped at red lights, there were always taxis for members of the military, the sick, the handicapped. I would catch the driver's eye and try to put on my friendliest and most pleasant face, then slip up to his window, open my handbag, and show him a five-dollar bill, telling him, "Oh, I'm going quite far." Then he would say, "I'm driving. Can't you see I'm busy?" "Yes," I would persist, "we'll drop this person off first, and then me." That's exactly what I did in Northport. "Afterward you can take me to the big white house," I told the driver. For I had seen, from the train, a three-story white colonial house like something out of a storybook.

The car stopped in front of the house, which had a magnificent garden stretching out around it. Since the gate was open, I went in as if the place belonged to me. A gentleman with a watering can in his hand looked at me with a smile. "Sir," I said, "this is very bold of me, I realize, but I am a foreigner. My husband, back in New York, is a writer. His name is Antoine de Saint-Exupéry—perhaps you've heard of him?"

"Oh, yes," he replied. "I've read his book *Wind, Sand, and Stars*—it's a best-seller. Would you like to come in?"

He ushered me into the living room of that house, which we later called Bevin House, I don't know why.

"I'm looking for a house to rent around here," I explained. "My husband can't endure the heat any longer. He had a very serious accident in Guatemala a few years ago, you know, and he can't parachute anymore because his elbow hasn't yet fully recovered. He has rheumatism in several joints and suffers from being forty-three years old. . . . They say he's too old to join the war effort with the Air Force. He's a pilot, too, you see."

"I know, I know all that. I've read *Night Flight,* and my wife even uses the perfume named after it: Vol de Nuit, by Guerlain, which we like very much."

These words were a balm to my heart; I was already looking at the ceiling, the décor, the rooms, the hallways, as if the house belonged to me.

"Do you live here?" I asked. "Does your wife come to spend the summer holidays with you?"

"Alas, my wife is handicapped," he said. "She cannot leave the hospital, and I have no children. I come here from time to time because we planted rosebushes and dahlias in the garden, and, as you can see, it's easy to go swimming. Look at the beach."

"And there's a pleasant little breeze, too. You know, in New York everyone is roasting."

"I love your accent," he said. "You speak like Salvador Dalí."

"So I've been told. He's a friend of ours. I'll introduce him to you whenever you like," I promised.

"Listen, Madame," he said then, "you can tell your husband that you have found your house. But make sure you tell him I won't rent it to him: I'm offering it to him at no cost. He can stay as long as he wants. Here is the key. This one here is for the front door, this one is for the gate. Would you like me to show you around?"

I called Tonio at once. "How much time does it take to reach that house from here?" he demanded.

"Well," I said, "in the train it took about three quarters of an hour, but it would take less time by car."

"Would you like coffee, tea, chocolate?" the gentleman asked me.

"Yes, I would love some chocolate," I said. "It's been a long time since I've had any. My husband will be here in less than an hour."

I began telling him about my life in Oppède. And whenever I started talking about that village, nothing could make me stop; the stones themselves seemed to speak through me, and the conversation could go on forever, or at least for hours.*

*In 1945 Consuelo published a book entitled *Oppède* (New York: Editions Françaises Brentano's), which came out in English the following year as *Kingdom of the Rocks: Memories of Oppède* (New York: Random House).

Tonio finally arrived with his secretary, his dog Hannibal, and his tape recorder. We toured the house from top
to bottom, and then our landlord, who had a train to
catch, left us there, adding, "It would give me great pleasure if you would invite me over one of these Sundays."

"You must come back whenever you want," I told him.
"You can live here with us: choose a bedroom—there are
so many . . ."

That house became the house of the Little Prince.*
Tonio continued to work on the manuscript there. I posed
for the Little Prince, and all of the friends who came to
visit us did too. Of course, when a drawing was finished, it
wasn't of them but of a bearded gentleman or some flowers or a small animal, which sometimes made them angry.
It was a house made for happiness. "Do you remember the
room in Buenos Aires, the one where I started writing
Night Flight?" Tonio asked me one day. "Do the same
thing for me here."

"Yes, Tonio, I'll find you a little cask with a golden
spigot, which we'll fill up with port. I'll give you thermoses full of hot tea, and I'll surround you with mint
pastilles, pencils of all colors, colored paper, and a large
table."

Tonio often left for Washington on the weekends. I
didn't know who he was going to see, and after a while it
began to make me anxious. He would call me on the
phone and come home on Monday, worn-out, without

The Little Prince was published in the United States in 1943 but did
not appear in France until after the war, in 1945.

saying a word. I never asked him what he was doing there. Later I found out: we were having lunch at the Café Arnold when an American general came over to our table.

"*Mon général,* may I introduce you to my wife, Consuelo? She is Spanish but speaks English."

"I speak French myself," the general replied with a heavy accent.

"Has your husband told you about the fine work, the extremely valuable assistance he is giving us every Sunday with our plans for the invasion—the day when we'll land in France?" he added. "He knows the sea like no one else; he's the man who knows how best to approach the Mediterranean coastline and even the Atlantic coast."

There was peace in Northport. All our sweet pleasures had returned.

27

TONIO DID NOT KNOW how to talk about himself, or did not want to. His way of seeing the world, of experiencing it, had undoubtedly come to him from his childhood. He never referred to himself, never talked about himself. He tried every day to grow, to use past experiences to increase the likelihood of success, not only for himself but for others. He didn't talk just to make noise with words or spew out hot air; he always said something that had meaning. He never allowed his physical and emotional suffering to interfere with the rest of his life; he put them completely out of his mind. He always gave himself over entirely to whoever was listening to him. I remember a line of his: "You must love others but without telling them so." It explains his character: he loved people but wasted no time explaining the attention and love he was capable of giving them.

For him, love was a natural thing. Those who lived with him found him hard to bear because when he left he took the whole of his being away with him, completely and utterly. But he was also capable of returning completely and utterly, without leaving a particle of himself anywhere else. His physical and psychological strengths were united, in harmony with each other, and almost inexhaustible. When I would scold him because he was working himself to exhaustion on mathematical equations that seemed alien and forbidding to me, he would answer with a huge laugh and then invariably say, "I won't be wearing myself out any longer when I'm dead!"

I loved him for his clumsiness, his poetic appearance, the way he had of looking like a giant who is concealing a sensitive soul. He knew how to move very heavy weights effortlessly, with the same grace he employed in cutting little airplanes out of lightweight white paper, airplanes he would then launch into the sky from our balcony over the neighboring houses . . .

He would forget that he was tall as a tree and was always, inevitably, knocking his head against doorways.

Every time he got into a taxi, he banged his forehead. He would smile and declare that he was only keeping himself in training for more serious accidents. Often he would say to me, "I think of myself as a handsome youth with curly blond hair, but when I run my hand over my head I have to face the facts: I'm bald."

His clothes were always wrinkled because he would lie down on top of them or sleep fully dressed—I never managed to press the folds back into his pants. He didn't untie the knot in his tie when he went to bed; he knew how to pull on one of the ends so that the knot would yield, the tie would loosen, and he could slip it off over his head. He often managed to lose his shoes within the confines of the bedroom. He'd ask his friends to help him look for them: the shoes might be on top of the fireplace, in his desk drawer, among his papers, or hiding under a stack of newspapers.

He wanted his pants and jackets to be all alike. He was always delighted to find pants that were just like the ones he'd been wearing except clean and new, and he would kiss me, saying, "Someday I'll go to the tailor myself and order some magnificent clothes: a navy blue suit, for example, which will look superb with my curly blond hair." And he would laugh. His shirts were always a certain gray-blue color, but for the evenings, our grand evenings out, he would wear white shirts, giving in to me on that one point. I never saw him wear suspenders. He loathed them as much as he loathed garters; he much preferred having his socks droop. When he discovered the electric razor, he was as proud as a child and exhibited it throughout the apartment. He shaved several times a day, and the sound of the electric razor became a comfort to him. It accompanied his musings.

At Bevin House, he was really very happy. We christened the estate "The House of the Little Prince." He spent a lot of time in the attic, which I fixed up for him. One day, the wife of André Maurois* asked me, "Who is the young woman who arrives at five o'clock every day? Your husband locks himself in with her up there. We see her only at dinnertime."

"She comes to teach him English," I answered.

In fact, I was the one who had convinced him to take lessons. "All right," he said at last, "but only if you put a notice out asking for a pretty young woman who speaks English well and will take up no more than ten percent of my time."

"I'll make it sound as appealing as I can," I said. "We'll give it to the Havas agency."

About twenty women responded—there was quite a traffic jam at our doorstep. We decided to skip the interviews. "Listen, just choose the prettiest one," he said. "You have better taste than I do."

"But I don't know if you prefer a brunette, a blonde . . ."

"I want the prettiest . . ."

So I chose the most stunning blonde in the group, who was holding a little cat in her arms. "But the cat might bother you," I noted.

*André Maurois (1885–1967): A prolific author of essays, novels, and literary biographies, and a member of the Académie Française.

"Oh, not at all," he said. "Ask the others politely to go away, but pay them for their gasoline, I don't know—something like five dollars per person . . ."

"One dollar," I said.

"Don't be miserly," he scolded. "You know we're soon going to die, and then there will be nothing more of us."

After I had explained all this to Madame Maurois, she asked, "How long has this been going on?"

"Since we rented the house. Several months already."

"And you've never gone upstairs to see what they're doing?"

"You know, I'm not indiscreet. I'm sure that if it were your husband, you would react in much the same way."

"Ah, non," she said. "Me—I'm going up!"

After a moment, I heard something like a rain of little stones rattling down the stairs. It was chess pieces. The empty box in your hand, you appeared, your shirt wide open, a little angry. I was a little angry too, and sad. That young woman had learned to play chess, but you, you hadn't even wanted to learn the colors of the rainbow with me.

I told the young woman she had not fulfilled the terms of her contract.

"It's all my fault," Tonio interrupted. "In any case, I no longer need to teach her chess, she's now a very good player. And I, for my part, will never learn English."

"Mademoiselle, how much severance pay do you want?"

"Please keep me on, I beg you," she answered, tears in her eyes. "I'll come for free!"

THE EXCHANGE OF OPEN LETTERS with Maritain* in the newspapers that winter was very painful for you. You felt misunderstood. It was a series of mistaken impressions that you couldn't seem to clear up. I didn't know how to distract you anymore. I suggested we take a walk through Central Park; we went to see the tigers, the lions, the chimpanzees—and even though you didn't much care for monkeys, I managed to win a smile from you as you watched them eating peanuts out of my hand.

All those weeks, since 1943, you'd been living with a cloud over your head, so you would pick up a large pair of scissors and make little airplanes. One day, a police officer came up to the house to tell you that you were littering the streets of New York City!

You smiled and told him, "I have an even better story than that. One day, after making a phone call, I forgot to hang up. I fell asleep and snored so loudly that they were afraid at the central exchange that something had happened in this building. They thought it was a fire and sent a whole ladderful of firemen!"

*On November 29, 1942, *The New York Times Magazine* published Saint-Exupéry's "Open Letter to Frenchmen Everywhere," in which he urged his compatriots to put their differences behind them. The letter was seen by many as an attack on Charles de Gaulle. Jacques Maritain, a highly respected Catholic philosopher, wrote an essay in response, accusing Saint-Exupéry of being vague and unrealistic, which appeared in an anti-Vichy weekly magazine, *Pour la Victoire*, along with a brief statement of rebuttal by Saint-Exupéry.

Another charming incident took place at Greta Garbo's house, which we had rented. Our neighbors were Mrs. Guggenheim, the mine owner, and her daughter Peggy, who was full of admiration for Tonio. She would lend me a hand with little things around the house. Our dog, Hannibal, a bulldog, was ill natured, but he very much liked Peggy, who was beautiful and blond: he would take her arm between his teeth and then wouldn't let go.

One day when we had some friends over—Jean Gabin,* Marlene Dietrich, Garbo—our refrigerator couldn't hold all the bottles of champagne, and Peggy had the idea of burying them in the garden, under the snow.

"Very well, young lady," said Tonio. "You do the work!"

When the time came to serve the champagne, Peggy announced, in front of the assembly of beautiful ladies— all with their white gloves on, even during the meal!—"I can't remember where I buried them. Does anyone want to go out and look with me?"

Gabin agreed to help her look for the bottles, which had been swallowed up by the snow. The two of them were freezing out there in the garden, and we could hear them laughing, especially Peggy, with that young laugh of hers. Then everyone went outside and joined in the hunt for the bottles: what a joyous moment in our lives!

That was how our stay in Garbo's house began. I was content, but I saw that you weren't at all happy. You wouldn't be happy, I knew well, until you had been autho-

*Jean Gabin (1904–1976): A beloved actor who appeared in many French films.

rized to rejoin your squadron—Group 2/33—to go back and fight, so that you could come under enemy fire once more.

At that time Peggy had taken in Max Ernst, whom she had snatched from the clutches of the Nazis. Then Max Ernst married Peggy. Without ever speaking of happiness or unhappiness, he would come to take refuge at our house. Like you, he was sad. You didn't like to have a lot of people over all at once, and I remember that one day you suggested to Max Ernst, "If you're alone, come to our place tomorrow evening."

He came, after having confided to Peggy, "I'm going over to Saint-Ex's, he's expecting me. He's only invited men—his wife will be the one woman there. He's getting ready to go off to the war, and he's a little worried about leaving her alone in New York."

I never complained about the loneliness I could foresee. Or the sadness to come. You had to leave, I knew that. "I have to come under enemy fire in order to feel washed, to feel clean, in this absurd war." Those were your words.

Tonio trained the bulldog, in anticipation of his departure. He would blow soap bubbles, and the dog would pop them against the pure white walls of Garbo's house.

"When I come back," he would say, "when I see you again, with your dog, I won't beat him if he doesn't recognize me. Instead I'll blow soap bubbles, and he'll know that I'm his master, who has returned."

28

O H Tonio, my beloved, it is terrible to be the wife of a warrior. Tonio, my love, my tall tree of a husband, it's decided: you're leaving. You know, Tonio, that you are my son, too. I know that you saw a woman before your departure and told her, "Thérèse, I will not kiss you. Because I will carry on my lips, until the end of the war, my wife's lips and her last kiss."

When you held me tightly in your arms, when you told me good-bye before flying off to Algeria, your voice stayed in my ears. I hear it now, just as I hear the beating of my own heart. I will always hear it. "Don't cry," you told me. "The unknown is beautiful when you are going off to discover it. I'm going to war for my country. Don't look at my eyes, for I'm weeping as much with joy at carrying out my duty as with pain over your tears. I could almost thank heaven for giving me a treasure to leave behind: my house, my books, my dog. You will keep them for me.

"Every day, you'll write me two lines, three lines— you'll see; it will be like a phone call, and we will not be separated since you are my wife for eternity. We will weep together across the distance of all the passing days during which we are not together, looking at the same things. *Petite fille,* don't cry, or I will cry too. I look strong because

I'm tall, but soon I'll be swooning, and then, if my commanding officer or my general is at the door, he won't be too proud of his soldier!

"Straighten my tie instead. Give me your handkerchief so I can write the next part of *The Little Prince* on it. At the end of the story, the Little Prince will give this handkerchief to the Princess. You'll never again be a rose with thorns, you'll be a dream princess who always waits for the Little Prince. I will dedicate that book to you. I can't forgive myself for not having dedicated it to you. I'm sure that while I'm gone our friends will be kind to you. When I'm here they prefer my company, but that's not particularly flattering to me. Those who love only the famous man in me make me sad. I will forget all those who don't extend all of their favors to you. When I come back, my wife, the two of us will be with the true friends of our hearts. Only them."

Oh, how I would like to lie here a little longer next to you, without saying a word. A rush of images from my childhood comes flooding into my mind at times like these. But we have to go. What time is it?

"Tonio," I said, "you're breaking my heart. You ask me to be nice to your friends who are staying behind, but since you received the authorization to go, not one of them has made any effort, even jokingly, to keep you here, to explain to you that fast planes require very young pilots. I forgive them their cowardice since they love you sincerely, they think of you as one of their own, going off to war, and they know it's what you wanted. It's what you need to do."

"*Pimprenelle*, don't make war on everyone, my love. Everything you've just said is true."

"Yes, I know. Perhaps I'd do better to show you how I organized your luggage."

"*Oh la la*, no instructions, please! You've given me too many handkerchiefs, pins, pills—and that underwear is too small for me."

"You'll lose weight," I said flatly.

"No, no, I'd rather get fat," he protested with a laugh. "But if I go mad, if I mix together all these pills, all these vitamins, into a nice explosive meal for a day when I have no bread, I'll start to swell up like the boa in *The Little Prince*! Don't be jealous of that band of doves in exile here who have cooed with me in French and have driven me, along with all our friends, to your door. I couldn't shake them off. Don't treat them badly. All rootless love is clamorous and clinging. Besides, I'm leaving: it's over. When I'm far away there will be other faces, other friends, and even other doves, you know. But this is different. My home is in your heart, and I will be there forever."

"Still," I said, "I can't exactly welcome them in with a smile. It isn't a party, your departure. And I have a fever."

"Ah! *Pimprenelle*, it's getting late and I have to catch my boat. It will go past our house tomorrow, perhaps even tonight. Take care of yourself. Write me, even if your letters are silly. I say silly because you are often mistaken in your judgments about some man or some woman. Don't forget what I told you: you're a better judge of men than of women. You are never mistaken about men, you're almost clairvoyant, but about women, you're always wrong!"

He left at last. I lay on the bed for hours in despair, as if paralyzed. I couldn't fall asleep. I listened for your submarine. I didn't hear any noise, but at every moment I could feel you going through the water, because you were not in those waters but in me, deep inside me. You know, Tonio, you are right, I was your mother, too.

Oh, how vain our little disputes seem to me now! How can I tell you—with everything I feel right now, thinking of you shut up inside that fragile vessel, though I know you are escorted by other ships—that I am protecting you? For I know you will reach your destination, my love, and I remember the secret you murmured in my ear when I was weeping hot tears, "Cloak me in your love, Consuelo, *ma Pimprenelle,* and I won't be touched by the bullets." I am making that cloak for you, my darling. May it enfold you for all eternity.

No, I didn't try to watch your boat go by through the waters of the Hudson that flow out toward the sea. You told me I wouldn't see you anyway, because of the fantastical reflections of the electric lights against the steely water. But you promised me you would hold me so tightly in your heart at that moment that I would feel your arms around me for the rest of my life. And you promised that if you didn't come back, the river would whisper to me about the strength of your kiss—and about you, about us.

Lake George, late June,
the day of your birthday

Tonio, my love,

I woke up at six o'clock this morning. I ran to the lake in my pajamas, to dip my feet in. The water is delicious. A reddish purple sun is rising from behind the neighboring mountain. I dream of you, my beloved. And I am happy to think of you, to dream of you. Despite the fear I feel, knowing that you are the oldest pilot in the world, mon chéri—imagine if all men were like you!

I have to run to the village, to a little Catholic church where mass is held at 7:30 every day, and it's the only mass—very few Catholics and very few Catholic priests here. I want to go sit in the church's empty pews today, the day of your birthday. That is all I can give you. So I'm running, my husband, I must get dressed—it's half an hour's walk to the church.

Good-bye for now. If I do not see you again on this planet, know that you will find me with the good Lord, waiting for you, truly you will.

You are in me as the vegetation is upon the earth. I love you—you are my treasure, you are my world.

Your wife,
Consuelo
June 29, 1944

[The same day Consuelo wrote this letter, Antoine wrote her a very somber love letter, with a note in the margin mentioning that he had just turned forty-four. A month later, on July 31, 1944, he disappeared while flying a reconnaissance mission over southern France. Neither his plane nor his body was ever found. In 1998 a bracelet engraved with the words "Consuelo" and "Antoine" was recovered from the Mediterranean.]

This book was set in Caslon, a typeface first designed in 1722 by William Caslon. Its widespread use by most English printers in the early eighteenth century soon supplanted the Dutch typefaces that had formerly prevailed. The roman is considered a "workhorse" typeface due to its pleasant, open appearance, while the italic is exceedingly decorative.